Red Chamber, World Dream

Red Chamber, World Dream

Actors, Audience, and Agendas in
Chinese Foreign Policy and Beyond

Jing Sun

University of Michigan Press

Ann Arbor

For questions or permissions, please contact um.press.perms@umich.edu

Published in the United States of America by the
University of Michigan Press
Manufactured in the United States of America
Printed on acid-free paper
First published March 2021

A CIP catalog record for this book is available from the British Library.

Library of Congress Cataloging-in-Publication Data

Names: Sun, Jing, 1974– author.
Title: Red chamber, world dream : actors, audience, and agendas in Chinese foreign policy
    and beyond / Jing Sun.
Other titles: Actors, audience, and agendas in Chinese foreign policy and beyond
Description: Ann Arbor : University of Michigan Press, 2021. | Includes bibliographical
    references and index. |
Identifiers: LCCN 2020046380 (print) | LCCN 2020046381 (ebook) |
    ISBN 9780472074860 (hardcover) | ISBN 9780472054862 (paperback) |
    ISBN 9780472128877 (ebook)
Subjects: LCSH: China—Foreign relations—20th century. | China—Foreign relations—
    21st century. | China—Politics and government—20th century. | China—Politics
    and government—2002– | Cao, Xueqin, approximately 1717–1763. Hong lou meng—
    Criticism and interpretation.
Classification: LCC DS779.37 .S86   2021 (print) | LCC DS779.37 (ebook) |
    DDC 327.51—dc23
LC record available at https://lccn.loc.gov/2020046380
LC ebook record available at https://lccn.loc.gov/2020046381

Cover photo by Kanegan on Flickr

To Meiqin, Colin, and Eva—My love for you knows no bounds.

Acknowledgments

I became a fan of China's classic epic novel *Dream of the Red Chamber* at a young age. In the late 1980s, when I was a teenager, a TV adaption of the famous novel dominated China's little screens for months. Many Chinese were somewhat familiar with this literature classic. But it was the first time people saw the famous story visualized with sights, sounds, and mostly young and dashing actors. Most Chinese families at the time had only black-and-white televisions—if they could afford one. This greatly reduced the visual effect of a TV drama rich in colors and ornate effects. But to me, also a young painter, it was a blessing in disguise—the TV drama became a giant coloring book that allowed me to use my imagination to fill in vibrant colors on the black-and-white screen.

Little did I know that the classic would provide inspiration for me more than three decades later to produce a book on Chinese foreign policy. But life makes unexpected and amazing knots. At the book's onset, I will not bother readers with the methodological connections between the novel and my own book. I will just state the thematic one: how seemingly powerful and affluent powerhouses can abruptly fall due to gradual decaying. This thematic connection is vivid and haunting at the same time.

How China writes its own story, to a great extent, will shape the story of mankind in the twenty-first century. As we are observing the Chinese story, we are also writing it. We are all in it. My analysis brings about many concerns. But it also highlights where hopes lie. Chinese people, like people everywhere, are champions of endurance. In the end, it is the human spirit that will brighten dark nights and ensure dawn's arrival.

For their help in making this book a reality, I first thank my family members in Beijing and Shanghai for their never-ending support delivered long-distance. In the professional world, I thank my wonderful colleagues at the University of Denver: Jesse Acevedo, Sara Chatfield, David Ciepley, Lisa Conant, Laurel Eckhouse, Seth Masket, Elizabeth Sperber, Nancy Wadsworth, and Joshua Wilson, among others, for their support. I would also like to express my gratitude to the multiple reviewers of my manuscript for their constructive and insightful feedback—all raised in the good spirit of helping me enhance its quality. I thank Edward Friedman, June Teufel Dreyer, Lowell Dittmer, Peter Hays Gries, Ming Wan, Ho-fung Hong, David Kang, Robert Sutter, and Lam Peng Er for their comments and criticisms on this and related projects. On the other side of the globe, I thank those Chinese scholars, journalists, and officials who agreed to talk with me, though I know they shall remain anonymous. My sincere appreciation also goes to Academia Sinica in Taiwan, particularly its director, Tse-Kang Leng, Dr. Yu-Shan Wu, Dr. Nien-Chung Chang Liao, and the wonderful coordinator Ya-Hui Huang. They all helped me have an immensely productive research stay in Taipei. As always, I thank my Japanese mentor, Dr. Kaoru Sato, for hosting my research stay at the University of Tokyo. At the University of Michigan Press, I thank Christopher Dreyer for being a calm, guiding hand in my experience of working with the press again—this time in the middle of a public health crisis. Christopher's consistent reassurance meant a lot to me during this confusing and difficult time. I also thank Anne Taylor for copyediting and Kevin Rennells for guiding me through the production process. Despite all the support I received from these sources, any errors remaining in this book are my sole responsibility.

Last but most importantly, I thank my family here in America for loving me and trusting me unconditionally. This book is for you—Meiqin (Piao-piao), Colin, and Eva. Thank you for making my life whole.

All of the Chinese, Japanese, and Korean names in this book appear in their original naming order of surname followed by given name, except when such names are from scholarly resources and the authors wrote their names in the western naming order of given name followed by surname.

Contents

Digital materials related to this title can be found on
the Fulcrum platform via the following citable URL:
https://doi.org/10.3998/mpub.11538783

1 • The "Chinese Dream"

Which Chinese Dream?

In such commotion does the world's theatre rage; as each one
leaves, another takes the stage.
—Cao Xueqin, ballad from *Dream of the Red Chamber*

Political Musing of an Ancient Chinese Dream

Dream of the Red Chamber, a novel written by Cao Xueqin in the eighteenth century, is commonly regarded as one of the Four Great Master-
works (*sida mingzhu*) in Chinese literature. The other three classics,
Romance of the Three Kingdoms, *Water Margin*, and *The Journey to the West*,
all belong to the same genre: They offer spotlights to emperors, lords, generals, rebels, and saints. They romanticize gory battles. They tell tales of
intrigue. They feature mysterious figures like Monkey King and his friends
Pigsy and Sandy, who are capable of polymorphic transformations.

 Dream of the Red Chamber, however, is about none of these. As a semi-
autobiography, the novel chronicles the rise and fall of one family—the aris-
tocratic Jia clan. As folklore goes, at its height, this prominent family's two
branches, the Ningguo House and the Rongguo House, boast wealth and
influence rivaling legendary gods governing heaven and ocean. Their man-
sions are made of white jade. They treat pearls as trivial as dirt and gold as
cheap as iron.[1] Eventually, though, the illustrious family falls out of favor
with the emperor, its grand chambers raided, its massive fortune confiscated,
and its once noble members executed, jailed, and enslaved. This plot would
mirror the author's life experience. As a boy, Cao witnessed his once prestigious family ostracized by the new emperor Yongzheng. With their properties seized and the family patriarch thrown in jail, the remaining members of
the Cao clan were forced to relocate to a suburb of Beijing. There, Cao

Xueqin would spend the rest of his life writing, drinking, drawing, and living in poverty. Historians are still debating his age upon demise—forty or forty-eight?[2] What is undebatable is that Cao died a broken man.

The novel has a second plotline: the coming-of-age story of Jia Baoyu, the family's young heir apparent. Buoyant and rebellious, the teenage boy forms a special bond with his cousin Lin Daiyu, a talented girl who has no qualms with love and hate. Baoyu, however, is predestined to marry another cousin, Xue Baochai. Baochai is as bright as Daiyu, but she is reserved and respectful of rules. Baochai thus better fits the traditional role model of a gracious, ideal lady. The novel, which details the romance, rivalry, and friendship among the three, ends with Daiyu's death, Baoyu's decision to become a monk, and Baochai's loss of her husband and life of loneliness and destitution.

Focusing on one family's fate and drawing on the tumultuous emotional world of teenagers, Cao's novel is markedly more delicate in both content and style than the other three great classics. Yet, *Dream of the Red Chamber* could be the grandest of all: by tracing the vicissitude of one family, it presents a tale of epic proportions—the rise and fall of dynasties and the universal truth embedded in such movements. At the beginning of the novel, as a story within the story, a Buddhist monk and a Taoist priest foretell readers what they are about to experience—they will be amazed, awed, and then stunned by witnessing the blooming and atrophying of an eminent family—and that such stories repeat themselves as eternal axioms throughout history.

The novel's grandeur also lies in its comprehensiveness: it depicts daily lives of Chinese society in the eighteenth century with a vast amount of details, presenting a panorama of poetry, medicine, cuisine, music, opera, festivities, architecture, painting, wedding and funeral rites, and so forth. It has become a treasure trove for scholars of various disciplines, who treat the novel as a collection of encyclopediac resources for examining Chinese culture and history. No wonder the study of this one novel has evolved into a stand-alone field known as redology (*hongxue*). None of the other three great books has stirred up such enduring and encompassing intellectual fascination.

It may sound a bit far-fetched for a political science book to start with the author's musing of a Chinese literature classic. But I will admit that my exploration of the political world has often been inspired and aided significantly by my roaming into the nonpolitical world. I suspect I am not alone in benefiting from crisscrossing between my home discipline and others or between the nonfictional and fictional universes. My first piece of reading at the graduate level at an American university was Gabriel Almond's "Separate Tables: Schools and Sects in Political Science."[3] In this piece, Almond laments how the political science discipline has been engulfed by theoretical turf wars: different schools and perspectives view one another in a mutually exclusive manner. The result is that the discipline has been taken over by theoretical extremists, as staunch disciples protect their "secret island of vulnerability" and hold rivals in contempt.[4] Almond concludes with a call for political scientists to view the infusion of different sects as a good thing that enriches the discipline and to resist the temptation to hold onto methodological purity. After all, political science should be "open to all methods that illuminate the world of politics and public policy."[5]

The "separate tables" metaphor stuck with me, as did Almond's call for bridging efforts to create a more nuanced, holistic understanding of political phenomena. Furthermore, one may elevate Almond's critique to the interdisciplinary level: infusion should happen not only *within* political science but also *between* political science and other disciplines. In fact, to prove that the study of politics matters, it is imperative that we reveal its looming shadow in other disciplines and vice versa.

It is in this light that I began my book on the contemporary Chinese Dream by recalling an ancient one imagined more than two hundred years ago. The fact is that *Dream of the Red Chamber* could be read as a political treatise. The defining feature of politics, namely, the quest for power, is a central theme that runs through its pages. Mao Zedong is probably among the novel's most prominent enthusiasts. According to his personal librarian, between 1958 and 1973, Mao checked out different editions of the book for a total of fifteen times.[6] Even during the legendary Long March (1934–35), when Mao had to abandon most of his possessions in the ardent 5,600-mile-long trek, he still kept the novel with him.[7] Mao regularly brought up the book in his conversations to audiences as varied as fellow Politburo members and his bodyguard and chauffeur. Proclaiming that the book represented the pinnacle of Chinese literary achievement, Mao urged everyone to read it at least three times.[8] When Mao's second wife, He Zizhen, dismissed the book as "soft and feminine" and filled with manufactured melancholies, Mao criticized her assessment of the book's message—rather, it was all about political power struggles. He also likened America and the Soviet Union, both superpowers at the time, as the two prominent branches of the Jia clan, stating that "being big brings its own problems."[9]

Mao even saw politics in the plotline that features teen romance. He applauded Jia Baoyu as "China's first great revolutionary" for his rebellious spirit. He also assigned class identities to the numerous characters in the book, detecting class struggles on every page. The chairman went so far as to get into a scholarly debate on the novel: in 1954, he wrote a letter to fellow Politburo members to support a paper written by Li Xifan and Lan Ling, two young college graduates.[10] The paper used Marxism to challenge Yu Pingbo, a famed senior redologist, on deciphering the book's hidden message. Yu saw the book as a sad hymn for a bygone splendid era. To Li and Lan, however, author Cao Xueqin was using his pen to vehemently attack feudalism. Major literature critique outlets snubbed Li and Lan's paper. It was later published by a journal housed under Shandong University. But thanks to Mao's promotion, the two authors became young heroes overnight. Yu, on the other hand, turned into a symbol of feudalistic academic authority. He was sent to a labor camp to receive reeducation. The book's impact on Mao was significant: he did not just read the book—he lived the book.

Dream of the Red Chamber could be of reference to not just political practitioners but scholars of politics as well. Its comprehensiveness also lies in its interpretive methodology. The novel includes forty major characters and more than four hundred minor ones. Chapter by chapter, Cao Xueqin describes a myriad of interactions of people at all levels: the family matriarch, the middle-aged male authorities, a highly competent female manager of the house, young princes and princesses, and numerous servants with varied degrees of influence. The book rejects making observations at just one level. By detailing actions among actors at all levels along the authority parameter, the book presents a dense network of interactions and power sparks on the nodes of this interactive network. Furthermore, by embedding a frame story—the Buddhist monk and the Taoist priest, who are not part of the two plotlines—the book uses their foretelling comments to highlight the significance of events upfront.

It turns out that long before Clifford Geertz coined the term "thick description," Cao had already skillfully applied this extensively interpretive method in this novel.[11] To put it another way, by observing actions among actors at all levels and providing a grand context through a frame story, *Dream of the Red Chamber* offers a comprehensive narrative of linkage politics unfolding in real time. The result is an "ordinary drama" chapter by chapter. The monk and the priest inform readers *what* will happen on page 1—a grand family's demise and destruction. By witnessing the everyday functioning of this organization, readers will become increasingly aware of *how* and *why* its death is inevitable.

Bringing Politics Back into Foreign Policy Analysis

One methodological implication that China's great book could offer to political scientists today is on levels of analysis. Understanding the big picture—or, to use a theoretical term, the "system"—can be achieved by observing actors, either individual or collective, at subsystemic levels. But the impact of actors' behaviors is not confined to the specific levels they are assigned to. It spills over all the time—just like the daily politics at the Ningguo and Rongguo Houses. As David Lampton contends in his study of contemporary Chinese leadership, such interactions form a network's many "nodes." A holistic, systemic approach to policy-making demands examining a cross-level network and the ways actors at different levels interact with one another horizontally and vertically.[12] Understanding the porous nature of levels of analysis would address caveats of reductionist theories like realism and liberalism, which highlight institutional properties of the structures. Meanwhile, a holistic approach rejects non-reductionist argumentation of Marxism, which examines agencies in self-contained class categories and predicts mechanical behaviors.

To be sure, observing has long been a crucial method for scholarly inquiries. But housing it under the concept of levels of analysis is relatively new. J. David Singer, in his seminal work in 1961, identified two levels of analysis on studying foreign policy making: the international system and the nation-state.[13] The systemic one views foreign policy making as possessing a high degree of uniformity across nation-states. States all act in a single-minded behavior to pursue national interest defined as power. A major proponent of this perspective is Kenneth Waltz. As a pioneering scholar seeking to make social inquires more "scientific," he updated realism by shifting its emphasis from competitive human nature to structures. To Waltz, international relations is a dark game. But they are not personal. The international system, with its defining structural feature of anarchy, compels all states to become "like units"—their needs and desires are essentially the same, regardless of their domestic ideologies and historical traditions. All states yearn for survival and security. In the absence of a world government, this universal yearning could only be realized through individual self-help. The one difference among states that matters is their means—in other words, how much power they hold to enable them to achieve the goals of survival and security.[14] Derivatively, great powers can afford to go it alone and defy international opinions if they deem their crucial national interest at risk. Weaker ones, by contrast, have to make peace with limiting their ambitions and jumping on the bandwagon of a great power.[15]

Such a pessimistic portrayal of international relations is not new. It has been told by classical realists of all ages: from Thucydides to Niccolo Machiavelli to Thomas Hobbes. What made postwar realism earn the "neo" prefix was a grander level of observations; Waltz, for example, dismisses the study of individuals (a level he termed "first image"), for human nature is abstract, unmeasurable, and mercurial. Instead, he shifted observations to the systemic level (a level he termed "third image"), where characteristics are simpler, stable, predictable, and, as a result, scientific.[16]

How about the "second image"—the study of nation-states? This level of analysis, as Singer suggests, has the potential of avoiding "inaccurate homogenization which often flows from the systemic focus."[17] In practice, though, the domestic level of analysis, influenced by the drive to make inquiries scientific, is still overtly structural. It replaces the emphasis on the singular systemic feature of anarchy with a binary categorization of strong states vis-à-vis weak states, depending on their relations to society. What exactly constitutes the "state"? There is no consensus—some scholars examined leaders and their perceptions, some analyzed the autonomy of the state as dictated by the political economy, while still others studied the characteristics of bureaucracy.[18]

The problem with this "second image" analysis, as Peter Gourevitch points out, is that it is fundamentally apolitical. It emphasizes procedures and institutions but divorces these components from the actual "content" of the interests as seen by political actors. Procedures and institutional arrangements alone become deterministic. As a result, a black-and-white dichotomy emerges: state-centered versus society-centered policy-making processes. As the study of decision-making mechanisms takes the driver's seat, the content of decisions no longer matters. The consequence, in Gourevitch's words, is that "somehow politics disappears."[19]

The departing of politics from policy analysis has real consequences. Political actors' preferences and orientations change, and such changes compel them to compete or cooperate. But by treating what actors want as fixed assumptions, "second image" analysis has become a subsidiary of the systemic level of analysis, a level it claims to challenge.[20] Actors are assumed to be essentially unitary rational entities that coherently configure and pursue goals. Substantively, this assumption is not true. Political struggles are real, and so are choices facing actors. It is imperative that scholars examine how normative expectations and structural arrangements can become weapons or obstacles as leaders, bureaucrats, and societal actors try to shape outcomes of their preferences through interactions.

One model that has attempted to fix this unitary, rational-actor assumption is the "two-level game" analysis. Robert Putnam coins the concept to describe how in international negotiations, government leaders need to carry out a second negotiation—that is, they need to strike deals with not just their foreign counterparts but also their domestic constituents.[21] This logic would be a natural derivative from a call for domestic coalitional studies that Goure-vitch made earlier: that is, how a myriad of domestic actors debate on policy alternatives and how some policies are legitimated while others are abandoned.[22]

A major contribution of Putnam's analysis is to open the black box of the state and problematize political struggles among domestic actors. But the two-level game model has its own limits. First, despite the rapidly growing body of literature utilizing the model, analysis has been mostly serving an empirical niche market—namely, explaining international negotiations. There is a narrow temporal scope as studies zoom in on inter- and intragov-ernmental meetings, as such events typically start and end with specific time windows. International negotiations and summits may indeed attract more media attention. But they constitute only a small part of foreign policy mak-ing. Much of the policy formulation and related political jockeying happen in more mundane and less dramatic settings. Such quieter places are also where political ascension or decay unfolds, however incrementally. Over time, though, it would become clear whether certain policy paths have led to success or failure, based on how they have shaped the country's position in relation to the world—the big picture, so to speak. In this regard, realities of international relations and foreign policy making are happening in a way not much different from the fictional tale told in *Dream of the Red Chamber*. Conflicts are occasional splashes. But it is the undercurrent that determines the flow of events.

The two-level game has another problem in selection bias: since domestic coalitional politics is the focus, cases have been predominantly about elec-toral democracies. This is understandable: only in such a setting are transac-tions between leaders and constituents more formal, transparent, and trac-table. Elections are powerful mechanisms. They act as compelling stimulants or deterrents as politicians assess their options. But what about political enti-ties that do not have meaningful elections? In those places, one cannot talk about leadership-constituency dynamism in the same sense as one can in an electoral democracy. The two-level game may still find its logic in such set-tings. But assessments are likely to require a longer time span, as power dyna-mism between leaders and masses is murkier and so are incentives and risks associated with policy options.

One latest challenge of the two-level game is to explain the unfolding trade war between China and America. The massive dispute is hurting the economic interests of both countries. The Chinese government also admits that in such straightforward economics there are no winners; everyone loses.[23] Meanwhile, though, by "everyone," it has become clear that Beijing's propaganda machine means *not* everyone, but America. The media have bombarded audiences with stories about how various American businesses, ranging from Apple and Boeing to soybean and pig farmers, will be hit hard by China's retaliatory wrath.[24] There has been little, if any, mention of how Chinese businesses have been hurt by the American measures. As a result, parallel rhetorical universes are emerging: in the universe of logic, both China and America lose. In the universe of outcomes, only short-sighted Americans bite the dust.

The two-level game model remains logically relevant but empirically muddier to detect in an autocratic setting. Chinese leaders will certainly have to grapple with domestic backlashes. Otherwise they would not have invested so much time and personnel in the frenzied negotiations with the Trump administration. However, since the public is denied access to information of sector-specific grievances, people would have a hard time weighing the pros and cons of policy alternatives, let alone offering input on how to negotiate with America. Public anxiety is real, but it has to find some creative outlets to manifest itself. For example, in the spring of 2018, Hu Angang, a professor at Tsinghua University known for his argument that China has already surpassed America "comprehensively," became a target of popular resentment.[25] Many netizens blamed Professor Hu for "misleading" the Chinese leadership to take on America prematurely. Hu, a pro-government celebrity intellectual not long ago, all of a sudden turned into a pariah. His name became a taboo word on search engines—a treatment typically reserved for enemies of the state like Nobel Peace Prize laureates Liu Xiaobo and the Dalai Lama. Meanwhile, on the American side, the media have offered various assessments, including those addressing the concerns, complaints, or even protests filed by constituents who could potentially be hurt by the trade war.[26] Even Beijing has contributed to this chorus by buying advertisement inserts in the Sunday edition of the *Des Moines Register*, trying to sway Iowan voters by touting the mutual benefits of US-China trade. The supplement did not forget to highlight President Xi Jinping's personal ties with Iowa, a state he visited as a young village chief in 1985. The strategy backfired—both President Donald Trump and Vice President Mike Pence quickly seized the opportunity and cited such advertising as evidence of Chinese meddling in US elections.

Argument and Method: In Search of Policy Making's "Human Factor"

In studying Chinese foreign policy making, I employ a tripartite analytical framework instead of a dichotomy of state versus society. The three groups of actors this book analyzes are leaders; bureaucrats (particularly diplomats); and societal forces that include prominent public figures, the media, and the masses. Each group shoulders its unique package of incentives and constraints. Two components go into such a package of policy possibilities: these actors' relations to regime legitimacy and their access to resources, both materialistic and emotive. This book's analysis is premised on these dual factors and their interplay. I contend that, jointly, the two factors have created various roles for political actors to play in Chinese foreign policy making.

Each chapter's analysis starts with a discussion on the actors' relations with regime legitimacy. This study rejects viewing legitimacy as a singular entity. Instead, it views the concept as a spectrum, extending from construction to implementation. Actors can then be placed on this legitimacy spectrum. If an actor stands closer to the creative end, power flows from the actor to legitimacy more than vice versa. Those who can credibly claim to be builders of legitimacy often acquire a more active, transformative role in policy making.

Departing from conventional wisdom, this book argues that this transformative role is not confined to leadership. As chapter 4 on the Chinese masses and foreign policy illustrates, the country's public has become more and more proactive, even assertive at times, in shaping foreign policy narratives. They do so because of their newly gained legitimacy as foreign policy constituents—thanks to their ever-increasing possession of wealth in a rapidly commercializing society. By contrast, if an actor stands closer to the implementing end of the legitimacy spectrum, power is inclined to flow from legitimacy to the actor. In this case, actors are no longer inventors. They are practitioners tasked with abiding by and substantiating the legitimacy bequeathed on them. This relationship has created a more passive, managerial role in policy making. One case to be analyzed in detail is China's highly professionalized yet institutionally tamed diplomatic corps. Another example is China's increasingly marginalized office of the premiership.

What resources does one possess and how should they be used? This question constitutes the second common thread linking political calculations at all levels. Resources for policy making could be both formal and informal. In the formal arena, one crucial resource is organizational arrangement. China has well-defined rules to designate which actors (individuals or collectives) are "core" and which are not. They also regulate the distances of various actors vis-à-vis the "core." This legalistic structure has led to competition among actors vying for preferred positions in the policy-making hierarchy. Resources could also be informal—norms, frames, identities, and values, and so forth. Indeed, insightful scholarship has been generated on leadership personality, ministerial character, and emotive leverages of the masses.

Actors, audiences, agenda settings, frames—all these terms suggest that a political analysis could be helped by fellow social science disciplines. In joining the separate tables, political scientists may find the dramaturgical approach from socio-psychological analysis particularly helpful. This approach stresses the importance of members interacting with one another as self, and identities are formed through rituals, routines, and presentations—a phenomenon that Erving Goffman terms "interaction order" in his pioneering work on interlinked self-presentation.[27] The dramaturgical approach, though, has a longer history of application than Goffman's theoretical summary of it. After all, William Shakespeare famously said: "All the world's a stage, And all the men and women merely players." He went on to say that all actors have their own moments of taking entrances and exits, which echoes Cao Xueqin's lament one century later about the bewildering yet sequential dramatic life in China. Goffman's contribution lies in expanding the presence of this role-playing phenomenon beyond theaters. He points out that it exists in reality. In social interactions, we all play roles. In this sense, we are all actors. Goffman further contends that through such role-playing, we are trying to manipulate others' impressions of us by utilizing a variety of tools that he calls "sign vehicles"—appearances, props, manners, and so forth.[28]

This dramaturgical approach quickly found its relevance in the study of politics—though political scientists lean on a set of vocabulary that replaces stage, props, and impressions with context, power, and perceptions. Political scientist Robert Jervis, for example, put such theorizing in International Relations (IR) analysis. He used cognitive psychological concepts like perception and misperception to examine political decision making. Jervis also examined the logic of images in IR, arguing that nation-states use verbal and nonverbal communication to cumulatively create a "behavioral profile" to influence recipients.[29]

The trend of embedding socio-psychological concepts in IR analysis is still going on, as exemplified by a new wave of scholarship that examines how norm-violating states challenge and transform moral discourse, how face-saving could be utilized as a tool for escalation management, and how high interaction density and common ethos contribute to the expansion of the European Union.[30] Jervis's latest book, *How Statesmen Think*, explores how emotional needs shape leaders' perceptions and misperceptions in international politics.[31] Scholars focusing on China have also applied these concepts—for example, Xiaoyu Pu explores how China, intensely conscious of its status, is searching for a coherent role at home and abroad; and Jessica Chen Weiss examines how the Chinese government uses nationalistic, anti-foreign protests as a signaling mechanism to demonstrate its domestic vulnerability to international audiences.[32]

This book is built on this growing trend. But it does more: it examines the political impact of socio-psychological factors at multiple levels in a tripartite, holistic framework. By doing so, it goes further than being another isolated project contained to one specific level of analysis. Its overarching theme is to bring politics back into foreign policy analysis. This mission methodologically requires a data-driven, inductive approach. The deductive approach, which starts with theoretical assumptions and then imposes them on empirical cases, works better at formulating and testing generalizable patterns. Although realism and its main contender, liberalism, disagree on arguments, they are methodological allies: both start with a few key terms that serve as assumptions—"zero-sum" and "self-help" for realists and "positive-sum" and "interdependence" for liberalists. Both camps contend that such terms are value neutral; that is, they are merely descriptions of the structural features of the international system. Yet, these allegedly objective terms have led to emotionally laden prospects: realists view the world in a profoundly pessimistic manner. Power struggles are eternal. Wars are ultimately unavoidable, and history would be, as Winston Churchill lamented, "one damned thing after another."[33] Mankind has made tremendous progress in running domestic politics: abolishing slavery, expanding suffrage, and protecting economic and social rights of minorities, to name but a few examples. Yet, when it comes to international relations, realists contend that we are no better than our ancestors thousands of years ago. What happened between Sparta and Athens has been repeated throughout history all over the world and will continue to do so in the future.

Liberalists, by contrast, are ultimately optimists. Liberalist philosophers, beginning with John Locke in the seventeenth century, saw great potential for human progress in modern civil society and a capitalist economy, both of which could flourish in states that guaranteed individual liberty. Modernity projects a new and better life, free of authoritarian government and with a much higher level of material welfare. Liberalist thinkers generally take a positive view of human nature. They have great faith in human reasoning. They are convinced that rational principles can be applied to international affairs. While acknowledging that individuals are self-interested and competitive up to a point, they also believe that individuals share many interests and thus engage in collaborative and cooperative social action, domestically as well as internationally, which results in greater benefits for everybody at home and abroad. Liberalists see cooperation as the only path for rational actors as they pursue prosperity in an interdependent world.

Whichever outlook one places one's faith in, the two perspectives are methodological partners—they both feature a deductive approach, an approach that imposes key terms and then points to the universal paths that such terms would dictate. This method has contributed to our understanding of international relations by highlighting generalizable patterns. By focusing on visible, quantifiable, and measurable indicators and on structures, they have conformed political inquiries to the postwar positivist trend of making social sciences truly "scientific."[34]

But such contributions have their own caveats. First, as the analytical framework focuses on structural properties and conclusions are foredrawn, teleological errors could happen. In the name of theoretical parsimony, "human factors" like personalities, perceptions, and preferences are often ruled out as intervening variables at best. Rationality is, after all, determined by impersonal structures. International relations, though conducted by people, are ultimately "just business," "not personal"—to borrow the famous quote from *The Godfather*. In the case of the movie, the plot reveals a quite different reality: many decisions made in the name of "business" are nonetheless immensely personal. When transplanted into social science inquiries, though, the "business, not personal" mantra would be more faithfully upheld. Human factors are often dismissed as unimportant or aberrant. The result is a mechanical, even robotic, portrayal of international politics.

A related problem is that an approach based on a foredrawn conclusion would blur the boundaries between scholarly analysis and political agendas. For a long time, those in favor of America having an engagement policy with China, liberalists predominantly, have adhered to the talking point that "if you treat China as an enemy, you are certain to have an enemy."[35] They employ this reasoning to challenge realists, seeing the latter's arguments as not only theoretically faulty but empirically dangerous. Predictions and yearnings have become two sides of the same coin.

But by criticizing realists as reckless, liberalists are committing their own teleological folly. Some liberalists, in a self-reflecting way, point out that the global surge of populist and nationalist sentiments, often supported by a racial, nativist undertone, is a backlash at liberalist policies.[36] Though liberalist analysis would point to an ultimately positive win-win scenario, average Joes in America and their counterparts in other countries cannot "feel it." And they cannot afford to go with simply having faith in a rosy prospect down the road. In a sense, making political analysis human again may start by acknowledging that people are risk averse and oriented toward the short term. Feeling marginalized and ignored, they resort to ballot boxes and other measures in an attempt to shape policy outcomes.

An inductive approach starts with a discursive mapping of actors and the content of their agendas. It does not reduce such agendas rigidly as derivative products of these actors' positions in the "system." After all, actors are not just puppets whose every move is pulled by strings that we call institutional arrangements. An inductive approach seeks to discern how actors formulate policies. In other words, it studies not just how actors implement policies. It starts by asking *what* actors want and *why*. Such problematizing invites questions on how actors calculate their benefits and gauge leverages vis-à-vis other actors. It also leads to the question of how actors interact with the relatively rigid institutional framework—when the framework could be used as a tool and when it becomes a barrier.

An inductive approach is thus more data driven. It aims at producing generalizable implications, too. But it does so by choosing a different path. For this project, I strive to show how certain themes—for example, actors' relations to legitimacy and their accesses to resources, both normative and materialistic—could shape their inputs in foreign policy making. And since such relations are dynamic, so are their roles and impacts.

These themes have a wider market beyond Zhongnanhai—the Chinese government's headquarters and thus the contemporary red chambers in Beijing. To trace changes over time, I see historicizing and contextualizing as crucial guidelines for my research. Practically, adhering to these guidelines translates into the extensive use of archival data and interviews. I carried out three rounds of fieldwork in China over a span of seven years from 2011 to 2018. I had three research sites: Beijing, Shanghai, and Changchun. To test the two themes' relevance in other settings, I also carried out short-term fieldwork in Japan in 2017. My research there helped me offer a discussion of the dual themes' wider application beyond China. This discussion takes place in the concluding chapter.

Archival data came in the form of declassified diplomatic files, memoirs written by leaders and their subordinates, media coverage, polls, and scholarly journals. I also subscribed to several public accounts on the WeChat platform—a mobile app that boasts more than a billion active users, mostly in China. These public accounts at WeChat would alert me to major news stories. Their utility did not stop there. They could also be used as political weathervanes. Securing access to sensitive stories often became a race against time with the Chinese censors. In fact, it would not be unusual for me to see some stories quickly evaporate in cyberspace, with only a government message popping up to announce vaguely that the story had been removed due to its "violation of relevant rules." On other occasions, the government might not even bother to offer an explanation. Readers would be led to a page with a hypertext transfer protocol (HTTP) code of 404—meaning "page not found." The Chinese public has become so used to bumping into this code that they have begun to use 404 as a verb and a selling point. Stories, sensitive or not, may be advertised as "Read quickly before it is 404ed!" to boost viewing. In any event, when such blatant censoring happens, the void or the 404 still serves as a canary in the coal mine, alerting me to varied levels of sensitivity that the government attached to these stories. The trace of a story could be as revealing as its content.

The contextualizing work was fulfilled by my use of interviews. My own journalistic background was certainly helpful in this regard. I did not use data solicited from interviews as primary sources of information. Rather, I used these opportunities to serve two purposes: first, interviews could alert me to subjects or arguments worthy of further research; second, they could be used as a confirming mechanism to help me double-check facts or sentiments that I collected from other sources. Most interviews were informal—to highlight my professional identity as an America-based political scientist interested in studying Chinese foreign policy would almost certainly make my job more difficult. My interviewees included officials (retired and current), journalists, and scholars. I also made use of the exchange network at my home institution here in the United States. I had a number of extensive conversations with visiting scholars from China. I found them to be more open when the conversations happened in the United States, even though I was still a stranger to them. There were also conversations carried out with former colleagues, family members, neighborhood association members, street vendors, and cab drivers. Though by no means scientific, such conversations did offer me a glimpse into popular sentiments, and they turned out to be surprisingly consensual. The last group, cab drivers, was particularly well known as barometers of popular sentiments to foreign journalists and scholars.[37] In many ways, they were the unofficial pundits on Chinese politics, only much funnier and more insightful. This point even seemed to be acknowledged by the Chinese government. The *Spring Festival Gala Show*, allegedly the most watched entertainment program in the world, has run multiple skit shows over the years featuring cab drivers as legendary narrators. When combined together, all these sources helped me present a multilevel, dynamic analysis of actors and their roles in Chinese foreign policy making.

Chapter Overviews

Leaders: When to Lead and When to Hide

In chapter 2, I examine the first actors, Chinese leaders. Plenty of studies have been conducted on the leaders' importance in policy making. In a country where electoral accountability does not exist, leaders seem all the more important. What I try to find out, though, are their dynamism and nuances: How do Chinese leaders exert their influence on foreign policy or, in some cases, refrain from doing so? What normative and structural factors shape their calculations? By assessing leaders' positions on the legitimacy spectrum and their uses of resources, I identify three types of leaders in foreign policy making: architects, disrupters, and managers.

An architect-type leader is a transformer. He is perceived as possessing a charismatic personality (I use the masculine pronoun because China is yet to elevate a female official to the position of head of the state or government). Such charisma may be either convincingly reflected by personal achievements or manufactured by a cult of personality. There is no clear demarcating line between the two. Even for leaders with a credible record of policy achievements, they often find a dose of personality cult helpful. Either way, a transformative, charismatic leader has become the personal embodiment of the regime's legitimacy. The arrow of influence flows from this person to regime legitimacy rather than vice versa. Leaders of this type also experience some major shocks, endogenous or exogenous, that compel them to establish new foreign policy paradigms. In other words, they need to come up with new ways of imagining their country's place in the world.

A transformative leader is not only a path trekker. The path he paves needs to be continuously walked on by future generations—that is, the institutional arrangements he puts in place and the norms and expectations he helps establish need to outlast his own time in office. His policies and, more importantly, his orientations and philosophies continue to define the scope of diplomatic adventures for leaders to come.

I identify two transformative Chinese leaders—Mao Zedong and Deng Xiaoping—with the current president, Xi Jinping, showing signs of becoming a third one. Mao's China started with major internal and external upheavals—the founding of a nation and the onset of the Cold War. Utilizing his towering authority, Mao designed a foreign policy paradigm with two conflictual dimensions: one consisted of highly interventionist policies driven by ideological fanaticism, and the other entailed cool-headed realist maneuvers based on situational ethics, alliance making, and a rejection of foreign intervention.

Mao's allegedly chosen heir, Hua Guofeng, would only become a blip on the screen. Paradoxically, though, Hua's timidity highlights the importance of personality—a crucial resource for actors at the individual level. Mao's eventual successor, Deng Xiaoping, built his legitimacy by charting China on the course of economic reform. On foreign policy, Deng's audacity was only half-hearted. He abandoned one dimension of the Maoist paradigm while reinforcing the other: the revolutionary fervor gave way to extreme pragmatism. But the realist dimension of situational ethics and an acute sensitivity to foreign intervention continued to dominate Deng's diplomatic thinking. In the wake of two new shocks—namely, the 1989 Tian'anmen Massacre and the end of the Cold War—Deng jolted China onto the track of market reform. The schism between the economy and politics would continue, as Deng imposed a new foreign policy orientation: to maintain low-profile diplomacy and to avoid claims of international leadership. As Deng's third chosen successor, Jiang Zemin, put it, the new foreign policy paradigm would be one characterized as "keep quiet and focus on making a fortune" (*mensheng fadacai*).[38] This wisdom, in the form of a twenty-four-character instruction, would define China's diplomatic behavior for the next two generations of leadership.

The 1989 Tian'anmen Massacre ushered in an era of rapid economic growth and political stagnation. Twenty years and two regular transfers of power later, a political backsliding would occur, as Xi Jinping entered Chinese leadership. In March 2018, China's nominal legislature, the National People's Congress, formally eliminated presidential term limits, thus paving the way for Xi to stay in office indefinitely. Deng had put the transformative policy of a mandatory retirement age in place to avoid repeating Mao's mistake. Now, the clock has been dialed back. Xi is widely perceived as the strongest leader China has seen since Deng and quite possibly since Mao. Given China's might, Western media outlets have come to label him the "most powerful man in the world."[39]

Xi's outsized persona is certainly a favorable condition for becoming a transformative leader—though in his case the strong-leader image owes in no small part to a new cult of personality. The existence of contextual shocks—the rise of populism and growing doubts about the global order based on liberal democracy—could also serve as good timing for the rise of assertive leaders. However, it remains to be seen how successful his efforts at abandoning Deng's leadership-avoidance diplomacy will be. Signs are mixed, and the staying power of his retrogressive domestic policies is under growing doubt. In fact, one unintended consequence of the trade war with America was a rare rebuke in 2018 that Xi faced at home on his strategy and leadership skills.[40] Such rebuking would emerge again in the early months of 2020. Following the death of whistleblower doctor Li Wenliang, a massive outpouring of anger dominated China's social media platforms toward the government's mishandling of the Covid-19 crisis. As numerous people voluntarily took part in China's allegedly first "online state funeral" for an ordinary hero, Xi all but disappeared from the official media. Government censors used to be quite efficient in getting rid of such stories. This time, however, for inexplicable reasons, they allowed this online uprising to survive for a few days, thus helping to expose the public's widespread frustration toward the government and its allegedly sole authority.

So, could Xi be a disrupter rather than a transformer? A disrupter-type leader shares a similarly lively personality with the transformative type. However, a disrupter may misperceive openings in foreign policy that are not there. Inadvertently, this person's exuberant character may boomerang back to become self-damaging, as political rivals use this as evidence of his running amok in foreign policy—an arena that emphasizes discipline and self-restraint. A disrupter ends up seeing not only his vision shelved and attacked but also his career cut short. China's reform-minded party general secretary Hu Yaobang would fit the image of such a tragic disrupter.

The majority of leaders whom China has produced are neither architects nor disrupters. They are transactional managers, focused on substantiating visions laid out by the architects. The Chinese political system has created two paths to becoming a transactional manager: one is by institutional design. China's dual-leadership structure, which permeates governable units at all levels, carves out a well-defined place for administrative technocrats. At the very top of the government echelon, this position would be the premiership. The traditional Chinese norms associated with a "grand chancellor" (*zaixiang*), the ancient equivalent of the modern premiership, have further reinforced the stereotypical framing of an ideal top career official: administratively competent yet politically timid. For technocrats, professing an unconditional loyalty to the political core is essential for their survival.

In recent decades this dual-leadership structure has evolved to further weaken the office of the premier. As the paradigm is set in stone by the architects, the political head, who is supposed to be a visionary figure, has stepped further into the field of policy formulation and execution—the traditional province of the premiership. This has created an identity crisis for premiers as they deal with an ever-shrinking autonomy. This tendency has become apparent under the reign of Xi Jinping; the party chief has been collecting one authoritative-sounding title after another. He has also filled important foreign policy posts with his loyal lieutenants, most notably Vice President

Wang Qishan and Vice Premier Liu He. With Xi expected to stay on for another decade or even longer, Premier Li Keqiang and his successors will be facing an ever-shrinking playing field vis-à-vis all the president's men.

Diplomats: From Plainclothes Soldier to Daughter-in-Law

In chapter 3, I examine the role of Chinese diplomats in foreign policy making. With China's rapid global ascendancy, a natural result is the country's growing diplomatic needs. One would expect this to be the golden era for the country's trained professionals charged with executing the country's foreign policy. However, Chinese diplomats are confronted with an uneasy reality. Yes, the country's diplomatic landscape has been expanding, and, yes, the Ministry of Foreign Affairs (MFA) has been accorded nominal significance, as attested to by the ministry's top position in the organizational structure of the Chinese government. Yet, Chinese diplomats are facing more and more challengers from lateral ministries and from society as they fight to maintain their policy influence. To say that the MFA is retreating in influence would be simplistic; this chapter portrays a ministry embattled but not retrenching. There are areas where its influence is shrinking, but there are also opportunities for MFA to expand its swagger.

The ongoing struggle of the Chinese diplomats starts with their boss—the foreign minister. I point to two recent undiplomatic moments featuring China's top diplomats, as they publicly lashed out at their foreign counterparts. The tendency to be assertive and acerbic on the global stage has now become almost a ministerial identity for the Chinese Foreign Ministry. In May 2020 at a press conference, the foreign minister openly embraced the moniker "wolf warrior diplomats" for himself and his subordinates. An individual-level historicizing will reveal, however, that such manning-up was artificial. Behind the attitudinal hardening of China's top diplomats is their rising sensitivity to heeding signals from the top. At the surface level, a question may be asked about why China's diplomats are becoming so brute. But at a deeper level the question flips, becoming one about bureaucratic timidity and paranoia.

Just like China's leaders, China's diplomats are carrying their own package of incentives and constraints in relation to legitimacy and resources. In recent decades, the MFA has been under duress from all directions. Multiple imbalances are all working to the disadvantage of diplomats: the first is institutional design. To be sure, the Chinese government has accorded the ministry pinnacle eminence: it has been consistently ranked as the top ministry in the government's organizational structure. The foreign minister, by default, is the top minister of any Chinese government. However, this ranking reveals, if anything, the amount of control and scrutiny the ministry will receive from the top rather than the influence it may exert the other way.

As in the case of leadership analysis, I also highlight the concept of legitimacy for diplomats. The foreign ministry's legitimacy is not only derived from the top—it also has been highly personalized. One leader in particular, Zhou Enlai, had a tremendous influence on defining ministerial norms and expectations governing China's diplomats. As the People's Republic of China's first premier and foreign minister, Zhou built a ministerial-level regime with the core identity of "plainclothes soldier" for Chinese diplomats. In practice, this translates into absolute loyalty and complete compliance to the party core—something Zhou personally practiced in managing his relations with Mao. Such demands have outlived Zhou's tenure. They remain the pivotal requirement for Chinese diplomats.

Such a holy obligation conceals an imbalance though: Chinese diplomats have received little in return for their unwavering loyalty. Coupled with their growing professionalism is a narrowing career path. Between Zhou Enlai and Wang Yi, the current foreign minister, the country has seen eleven ministers come and go. Using their pre-ministerial backgrounds as an indicator, one may place these diplomats into three categories: revolutionaries, young underground party activists, and career diplomats. With each generational change, Chinese foreign ministers see their distance from the party core slip away further: from premier and marshal to vice premier and now to state councillor.

Today, the clout of the Chinese foreign minister is not comparable to that of his Western counterparts, most notably the US secretary of state. However, the situation is changing, which could benefit top diplomats, as Xi Jinping crowned himself the "chairman of everything." In 2013, Xi Jinping set up the National Security Commission (NSC) to replace the ad hoc "leading groups" to handle major security issues. A first look at the Chinese NSC may reinforce the impression of the marginalization of Chinese diplomats in comparison with their American counterpart. The White House ranks the US secretary of state as the third most important member of the National Security Council, only after the president and vice president but ahead of the secretaries of treasury and defense.[41] The ranking is clear: America's top diplomat should definitely be among the core decision makers. When this fails to happen, it is a clear signal of political troubles. For evidence, one only needs to look at the fate of Secretary of State Rex Tillerson. By contrast, Tillerson's successor, Mike Pompeo, is not just a member of the National Security Council but also widely considered a close confidant of President Trump.[42]

Unlike its American counterpart, the Chinese NSC's membership is secretive. When founded in 2014, its publicized roster listed only four people: President Xi Jinping, Premier Li Keqiang, the chairman of the National People's Congress Li Zhanshu, and the director of the General Office of the Chinese Communist Party Ding Xuexiang. Both Li Zhanshu and Ding are regarded as Xi's loyal aides. It is not clear whether their presence in the NSC is due to the offices they hold or the personal trust they secured from Xi. Either way, the public roster does not offer a permanent seat to the foreign minister.

However, such unprecedented condensing of authority into one person's hand could be a blessing in disguise for Chinese diplomats, at least the top ones. As politics goes personalistic, a new role could be carved out for China's senior diplomats—diplomatic confidants for the one man. Sixteen years after Qian Qichen, a foreign minister popularly known as China's "diplomatic godfather," retired from the vice premiership, former minister Yang Jiechi finally ended the promotion drought by joining the Politburo in 2018, thus entering the rank of "national leadership." Since then, Yang has played the role of Xi's "personal envoy" by default on dealing with sensitive issues. Such a post-ministerial portfolio could mean a new spring of career enhancement. On the other hand, Yang and his future successors will continue to face intragroup competitors like Vice President Wang Qishan and Vice Premier Liu He in the fight for influence. The best that China's top diplomats could hope for would be a key yet murky position of councillor to the chairman.

Another battle confronting the MFA comes laterally from other ministries. They have begun to conduct their own diplomacies that better fit their own administrative responsibilities. The MFA's most formidable competition comes from the soldiers in uniform, the People's Liberation Army (PLA). Since making its debut in 2002, the Chinese military has been getting busier in carrying out its own diplomatic missions, primarily in the form of performing joint military exercises and sending delegates to international security conferences, most notably the annual Shangri-La Dialogue in Singapore. The PLA boasts a nationalistic indoctrination, a more rural demographic structure of recruits, and a revolutionary legacy based on direct lineage to the founding of the party. All these qualities would seem to put the soldiers in uniform on a path of value-based collision with the soldiers without uniform. In this competition for influence, people holding guns have a natural advantage over people holding pens. However, the MFA has its own strength in diplomatic experience and local knowledge possessed by its large staff stationed around the world. It comes as no surprise that the MFA rather than the PLA played a key role in coordinating the safe withdrawal of Chinese citizens from war-torn regions like Yemen and Libya.

One more source for the MFA's exhaustion comes from below: an overstretched ministry trying to satisfy rising demand from the masses, as people head to the world beyond China in ever-growing numbers. As more and more Chinese can afford to travel internationally, unbound by disciplines, the MFA is losing its materialistic allure as well. It has to battle a brain drain problem, as young talents are shunning or quitting the ministry. The ministry's morale has been further hit in its role as default scapegoat when the public voices its ire about Chinese diplomacy. This carries a dose of irony, for Chinese diplomats' actual influence on policy making is fading.

All these battles have put the MFA in a struggle to maintain momentum amid multiple contests. By borrowing a metaphor from a Chinese diplomat, chapter 3 concludes that the Chinese diplomats start working as plainclothes soldiers but end up behaving more like daughters-in-law in a traditional Chinese family: dutiful, loyal, obedient, serving multiple masters with conflictual agendas, and willing to take the blame if something goes wrong. Yet, also like many Chinese daughters-in-law, the MFA has been searching for ways to resist, rebel, and reclaim its pride and influence in a big family.

Celebrities, Masses, and Foreign Policy's Commercial Logic

Chapter 4 turns to societal forces and their growing impact on Chinese foreign policy. Like the preceding chapters, the analysis centers on the themes of legitimacy and packages of incentives and constraints. It first dissects the concept of "Chinese public." Before China's economy went market, the idea of "public" was a simple one; except for those who had the fortune of working at foreign-related systems (*duiwai xitong*), foreign policy was largely irrelevant to the overwhelming majority of Chinese people. China's polity ceremonially gives foundational legitimacy to "the people." In practice, though, the masses were strictly on the receiving end of the legitimacy spectrum. During the Mao era, this imbalance was pushed to the extreme: people's purpose of living their lives would lie in serving the chairman. Under the slogan of "many hands make our job easy" (*renduo haobanshi*), Mao was using China's almost inexhaustible manpower to carry out missions ranging from staging massive welcoming ceremonies to spreading revolutions across the globe. Some jobs were trivial, while others involved life-and-death consequences.

During the Deng era, the zeal of planting red flags around the world waned. A paradoxical transformation occurred: as China opened up, the public's presence in diplomacy atrophied. Deng called on the whole nation to turn its attention inward. "Catch up, or China's membership on the globe will be stripped," he warned.[43] Diplomacy returned to its elitist cocoon. In retrospect, this would be the golden era for Chinese officials in the country's foreign-related system, as they were among the few to have the privilege of traveling internationally and having access to sought-after commodities only available at government-run special stores.

As the country's economy took off, its diplomacy finally became relevant to the public on a personal level. Diplomacy was no longer just a mission. It became a service that the public could consume. The old role of the masses serving as a mobilization tool would stay. In other words, the masses would remain the droplets in the government's use of the "human wave" tactic. But people have been acquiring new roles too. Indeed, the word "public" itself has experienced stratification or can be used in plural forms: the masses as customers ready to consume the Chinese power they have produced; publicity hunters who seek fame and notoriety by sensationalizing diplomatic issues; and the media caught in between an information-yearning public on one side and a paranoid leadership on the other. The media have been utilizing the gap between spreading the words and abiding by propaganda principles to make a profit without being penalized.

A few cases reveal the public's role both as patriots and as constituents of Chinese diplomacy in this new era. The interplay of these two roles has led to unintended political and economic consequences. The first role, as patriots, is about the interplay between the people and the state centering on the theme of nationalism. Much study has been done on this topic.[44] One conventional wisdom is that the Chinese government has intensified its nationalistic indoctrination in the wake of the 1989 Tian'anmen Massacre. The end of the Cold War two years later added more urgency to the task. History-based studies, however, have shown that patriotism as a sentiment had a consistent presence among the Chinese masses.[45] Seen from this perspective, the public has not changed. It is the government that has adjusted its tactic. It used to view such sentiment with suspicion and hostility. After 1989, however, to find a source to rekindle its legitimacy, the government stole the show. It packaged and congratulated itself as the nation's tested savior. Meanwhile, the Chinese authorities pulled off the feat of nailing Jell-O to the wall—that is, they tamed the internet and turned it into a powerful tool for nationalistic propaganda.

My own examination shows multiple possibilities for state-public interactions over contentious diplomatic issues. The public, assisted by profit-driven media, can now play a "catch me if you can" game with the authorities. Yes, the media need to eventually abide by the party's propaganda instructions. But central planning has never done a good job of predicting contingencies—not in the past and certainly not now. The Covid-19 fiasco would be the latest example to support this point. The fact is that stuff happens. Technology has offered the public many access points to alternative information and spread it with lightning speed. The Chinese media have developed a pattern of first chasing the economic logic by covering these contingencies before they succumb to the political one of unifying their voices. In a sense, they have managed to have their cake and eat it too.

In addition, the state and the public are not always antagonistic toward China's rapidly growing social media platforms. The authorities need to use social media outlets as "input institutions" to gauge public sentiment. In this process, it has to tolerate some social space to exist. Susan Shirk once described how the Chinese state was walking on a tightrope of both needing *and* containing nationalism. This acrobatic act has created a "fragile superpower."[46] More than a decade later, such fragility has become all the more apparent.

As Chinese people's connections with the world have widened, they have also become constituents demanding services from the government. In this process, though, the public has inadvertently become teachers to the government, exposing the latter's ignorance or clumsy handling of policy issues— once again thanks to social media. One example is the latest flip-flop by the Shanghai municipal government on revoking *hukou* (family registration) for overseas Chinese. The government's initial response to public protests was to hold its ground. Yet, overwhelming public outcry that spread virulently over social media exposed the proposal's illegality. The public eventually shamed the government into retracting it.

Enduring patriotic sentiment, when coupled with the public's rising economic might, could produce all kinds of political possibilities that are tricky for everyone. In this light, I point to some new realities: the public as vigilantes voluntarily policing Chinese foreign policy and as consumers consuming patriotism as a form of entertainment. The case I use to illustrate the role of vigilantes is Beijing's "One China" policy toward Taiwan. After Tsai Ingwen's electoral victory in 2016 as Taiwan's first female president, she rejected Beijing's demand to accept the "One China" position as the precondition for cross-strait negotiations. Not surprisingly, then, Taiwan has become the new Japan to China, a popular and safe target toward which the public can unleash anger, hatred, and ridicule. A few recent incidents have occurred where Chinese, either overseas or at home, have challenged foreign businesses for commercial content deemed to violate Beijing's "One China" policy. Such popular assistance is not always welcomed by the Chinese government. Sometimes it can bring chagrin. For example, evidence has surfaced that some individuals are using such campaigns to choke commercial adversaries or personal foes. Even when the government realized this, it had to play along to protect its principled image—a textbook example of the tail wagging the dog.

Consumer identity in the public's relations to diplomacy, on the other hand, has added real monetary profits to all parties involved. By analyzing pro-government pundits and their followers, the viral popularity of China's anti-Japan TV dramas, and the latest big-budget movies lionizing China's rising impact, I point to an emerging economic ecosystem built on commercial logic: consumable patriotism. A booming mega-business is serving the economic interests of a plethora of actors at all levels: individual entrepreneurs, consumers, and local governments. One agent that could be troubled by the virulent commercial patriotism, though, is the central government. An explosive growth in patriotism-related movies has pumped up popular adrenaline. Chinese tourists are beginning to see every inconvenience they experience overseas, for example, flight or cruise delays, as an insult to China. An easily irritated public is likely to bring new headaches to an already exhausted bureaucracy and a permanently paranoid leadership.

Beyond China and Rethinking the Dream's Meanings

In the concluding chapter, I go beyond the Chinese context to detect the interactive pattern among leadership, bureaucrats, and society in other countries' foreign policy making. My generalizing effort begins with dissecting Chinese president Xi Jinping's pet slogan—the "Chinese Dream" (*zhongguo meng*). I contend that due to the phrase's vagueness, the Chinese Dream allows flexible and even conflictual interpretations. One may place numerous interpreting efforts on a range, with assertiveness and accommodation as its two ends. On the assertive end, the Chinese Dream is unapologetically Sino-centric, chauvinistic, and even racially nativist. It imagines a new world in which China replaces America as the sole global hegemon and other countries kneel down to the Middle Kingdom. On the opposing end, the Chinese Dream is based on a selectively benign interpretation of the Confucian concept of *Tian Xia*—all under heaven. It envisions a world of "huddled masses" under an open international order. China would be simply one in a crowd but would take pride in ushering in this new era of an accommodating *Tian Xia*. The Chinese government's official interpretation of the dream lies somewhere in between. It bends and welds the two interpretive ends—Sino-centrism in substance but packaged in an open, benevolent rhetoric. One diplomatic practice based on this amalgamation is the Chinese government's growing emphasis on *dandang*—the courage to take

the lead in a world from which America seems to b
ing. Despite that the Chinese Dream sounds suspi
famous motto—the American Dream—the two ;
ingly put their dreams on a collision course.

Furthermore, if we focus on the word "dream," we
sal truth embedded in this catchphrase: that is, if we c
lective pursuit of a grand vision and a search for a cr
among peers, then we live in a world of dreamers. As
destiny interacts with that of another, it leads to all kind; _merging and colliding possibilities.

Any nation's grand pursuit of its rightful place in the world is shaped by
two forces: one is emotive. It is about an impassioned imagination of a future
worth fighting for. The other force, however, has to be non-emotive. It needs
to be based on a cool-headed, cost-benefit calculation of how to get there.
These two forces do not always act in tandem. When they do not, a nation
feels anxious and torn.

Australia is a case in point. On the one hand, China has become Australia's most important trading partner. To a great extent the emergence of
boomtowns in Australia owes to China's rise.[47] In the 2018–19 fiscal year,
Australia's export revenues to China alone amounted to nearly one-third of
its overall exports. The value, which stood at US$99.9 billion, would be more
than two and a half times of what Australia sold to Japan, its second biggest
export market, and close to seven times of its exports to America.[48] The
China factor, on the other hand, has not only brought in profits but also
stirred up anxiety and created schism. As Australia's economic dream is
merging closer with that of China's, the country's value-based dream is pulling it in the opposite direction. China's ever-stronger commercial pull has
aroused Australians' concerns about their country's political integrity and
security. Such angst was most vividly captured by a dramatic moment when
the Australian prime minister Malcom Turnbull, mistakenly quoting Mao,
publicly warned Beijing that "Australian people have stood up."[49] Turnbull's
warning, delivered in Chinese, found a largely amused audience back in
China. It became a popular target of mockery and reinforced the Chinese
impression of Australia's secondary importance on the international stage.

My examination then turns to Japan, the concluding chapter's core case. I
investigate what roles Japanese leaders, bureaucrats, and the masses have
played in shaping their country's foreign policy. The purpose here is not to
offer a case analysis with the same depth that the Chinese case carries. Rather,
the purpose is to test the wider implications of the tripartite analytical framework. It offers an empirical hint at future research projects.

three groups of Japanese actors, their roles in foreign policy are
shaped by their relations to legitimacy, coupled with incentives and constraints imposed by norms and institutions. Take leadership, for example:
the three roles that the Chinese leaders have played can all find their Japanese
recruits. However, postwar Japan experienced a markedly different sequence
of contextual shocks: defeat, democratization, and the US-Japan Security
Alliance. The country's grand path was officially imposed by an external
power—this fact created unique political openings for and constraints on
the Japanese leadership. The country had fewer opportunities for creating an
architect-type leader. In fact, Yoshida Shigeru would be the lone Japanese
equivalent. His agenda was to transform Japan into a "good loser"; this translated into Japanese practices of offering deference to the institution, namely,
the US-Japan Security Alliance, but manipulating its content whenever possible to restore Japan's own policy autonomy. The Yoshida Doctrine, with its
two pillars of alliance with America and a mercantilist focus on international
trade, has continued to serve as the foundation of Japanese foreign policy to
this day. Yoshida's policy legitimacy has proved to be enduring.

While Japan has had fewer political architects, it has produced more
disrupters. Institutional design matters; being an electoral democracy
means lower risks for leaders who choose to rebel. For Chinese disrupters
like Hu Yaobang, "down and out" was the only consequence. Furthermore,
a Chinese leader's career demise and his physical demise could become disturbingly connected. For Japanese disrupters, thanks to democracy and
peaceful transfer of power, they could choose to be "out" without worrying
about "down." I then offer a dichotomy of two subtypes of Japanese disrupter: policy driven and personality driven. The leadership analysis ends
with a discussion on why, like China, the majority of Japanese leaders have
been managerial.

Moving on to the second group of actors, I show that Japanese diplomats
constitute a sharp contrast to their Chinese colleagues: they are nobody's
daughters-in-law. Unlike Chinese diplomats, whose legitimacy is derivative,
Japanese diplomats have long mastered the art of leading from behind. They
operate in a system under which one political party, the Liberal Democratic
Party, nominally reigns but allows the bureaucrats to rule.[50] Japanese bureaucrats' faith in their own independent legitimacy thus stems from their traditionally high degree of autonomy. I then use two cases, the stalemate in
Japan-Russia relations and the alleged "China School" sect of the Japanese
Foreign Ministry, to illustrate the constant tensions between the political
leadership and the diplomatic corps, as the two jockey to gain the commanding height of foreign policy making. Resentment by political leaders toward

bureaucrats has become bipartisan—governments led by both the Democratic Party of Japan and the Liberal Democratic Party have attempted to challenge "bureaucracy-centered" policy making (*kanryo seiji*). Prime Minister Abe Shinzo's plot of bypassing the foreign ministry to forge a personal bond with Donald Trump serves as the latest example.

The roles of the Japanese public in foreign policy are also quite different from those played by its Chinese counterpart. Both norms and structures account for such differences. The Japanese live in an affluent democracy where politicians' fates largely depend on how well they respond to constituents' local needs and desires. As in many other postindustrial democracies, voter attention to local issues in Japan far exceeds that to foreign policy.[51] The Japanese public is also less emotionally committed to the contentious issues Japan is having with China and South Korea, partly thanks to an awareness of alternative arguments even when people are not following them closely.

The Japanese public's roles in foreign policy are thus more latent. Paradoxically, though, such roles could be more powerful. After all, being an electoral democracy means the people are a more meaningful embodiment of legitimacy. They have real, institutionalized leverage vis-à-vis politicians and bureaucrats. At the macrolevel, a majority of citizens want to see their country maintain the delicate balance between strengthening the US-Japan alliance and upholding constitutional pacifism. At the microlevel, citizens exposed to alternative narratives have carried out their own personal-level diplomacies. Some endeavors, like the consistent presence of Japanese volunteers in China even in difficult situations, are enriching relations by making diplomacy human again.

This is not to say that the Japanese public's roles are uniformly positive. I point to two challenges confronting the Japanese public, one structural and the other normative. The structural one is Japan's looming demographic crisis. Put bluntly, the country is running out of young people, to whom the torch of fostering people-to-people exchange is supposed to be passed on. Even more worrisome is that the country is running out of young minds: as the Japanese ambassador to China Niwa Uichiro laments, even for Japan's young people, many are showing signs of becoming increasingly inward looking and timid of competitions.[52]

This book starts with the musing of a classic Chinese novel, *Dream of the Red Chamber*. It ends by returning to this great book. The "dream" in the book's title is not about imagining a future worth pursuing. It is about lamenting a past lost in perpetuity. Dreams could thus be either future oriented or past oriented. The line separating these two paths is not always clear. What has been happening to China, America, Russia, and the European Union, among other places, tells cautionary tales that tensions are abound and political backlashes are real. How can a leader's dream not become a nightmare for his people? How can a nation's desire for greatness not instill terror into others' minds? Tangled in layers of interest and conflict, a world of dreamers is still searching for an answer to this ultimately moral question.

2 • Architect, Disrupter, and Manager

Leaders and Foreign Policy

To Kunlun Mountain now I say, neither all your height, nor all your snow is needed. Could I but draw my sword o'ertopping heaven, I'd cleave you in three: one piece for Europe, one for America, and one to keep in the East. Peace would then reign over the world—the same warmth and cold throughout the globe.
　　—Chairman Mao Zedong, *Kunlun*

Foreign media call me "China's Gorbachev" or "Economic Tsar" or whatever. I am very unhappy with all these monikers.
　　—Premier Zhu Rongji

Who's Hu versus Xi's the Boss

If there were a Guinness award for the most awkward handshake in history, the one between Abe Shinzo and Xi Jinping would likely claim this title. On November 10, 2014, these two leaders met in Beijing on the sideline of the Asia-Pacific Economic Cooperation (APEC) annual summit. On the same day, Xi welcomed a number of other foreign dignitaries. He and those guests looked ebullient as they warmly shook hands. Behind them, the flags of China and the guest countries draped neatly alongside traditional Chinese paintings.

Alas, the visiting Japanese prime minister was in for special treatment. The Xi-Abe summit looked different than Xi's interactions with the other guests; in fact, it looked like a funeral. There were no flags and no artworks, only a dark blue velvet curtain to ensure that the beautiful paintings would be covered. The Chinese host obviously wanted the meeting place to look as unimpressive as possible. Abe approached Xi, extending his hand. As the handshake began, Abe appeared to be saying something to Xi. Instead of responding to Abe or at least acknowledging that he was listening, Xi abruptly looked away, almost closing his eyes. Abe got the message. Both men stared sternly into the cameras and let a barrage of flashlights capture their so-called handshake or, more accurately, two hands locked lifelessly together.

From the barren background to the frozen handshake, Xi was using every specific to tell the world he did not want to meet Abe. The meeting had to happen simply because China was always a merciful host. But through all the details, Xi was announcing to everyone that he had nothing but disdain for the Japanese prime minister. He succeeded: the handshake became bigger news than the meeting itself. Both the Chinese and the Japanese media lined up pictures of a beaming Xi meeting with other foreign heads of state to prove the point everybody knew—what happened between Xi and Abe was not normal. The moment quickly morphed into a global sensation. Even late-night TV host Jon Stewart weighed in, using profanity-laced language to tell his American audience that if they think America's relations with Russia are awkward, look at the meeting between China and Japan, because *that's* how bad two countries' relations could become.[1]

The ungentlemanly moment also hinted at things that would grow clearer in forthcoming years: Xi's personality and authority. Chinese leaders rarely display hostility at diplomatic occasions. In fact, they rarely display any emotion. In their stiff and wooden demeanor, they are heeding the teachings of Zhou Enlai to the extreme. After all, Premier Zhou, who died in 1976, is still viewed by many as the most competent diplomat the People's Republic has ever produced. Zhou once reminded his subordinates, "There is no such thing called a trivial matter in diplomacy" (*waijiao wu xiaoshi*).[2] Since every moment is a major moment, those who are in it need to exercise extreme caution. In practice, this translates into timidity. As Prince Charles mocked in his dairy, Chinese officials struck him as a "group of appalling wax works."[3] Yet, being waxy is politically safe.

Even when unexpected incidents occur, Chinese leaders' intuitive response is to follow the script to the letter. For example, on April 20, 2006, a Falungong activist entered the White House South Lawn with a press credential. There, President George W. Bush was welcoming Chinese President Hu Jintao with pomp and ceremony—something the Chinese side had requested for years.[4] As Hu was delivering his propaganda speech praising the China-America friendship, the activist began screaming at him. She yelled that his days were numbered. She also demanded him to pay with his blood for the persecution of Falungong followers. Hu went on as if he were in a parallel yet tranquil universe, not sensing anything wrong. But everyone else, caught in the midst of Hu's speech and the protestor's shrieking, knew something *was* wrong. President Bush, who was not particularly known for his wit, patted Hu on the back and said, "You're OK."

The Chinese president turned out to be anything but OK. Hu was not in a parallel universe after all. He knew exactly what had happened. Hu attempted to leave the podium the moment he was done with the speech, forgetting that President Bush had yet to deliver his welcoming remarks. To make Hu stay, Bush grabbed his arm and accidentally ripped the Chinese president's suit sleeve. This was certainly *not* the grand welcome ceremony the Chinese had asked for. As a minor comfort, China Central Television, by using the broadcast delay technique, blocked this embarrassing moment to the Chinese audience.

Here is the sad point: Chinese leaders were not born wooden and stiff. They evolved into the epitome of boredom because they needed to survive. Again, Hu serves as a revealing example—as a young man, he used to be a lead dancer at college. In the online world, a widely circulated video shows Hu in his early forties hosting a Chinese New Year's gathering. He sprints to the stage and offers a passionate welcome speech to attending party elders, beaming radiantly. Chinese netizens were amazed by how lively and happy Hu once looked. They could not help lamenting how politics weathered a person.[5]

Hu's timidity was thus acquired. This trait became more pronounced as he climbed higher up the political ladder. Though groomed to be China's future leader at the relatively young age of forty-nine, Hu never seemed confident, thus earning him the nickname "petty daughter-in-law" (*xiaoxifu*) among Chinese netizens.[6] Like a timid daughter-in-law, his job was not to lead but to obey. The display of emotions is not just unnecessary; it could also be risky. Hu and other daughter-in-law-type leaders are inclined to following the script, even when the script is collapsing. To be sure, there are moments when they disagree with foreign counterparts, but when that happens, they tend to stick to the talking points in public: cooperation, common interest, and mutual respect. This "shut the door and let's talk" tactic (*guan qi men lai tan*) makes sense. It is human to err. But since Chinese leaders never make mistakes, they can only be human behind closed doors.

Then entered Xi. His act of openly humiliating a foreign guest would have made Zhou Enlai roll over in his grave. But Xi does not seem to care. Four more years had to pass before Xi eliminated the presidential term limit, a move that sealed his status as China's most powerful leader since Deng Xiaoping and quite possibly since Mao Zedong. But by 2014, Xi was already feeling safe about adding his own color to the boring game called Chinese diplomacy. Indeed, Xi's open snub of Abe was not the first time he stirred up international controversy. In 2011, when visiting Mexico as vice president, he used a slang to describe Western critics who condemned China's human rights as "well-fed foreigners who have nothing better to do."[7] In Beijing dialect, this slang is typically associated with the image of a neighborhood hooligan who has too much time on his hands and ends up using this luxury to annoy everyone. After delivering this not so subtle zing at America and its Western allies, Xi went on: "First, China doesn't export revolution; second, China doesn't export hunger and poverty; third, China doesn't come and cause you headaches, what more to be said?"[8]

This unusual blurt happened at a time when Xi was still under the tutelage of the third generation of leadership headed by Hu. At the time, this hardline rant triggered a fervent online discussion: Was Xi's colloquial remarks premeditated, or was he running amok? Seven years later, the message became clearer: Xi was no daughter-in-law. He was ready to be the boss.

The Rise, Fall, and Resurgence of Studying Leaders

There was a time when the world stage of diplomacy was filled with figures like Xi. In a sense, the study of international relations began as a study of leaders—kings, princes, popes, generals, and other larger-than-life individuals. Some accomplished amazing feats. Others committed disastrous follies. Either way, their personal choices and characters became the destinies of their people.

Classical realism, the oldest school of thought on international relations, put a tremendous emphasis on leaders' wisdom. In the words of Niccolo Machiavelli, a leader—or a prince in his time—needed to be both a lion and a fox.[9] In other words, a leader needed to be both strong and cunning, ready to fight and deceive to protect his subjects. Values that would make someone a nice person—for example, compassion, honesty, tolerance—would make this very person a most irresponsible leader in international relations. A great leader is thus someone who knows when *not* to be good. Machiavelli's advice was offered not just for princes of powerful kingdoms. In fact, dark wisdom would matter even more to leaders governing smaller and weaker territories. To them, all was not doomed. The path to survival lay in having an acute sense of their kingdoms' place in the jungle, forging alliances, and biding time for their future rise.

Realism remains one of the most influential theories in the study of international relations. Even to those who reject realist thinking, they often need to define their perspectives in relation to realism: that is, how their analysis has emerged as a meaningful critique of realism. Meanwhile, realism itself is not static. It has undergone major transformations. Under the influence of a behavioral revolution, a new generation of international relations scholars began to question the utility of studying human nature. Their interest was in finding the structure of the international system. One change, as a result, was that leadership studies fell out of favor.

Kenneth Waltz, a pioneering scholar of the postwar neorealism school, shared classical realists' unwavering faith in power. But to Waltz and his fellow neorealists, power is not something to be generated or amplified through a leader's calculation. Power is an objective fact observable through "static indicators."[10] Neorealists are hence also known as structural realists. To them, international relations are impersonal. They run like clockwork. The core piece of the machine is anarchy—the absence of world government. All states are busy taking care of themselves, yet no one is taking care of the system.

Neorealists shed anarchy's negative connotation. The term no longer means the dark province where mayhem reigns and death lurks. Rather, anarchy is the most foundational certainty, the basic law governing interactions among states. And laws are good—they create assurances, cooperative or destructive, and assurances lead to peace. Laws are good also because they are independent of individual desires. All the states are like-units—they are essentially the same living entities performing identical functions of survival. The only difference is how much power one possesses. To use an avian metaphor, one state would be a sparrow and the other an eagle, yet birds are birds. As the Chinese proverb puts it, "A sparrow may be small, but it has all the vital organs there" (*maque sui xiao, wuzang juquan*).

In a sense, neorealists relieved leaders of the burden of leadership, for international relations looked increasingly like a user's manual, and not even a thick one: anarchy on page 1 and knowing your friends and enemies on page 2. Following them does not require a whole lot of visionary power. It only requires rationality or, in other words, sanity.[11]

Fast-forward to the world today, and anarchy is still with us, but the clock known as international relations is running on very different time from the one that Waltz described in his groundbreaking work in 1979. A number of reasons account for the resurgence of the study of leaders. First, even as neorealists sought to impersonalize the study of international relations, they were not observing our world from the stratosphere. We are all products of our time. There is a reason why neorealism quickly gained influence during the Cold War—a reason revealed by John Mearsheimer when he lamented that we would soon come to miss the end of the Cold War: a world of bipolarity, a world of black and white, where everyone was keenly aware of who were the enemies and who were the friends, along with what their interests were and were not.[12] Indeed, to neorealists, calling the years between 1947 and 1991 the Cold War would be misleading. They were really the years of Cold Peace.

Neorealists were right: the world during the Cold War was indeed filled with certainties, the most effective one being mutually assured destruction (MAD). In such a MAD world, there was not much room, or need, for leadership creativity. Neorealists were also right in foreseeing that bipolarity's demise would open the gate to a flood of uncertainties and contingencies. Debates are still going on about the exact nature of the world today, whether unipolarity, multipolarity, or bipolarity 2.0. Boundaries among friends and foes, domestic and international politics, and opportunity and crisis are all becoming increasingly obscure. Popular anxiety is surging, so is the demand for leaders' ability to see and lead.

In fact, even during the Cold War years, the study of leaders never should have faded. To neorealists, because everything was mechanical, power became almost hereditary. To continue the avian metaphor, the huge discrepancy in size between a sparrow and an eagle determines the very different ways the two birds behave. However, one thing that cannot happen in the animal world but has happened in the human world is this: while a sparrow and an eagle can never trade places, the vicissitudes of states in relation to one another have never stopped. A weak state (i.e., a sparrow) may become a strong, soaring power (i.e., an eagle) in a relatively short period of time. Other states, though, would decline and decay so much that they would have to make peace with shrinking ambitions. As a case in point, Japan's diplomatic veteran Tanaka Hitoshi admitted that he, like many of his cohorts, never thought China would become a "big" country.[13] It would not be unreasonable to deduct that for Japan's policy elites in the 1970s and 1980s, China was no more than an oversized sparrow. As a counterexample, even as he was attempting to rekindle his people's hope, Japanese prime minister Abe admitted there is a widely shared sentiment that the sun has set on Japan's future.[14]

The change in power dynamics between Japan and China is not one between a sparrow and an eagle. However, it is true that China's global ascendancy has been meteoric in the past three decades and that Chinese leaders have played a key role in making this happen—though now it looks like they could also be key to stalling it. As another example, much study has been conducted on the political engineering by Nelson Mandela. His vision of transforming South Africa into a "Rainbow Nation," substantiated by policies ranging from setting up truth and reconciliation commissions to enshrining diversities of all sorts, guided the country's relatively smooth transition into a democracy.[15] Furthermore, these policies have offered inspiration for reconciliation projects in other parts of the world. The post-Mandela South Africa has failed, however, to live up to the great expectations his presidency excited. As scholars and media pundits lamented South Africa's downward drift, they identified incompetent leaders as a key reason for the country's stumbles.[16] For good and bad consequences, leadership matters.

We expect leaders to act decisively at uncertain moments. Neglecting leadership studies leaves us ill-equipped to explain the dynamic movements of their countries in the "system"—a concept that structuralists hold dear. But the system is anything but imperturbable. Even when it seems quiet, it could be a volcano in dormancy, with eruptive forces seething underneath. For an example one needs to look no further than the European integration experience. The expansion of a seemingly impersonal "system" may have seemed unstoppable. But it ended up helping the resurgence of leaders and their very personalistic style of politics. In retrospect, even during the heydays of European integration, scholars noticed the dilemma of a "democratic deficit": politics in the European Union was so institutionalized at a supranational level, Eurocrats gathered such tremendous power yet were not held accountable to electoral interests in member states, the EU governance was so devoid of emotions and sentiments, eventually a very emotional backlash would occur.[17]

This fear is now a real-time reality show: amid raw emotions, one major player, Britain, has left the organization. For those who are still in, some are experiencing democratic retrogression. Europe is witnessing the rise of illiberal, xenophobic leaders like Viktor Orban of Hungary, Milos Zeman of the Czech Republic, Andrzej Duda of Poland, Sebastian Kurz of Austria, and Matteo Salvini of Italy, among others. Isaac Newton's third law of action and reaction, it turns out, applies to international relations as well. What Newton did not foresee, though, is that one could punch his own face with one hard blow after another just to feel the pain. What a regret he missed the EU era.

Counting Chinese Leaders: Not Math but Art

A study of leaders needs to start with a mapping of cases—who are the leaders? The answer is not as simple as it seems, especially for China. There, the counting of leaders is an Orwellian art rather than a simple tally. The country's official chronology looks impressively neat—it uses the unit of generation to sort leaders into groups, and the country has produced five generations of leaders: Mao Zedong, Deng Xiaoping, Jiang Zemin, Hu Jintao, and Xi Jinping. As a corroborative note to this official counting, five floats, each a giant portrait of these leaders, passed by Tian'anmen Square in the country's massive celebration of the 70th anniversary on October 1, 2019. However, there are black holes in this otherwise neat universe of stellar leaders. These black holes are reserved for disrupters and underperformers. They were purged and forgotten as if they never really existed. Hence, a more accurate title for the officially recognized five leaders would be five survivors. The five floats were a celebration of their very existence.

The aim of this chapter is to detect patterns of how Chinese leaders influence foreign policy making. Given this purpose, I find it neither possible nor desirable to discuss each and every leader counted and uncounted in the official chronology. Instead, I identify cases that would distinctly fit into some leadership roles, with an eye on borderline candidates. The assessment is conducted by examining the interplay of factors identified in the preceding chapter: leaders' relations to regime legitimacy and their idiosyncratic packages of resources and constraints. In the latter group I particularly highlight personality and contextual contingencies. The list that such an analysis generates is indicative rather than exhaustive. My purpose is to create a thematic palette on which a particular leader may be portrayed (fig. 2.1).

As figure 2.1 demonstrates, I place Chinese leaders into three groups related to their roles in foreign policy making: architects, managers, and disrupters. These labels are not value laden. I employ them to weigh the varied impacts these leaders have exerted on Chinese foreign policy. I define architect-type leaders as those who either created or fundamentally changed norms, identities, and expectations associated with their country's foreign policy and whose changes are sustaining. An architect is not necessarily progressive. The rules and institutions an architect-type leader constructs could be revisionist in nature. The key here is a leader's ability to make paradigm changes and ensure these changes outlive his tenure.

Manager-type leaders, by contrast, focus on improving, enriching, and consolidating existing arrangements rather than building something anew. Their legitimacy is often derivative, sensitive to their performances of materializing the norms and expectations that architects laid down. The goals that managerial leaders set to achieve are different from those of architect-type leaders. To use a comparison familiar to people in the business world, the difference between architect-type leaders and manager-type ones is one between being transformative and being transactional.[18]

Leaders' Roles on Policymaking Spectrum

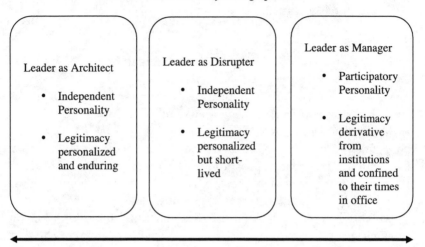

Fig. 2.1. Factors shaping leadership roles in foreign policy

A third possibility is a disrupter. Disrupter-type leaders are not necessarily underperformers. In fact, when it comes to personality and ambition, disrupters often come close to architects. During their tenure, they often managed to shatter norms and destabilize existing policies. However, either they failed to replace what they had destroyed with functioning new policies, or the new courses they charted were quickly abandoned once they left office. In a few extreme cases, disrupters paid a costly personal price for the vision they championed.

Of the three types, transformative architects are the rarest. This is understandable—a state that constantly witnesses one transformer after another is one where something major is persistently wrong. Indeed, what makes a leader an architect is the stability he bequeaths to future generations. Both the norms and the policies he puts in place will be institutionalized, enduring after his physical departure. The rarity of architect-type leaders also means that the mainstream type for the majority of leaders is thus competent manager. The third type, disrupters, is unique: in the Chinese system, it is not a role by choice but by consequence.

These three types are not mutually exclusive. Instead, they create a continuum of tints and shades on the leadership spectrum. Even for architect-type leaders, their job invariably has a manager component to it. Some architects have also at times become disrupters to the very norms and institutions they previously built. Likewise, manager-type leaders may prepare the stage for the rise of the next architect.

Architects: From Monkey King to Chinese Dreamer

Character is destiny. For transformative architect-type leaders, their personal characters have shaped the destinies of their people. As the Chinese proverb goes, "Times produce their heroes" (*shishi zao yingxiong*). The word "times" (*shishi*) paints an unmistakable image of disarray, misfortune, and confusion, often of epic proportions. The "times" are never supposed to be peaceful. For better, more prosperous eras, the Chinese would use the term "*shengshi*," which literally means "glorious world." Since the late 1990s, the country's propaganda apparatus has constantly used "*shengshi*" to remind its people how good their lives have become and how grateful they should feel to the government, the party, and the leader.

What is unique to architects, though, is that they are not only the products of their times. They are also the creators of new eras, hence the latter half of the proverb—"Heroes make their own times" (*yingxiong zao shishi*). A chaotic time is bad for everyone except transformative leaders. Rising from mayhem, they succeed in reshaping the world to their own preferred vision. In doing so, architect-type leaders create a new paradigm consisting of both norms and policies. This paradigm, which carries their strong personal colors, constitutes the foundation of legitimacy on which future leaders govern. Using these criteria, Mao Zedong and Deng Xiaoping fit this type. Xi Jinping, the current leader, is yet to make the cut despite the media framing him as among the most powerful people in the world. The revisionist nature of his policies invites suspicion about the endurance of his legitimacy.

Mao's towering charisma is widely acknowledged. To borrow the words of Jonathan Spence, this is a leader "who loved to thrust himself forward into the limelight, and never shrank from taking credit for China's perpetual upheavals."[19] As a native speaker of Chinese, I first sensed Mao's commanding authority through a linguistic lens—that is, by trying to understand what the chairman was trying to say in the first place. Mao spoke Chinese with such a thick Hu'nan accent that it was often unintelligible to me. I am certainly not alone—there are many accounts of people who met Mao and later admitted they had great difficulty in understanding him.[20] Fortunately, China's largely unified writing system could decode numerous accents and dialects into a common written language. But a new problem emerged—as I was reading the transcript of Mao's conversations with foreign guests, I often found myself getting more confused, unable to trace his thinking process. Sporadic ideas on unrelated topics seemed to sprout out all the time. The following conversation between Mao, Zhou Enlai, Henry Kissinger, and Richard Nixon during the latter's historic visit to China in 1972 serves as an example:

PRIME MINISTER ZHOU: Dr. Kissinger doesn't run for President because he wasn't born a citizen of the United States.

DR. KISSINGER: Miss Tang [*Tang Wensheng, Mao's interpreter, who was born in America*] is eligible to be President of the United States.

PRESIDENT NIXON: She would be the first woman President. There's our candidate.

CHAIRMAN MAO: It would be very dangerous if you have such a candidate. But let us speak the truth. As for the Democratic Party, if they come into office again, we cannot avoid contacting them.

PRESIDENT NIXON: We understand. We will hope that we don't give you that problem.

CHAIRMAN MAO: Those questions are not questions to be discussed in my place. They should be discussed with the Premier. I discuss philosophical questions. That is to say, I voted for you during your election. There is an American here called Mr. Frank Coe, and he wrote an article precisely at the time when your country was in havoc, during your last electoral campaign. He said you were going to be elected President. I appreciated that article very much. But now he is against the visit.

I remember this conversation well, for when I was an undergraduate at Fudan University, my rebellious young political science instructor used this episode as an example of Mao's already quite incoherent and incomprehensible thought process—in just two exchanges Mao changed topics four times. The instructor also showed us the official narrative. As a documentary described it, "Chairman Mao is in complete control of his conversation with Nixon, just like a steed freely roaming the sky."[21]

More than twenty years later, as I revisited this conversation, I still found myself bewildered. I further wondered that if I, a native speaker with training in political science, could not follow the flow of the chairman's thoughts, how could his guests not get lost in translation? Maybe both my instructor and the official narrative were right—as incoherent as he sounded, Mao *was* in complete control. Even when his guests had doubts about what the chairman was trying to say, no one had any doubts about his supreme authority.

A charismatic personality is an innate psychological quality that could prepare one leader for prime time and cause another to go down in flames. A poet, calligrapher, and voracious reader of Chinese classics, Mao displayed his charismatic character through all of these venues. Topics of his poetry, written in the traditional romantic genre, range from mocking emperors to chopping down mountains with a sword to offering tender verses for his spouses. His unique style of calligraphy, still widely displayed in China more than that of any other leader, was described by Chinese admirers as "free-spirited" and by the British Museum as "wild" and "intimidating."[22] Though he typically spent his time reading nonfictional history books, Mao loved fiction as well. Besides *Dream of the Red Chamber*, another great book Mao repeatedly quoted from was the Ming Dynasty mysterious novel *Journey to the West*. He stacked five different editions of the novel in his bedroom and penned down extensive remarks throughout their pages.[23] When commenting on affairs at home and abroad, Mao on many occasions mentioned the Monkey King, a heroic rebel in the novel. The Monkey King announces himself as the "Great Sage Equal to Heaven" (*Qitian dasheng*). He fights all the way up to where the Jade Emperor lives and causes great havoc.

By constantly bringing up the Monkey King with an admiring tone, Mao left no doubt as to who he perceived as the real, human Monkey King—himself. Throughout his tumultuous life, Mao saw Jade Emperors at every turn: Chiang Kai-shek, America, and the Soviet Union, among other captive evil spirits (*niugui sheshen*) like Japan and South Vietnam. In stirring up one maelstrom after another, Mao secured his paramount authority by not only leading but also participating. One only needs to think of the costly price his family paid: his first wife and younger brother were executed, his oldest son was killed by American bombing, the youngest son died of dysentery at the very young age of three or four, and the only surviving son was beaten severely by the Shanghai police and became schizophrenic. As Mao lamented: "Chinese tradition only honors sons as inheritors. Daughters do not count. One of my sons was killed, another gone crazy. It seems to me I do not have any male heir left."[24]

Mao's policies were brutal and their consequences calamitous. Yet, his revolutionary passion and all his personal sacrifices made his authority genuine and his legitimacy enduring. To him, the title of the nation's founding father was earned rather than bestowed. Not only Mao's followers but also neutral observers seem to acknowledge this point. Upon his death, the *New York Times* referred to him as "history's great revolutionary figure."[25] A few years prior to his death, all mainstream Japanese media outlets, including conservative ones, offered lavish praise to Mao's China, seeing it as a moral example for Japan to follow.[26] However misleading, Mao kindled real passions at home and abroad. As a contrasting example, Josef Stalin could arouse only fear.

Mao's influence on Chinese foreign policy is far-reaching. In fact, such influence may even be greater than the one Mao exerted on domestic politics. Deng Xiaoping built his own brand of transformative leadership by abandoning most of Mao's policies. However, at the orientational and strategic levels, many of Mao's thoughts on foreign policy have withstood China's tremendous transformations since his death. With Xi Jinping dialing the clock back to totalitarian time, Mao's ideals and practices may even experience a second spring.

Mao built a diplomatic paradigm with two somewhat conflicting dimensions: the Monkey King dimension, where China proclaimed itself a warrior of the suppressed, destined to topple down the old-world order. In practice, this would be translated into highly interventionist foreign policies with a fanatical passion. On the other hand, Mao was the country's first great balancer. He possessed all the moves that made him a staunch realist: situational ethics, about-faces on policies, and alliance making. Machiavelli was a contemporary of Wu Cheng'en, the Chinese author of *Journey to the West*. Though the Italian would never hear of the Monkey King, he would have definitely seen Mao as a canny fox who knew when *not* to be good. At a time when China was weak and brutal, Mao made his country appear more important than it actually was. Although Mao shut China's door to the outside world and impoverished his people, he affected the world through moral appeals and mobilized an army of followers, both figuratively and substantively, far beyond China's borders.

In retrospect, these two dimensions were not equal: successive Chinese leaders since Deng Xiaoping have largely dismantled or suppressed the interventionist dimension of Chinese foreign policy—until now. The realist dimension, on the other hand, is so deeply entrenched that it has become an instinct in Chinese foreign policy. As a paradox, these two dimensions constitute two sides of the same coin: the intervention in other countries' affairs and the adamant refusal to allow the meddling of foreign influence in its own affairs. This double standard continues to guide Chinese diplomacy today.

Mao was already a revolutionary icon during his time. Before the concept of "soft power" was even coined, Mao was already a skilled practitioner of diplomatic wooing. He awed audiences near and afar, and he turned such awe into a larger-than-life presence not only for himself but also for China. Mao's agenda stemmed from his faith in the genuine urgency of liberating the suppressed. In answering American writer Edgar Snow's question of what socialist revolutions elsewhere could borrow from the Chinese experience, Mao wondered, given the rapidly expanding gap between the Third World and more affluent countries, "Will time wait for the Soviet Union to demonstrate the superiority of the socialist system—and then wait a century for parliamentarianism to arise in the underdeveloped areas and peacefully establish socialism?" Mao's answer was that his patience was running out.[27] If Moscow was too timid to lead a global revolutionary offense, China would take charge.

Southeast Asia bore the brunt of Mao's interventionist fervor. Even China's own scholars and diplomats admitted that Chinese foreign policy toward the region during the Mao era was "overly ideological."[28] Southeast Asia served as the front of Mao's ideological crusade. China's interventions started with a strong anti-America message: recipients of Beijing's aid included both communists in Indochina who were openly fighting America and clandestine militia groups in Thailand, Malaysia, Burma, and the Philippines, among others. Beijing was not shy about its purpose: to overthrow allegedly pro-America governments in the region. An editorial by the *People's Daily* that justified Chinese intervention in Thailand was revealing in this regard: it proclaimed that China had a "righteous and irrefutable responsibility" (*yiburongci*) to assist Thai people's armed struggle "against American imperialism and its tail-wagging Thai dogs."[29]

Frustrated by the appeasing Soviet Union under Nikita Khrushchev, Mao further expanded China's instigation from "Lean to One Side" to "Hit with Two Fists"—now both America and the Soviet Union were targets. As Mao saw enemies everywhere, in the end it was Beijing that suffered the severest debacle: a military coup occurred in Indonesia in 1965. It overthrew the Sukarno government, which had been on increasingly friendly terms with China. Military officers led by Major General Suharto wiped out the communists, expelled Chinese diplomats, and cut off relations with Beijing altogether. Ensuing mass killings claimed numerous lives, with most estimates ranging from five hundred thousand to one million.[30] Chinese interventions in Thailand, Burma, Malaysia, and the Philippines suffered similar fates. By the late 1960s, realities on the ground would be quite to the contrary of what Mao would want his people to believe—a 1968 *People's Daily* map illustration showed major players in the region (Burma, Thailand, the Philippines, Laos, Vietnam, Malaysia, and Indonesia) as all being engulfed by "armed" and "anti-imperialist" struggles. The world situation, as the map title suggests, was "splendid."[31] The reality, though, was a whole different story. Although governments in the region might be ambivalent about choosing sides between the Soviet Union and America, they had a consensus on whom to kick out—China. Revealingly, the region's distrust of China was so deep that it refused to let its guard down even after Deng Xiaoping jolted the country down a different path. Trade connections prospered, but the region was slow to resume political ties with China. Singapore would be the last Association of Southeast Asian Nations member to normalize relations with China. It did not do so until 1990. For many in the region, the trauma was too acute to be brushed aside.

Southeast Asia is but one example. In the 1960s, Mao put leaders in Africa into three ideological groups—left, centrist, and right—depending on their attitudes toward America. In the 1970s, African leaders' attitudes toward the Soviet Union became the litmus test. Those who were loudly against Moscow would receive the most generous aid. A Chinese diplomat at the time recalled the experience of setting up "Mao Zedong Thought propaganda units" and local "Green Guards" to overthrow the host governments.[32] The amount of Chinese aid to Africa was remarkable, particularly in light of the fact that the Chinese economy was much smaller than what it is today. Between 1956 and 1976, China offered aid to thirty-eight African countries totaling US$21.7 billion. Proclaiming Chinese aid to be "generous and unselfish" (dafang kangkai) and "having no consideration on costs" (buji chengben), China experienced a fiscal hemorrhage. By 1973, Chinese foreign aid consumed 12.43 percent of the government's total expenditure. Aid to Africa alone reached the amount of US$182 million, compelling Deng Xiaoping to scale back aid in 1975. As one Chinese scholar reflected, it was a period of China "hitting its own face swollen to appear fat" (dazhonglian chongpanzi), that is, offering foreign aid beyond what it could afford.[33]

Financial burden was not the only dire consequence China had to confront. Chinese money was simply squandered in many cases. It did not buy Beijing the political allegiance it had hoped for. Chinese diplomats on the ground soon realized that the recipient countries had no qualms with receiving the aid without following Beijing's preferred agendas, resulting in a situation of "major betrayals by major recipients, minor betrayals by minor recipients, and no betrayals by those who did not receive anything."[34]

Given its costs and disastrous results, it is no surprise that Deng abolished the interventionist dimension of Mao's diplomatic paradigm. But he and other Chinese leaders continued to uphold the realist, interest-based one. In January 1949, still nine months away from announcing the founding of the People's Republic, Mao laid out metaphorically the new country's three basic diplomatic principles:

1. Set up a new kitchen.
2. Clean the house and then invite guests.
3. Lean toward one side.

As Mao elaborated, the "new kitchen" metaphor referred to cutting off diplomatic relations with all those who recognized Chiang Kai-shek's nationalist government; the house-cleaning metaphor referred to the need to eliminate foreign influence before resuming connections; and the leaning metaphor meant forging an alliance with the communist bloc led by the Soviet Union.

The first two principles still govern Chinese diplomacy today. Sensitivity to foreign intervention was built into the new country's diplomatic genes from the very beginning. The "lean toward one side" principle would suggest China's one balancing act after another. To Mao, China's independence was his only consistent pursuit. Yet, realizing how weak and poor the country was, he would forge, abandon, and switch friendships with great dexterity. Shaking hands with the president of the country that killed his son, Mao told Richard Nixon: "I was only creating some loud sounds by saying things like 'down with American imperialism.' . . . If you were really down and out, we no longer had any friends."[35] Mao went so far as to say he liked rightists and the Republican Party, a point elaborated by Nixon that in America, "those on the right can do what those on the left talk about." When Kissinger pointed out that the left were also "pro-Soviet," Mao answered: "Exactly that."[36] Throughout multiple conversations between the three men, Mao repeatedly brought up two countries with great concern: the Soviet Union and India, two powers he had once built alliances with.

China's independence became Mao's most consistent goal. Everything else became relative. With a dose of irony, this would apply to the independence of other places as well. In the country's pre- and post-victory, Mao offered very different thoughts on issues like Taiwan's and Tibet's independence. When meeting with Snow in July 1936, Mao put Taiwan on an equal footing with Korea: "After we regain all the lost territories and achieve independence, if Korean people want to break the chains put on them by the Japanese imperialists, we will fervently support their struggle for independence. This stance applies to Taiwan as well."[37]

This flexibility would apply not only to Taiwan; Mao's first experience of drafting a constitution happened in November 1931. The Jiangxi Soviet under his leadership ratified a constitutional guidance that acknowledged the rights of all ethnic minorities to choose whether to stay in or leave the Chinese union. Both Taiwanese and Tibetans were explicitly identified as those who deserved this right.[38] Mao's later attitudinal change on both issues attests to his realist nature: the strong does what it has the power to do, and the weak has to endure what it must endure.

"Everything Is Set. All We Need Now Is Wind Blowing from the East"

Common wisdom would see Deng Xiaoping as another transformative leader. China today, except for Mao's portrait and body still being worshiped in downtown Beijing, is a product of Deng's rather than Mao's vision. This narrative is embraced even by the Chinese media, as Mao and Deng split the award for making China great again: "Chairman Mao made Chinese people stand up; Comrade Deng Xiaoping made Chinese people prosperous." With Xi Jinping trying to elevate himself to the same height, the *People's Daily* now adds a third recipient: "General Secretary Xi Jinping made Chinese people strong."[39]

China's official narrative refers to Deng as the "grand architect of Chinese reform." He replaced Mao's ideological purification campaign with one that emphasized extreme pragmatism. In assessing Deng's influence on Chinese foreign policy, though, one needs to pay attention to two continuities: the importance of personality in handling internal and external shocks and the foundational status of realism as the guiding principle. On these two issues, Deng continued to walk on rather than depart from Mao's path.

The emergence of a transformative leader hinges on two conditions: major contingencies and personality. Deng's rise to prominence had both conditions in place. The contingency was self-inflicted: China was near the edge of regime collapse due to Mao's disastrous campaigns, particularly the Cultural Revolution. The dire situation, as Deng put it, was one in which, unless China launched major reforms, the country "would be stripped of membership of the Earth" (*kaichu qiuji*).[40] It was a life-and-death moment for the country and the party.

In Chinese history, whether a leader could rise up to such a life-and-death moment could decide the fate of a dynasty. In the novel *Romance of the Three Kingdoms*, written by Luo Guanzhong, the great strategist Zhuge Liang designs a plot of setting up fire to defeat the massive fleet led by Cao Cao. As all preparations are put in place, Zhuge Liang tells his alliance partner Zhou Yu: "Everything is set. All we need now is wind blowing from the East [to start the blaze]." For countries standing at historic crossroads, leadership personality could be that precious east wind.

In the crucial year of 1976, Deng was not the east wind foreseen by Mao. In fact, to crush Deng for the third time would be the chairman's last campaign. Mao's allegedly chosen heir, Hua Guofeng, however, served as a negative example of how personality could make or break a leader at history's major junctures. Hua was everything Deng was not—timid, awkward, and someone who only felt safe by imitating Mao, including his physical appearance. The arrest of the conservative Gang of Four in 1976 exhausted whatever shred of courage Hua possessed. He quickly turned all his efforts to blocking Deng's political comeback.

As a guerrilla fighter and later the village party chief of Mao's hometown, Hua had little international exposure. Coupled with his rigid upholding of Mao's words, this would be a recipe for one diplomatic embarrassment after another. Singaporean prime minister Lee Kuan Yew vividly recalled such a moment during his visit to China in 1976, when during a meeting the then vice premier Hua handed Lee a book by Neville Maxwell titled *India's China War*, a pro-China account of the two neighbors' hostilities in the 1960s. Hua told Lee this was the "correct" version of the war. Lee declined the gift. He handed the book back and said: "Mr. Prime Minister, this is your version of the war. There is another version, the Indian version. And in any case, I am from Southeast Asia—it has nothing to do with us."[41] An awkward silence ensued. Zhang Hanzhi, Hua's interpreter and the wife of China's foreign minister Qiao Guanhua, stood up and left. Qiao, according to the participant who produced the written record, suddenly began packing some documents and probably by doing so did not have to look up.[42] Lee left the meeting with a very unfavorable impression of Hua, telling fellow delegation members that Hua's appearance and demeanor reminded him of a communist spy chief.[43]

This would not be the only occasion when Hua caused diplomatic chagrins. A retired Chinese diplomat admitted that he had no confidence in Hua's ability to handle questions from foreign press. On Hua's trip to Japan in 1980, this diplomat phoned a chief editor at the *Yomiuri Shimbun*, someone he knew would be representing Japanese journalists to ask questions the next day. This was a time when Japan and China were undergoing the honeymoon period of their relations. In the spirit of friendship, the editor offered a list of questions to the Chinese diplomat. Hua was thrilled at getting the list in advance. Yet, the next day, the same editor asked a question about a political star named Zhao Ziyang and his future—a question not on the list. Hua berated the Japanese journalist for asking an unexpected question.[44] On the same trip, Hua almost caused another major awkward moment by attempting to take a stroll at the hotel garden in his Japanese-style pajamas.

Stopped by his aid at the last minute, Hua expressed confusion why this would be a problem.[45] In the limited number of memoirs written by those who knew Hua, a consensus emerged: Hua was a "simple," "nice" man—code words for someone unfit to lead. A transformation would happen, but not in his name.

The east wind that China needed eventually came with the third resurgence of Deng Xiaoping. Despite his rural background, Deng spent seven years in France and the Soviet Union during his youthful years. It was in Europe where the teenaged Deng completed his transformation into a lifelong communist. This would be in sharp contrast to Hua Guofeng, whose only experience of dealing with foreigners was fighting the Japanese. The two leaders' paths continued to differ after the founding of the People's Republic. Unlike Hua, Deng had much more experience working at the top of the party, in government, and for military apparatuses. His ability to endure the ups and downs in life has become legendary, earning him the nickname "roly-poly man" (*budaoweng*).

The same Lee Kuan Yew who humiliated Hua had a quite different relationship with Deng. The two had a rough start. Apparently, Deng and his delegation became annoyed during their 1976 visit to Singapore, when Lee repeatedly warned the Chinese not to interfere in Southeast Asian affairs. As reporters noticed during a banquet, after Lee belabored the point that Singapore was very different from China despite its ethnic Chinese majority, the Chinese delegation members used pencils to cross out the word "friendly" in a sentence that originally read "His Excellency Prime Minister's friendly speech" in Deng's prepared remarks.[46]

Yet, Deng was a learner. Suspicions voiced by Lee and other Southeast Asian leaders made him keenly aware of the burden China had to let go of. During the same visit, when Lee brought up the request that China end its effort of spreading revolution, Deng simply asked back: "What do you want me to do?" Surprised, Lee asked China to stop its broadcasting programs to communist militias and to cut off its support to these groups. Both requests were honored within two years.[47] In 1980 at a campaign rally, Lee praised Deng effusively, calling him a "great man" with an "open mind" and "common sense." Almost thirty years later, Lee still harbored admiration for Deng. In a television interview, Lee named him along with Winston Churchill and Charles de Gaulle as the three statesmen he held in the highest esteem.[48] In 2010, with Vice President Xi Jinping at his side, Lee unveiled a commemorative sculpture of Deng in Singapore. This was a rare acknowledgment of Deng from a leader known for his acute sensitivity to Chinese influence.

Deng's transformation of China has been well recorded and analyzed by numerous outlets. He is rightfully accredited as the leader who opened the country and laid the foundation for its global ascendancy. Deng's legitimacy in this regard is still robust. Employing extreme pragmatism, Deng changed Chinese foreign policy by shrinking the country's ambition—the opposite of Mao's lifelong campaign. In his metaphorical language, Deng mocked his own country: "China is not a beauty, and it should not insist on being referred to as one."[49] The pattern of interactions between China and the world, particularly the advanced part of the world, evolved from one of China attempting to affect the world beyond its means to one of China selectively letting the world affect itself. However, the other pillar supporting Mao-era Chinese diplomacy—namely, realism—remained intact. A new generation of Chinese officials, many of whom had exposure to living and learning in the West, became even better at reframing China's situational ethics to justify the government's legitimacy.

Deng also inherited the chairman's sensitivity to national independence. His diplomatic practices in this realm could be loosely divided into two phases: pre- and post-1989 Tian'anmen Massacre. Prior to this incident, Deng was on the offensive, attempting to formally end the chapter of historical humiliation imposed by Western powers. The climax of such efforts would be the negotiated return of Hong Kong from Britain. In 1984, Margaret Thatcher went to Beijing. Even to this day, the Chinese media are still entertaining two episodes associated with the Iron Lady's trip: Deng Xiaoping's warning to Thatcher that he would be no better than the traitors of the Qing Dynasty if he agreed to let Britain stay in Hong Kong beyond 1997 and the British prime minister's fall on the steps of the Great Hall of the People after the meeting. Thatcher's stumble has been gleefully discussed by numerous Chinese media outlets as a British surrendering gesture and symbolic sign that Deng crushed her.[50] Even as late as 2018, if one typed Thatcher's name in the search bar in Baidu, China's top search engine, the site would suggest the word "fall" (*shuaidao*) following her name.

Chinese dramatization notwithstanding, in the words of a British diplomat, the formidable Iron Lady, who had stalwartly defended the Falklands, "met her match with the tiny, owlish Chinese leader Deng Xiaoping."[51] Despite Thatcher's warning that any unilateral action by China would be a violation of international law, "the diminutive Chinese leader got what he wanted,"[52] a result about which Thatcher in later years expressed regret and sadness.

After 1989, Deng's sensitivity to foreign interference remained. But he changed tactics. Roughly at the same time as he pushed China to market reform, Deng issued a twenty-four-character guidance to Politburo members, urging the whole nation to bide time, hide capabilities, and never claim leadership. Deng's words quickly received biblical status. Briefing sessions avalanched throughout China, informing citizens at all levels of Deng's instructions. "More hands make our job easier"—the party's heirloom wisdom also adapted to the post–Cold War new realities. Deng's words became the survival guide for the next two generations of Chinese leadership. The last point of never claiming leadership was a direct warning not to return to Mao's path of setting up fires around the globe. In 1992, leaders, officials, and many Chinese citizens still had fresh memories about the Mao era. Now, traumatized by the death of the "Big Brother" Soviet Union, many felt Deng's advice justified and timely.

It would be difficult to overstate the importance of Deng's twenty-four-character guidance. It was the foundation to a plethora of Chinese diplomatic practices in the next two decades, from major to trivial: biding time and hiding capabilities inevitably led to China's being mum or ambivalent about contested issues in which it had no direct involvement, leading some Chinese citizens to joke that the only vote China's ambassadors would carry to the UN Security Council meetings was "abstention." Even the *Phoenix News*, a Hong Kong–based pro-China media outlet, likened the Chinese government to a "rabbit that never hurts a fly" at the UN.[53] The "never claiming leadership" advice also had a major impact on how leaders would behave on the international stage. Leaders like Hu Jintao may have treated it as a survival manual not only for China but also for themselves. Yet, when leaders were shunning the exercise of leadership, looking stiff and uneasy would be a natural byproduct.

How to Say "Covfefe" in Chinese?

Is Xi Jinping the third transformative leader of the People's Republic? He is certainly enjoying a level of authority that no recent Chinese leaders have managed to claim. To gauge such authority, one way is to observe how societies respond when leaders make mistakes. On May 31, 2018, Donald Trump tweeted from the White House, "Despite the constant negative press covfefe," and the sentence abruptly stopped. The tweet quickly went viral. To this day it remains one of the most popular presidential tweets. Journalists, media pundits, and comedians all participated in a fiesta of guessing the meaning of "covfefe." Unable to block media coverage, Trump joined the amusement by wishing people good luck in this guessing game. About one year later, at the Belt and Road Summit in Beijing, the Chinese president Xi Jinping misspoke the word "*jingzhan*" (greatly skillful) as "*jingshen*." The latter does not exist in Chinese vocabulary, and Xi made this mistake probably because he confused two visually similar Chinese characters: only three strokes of difference exist between "*zhan*" and "*shen*." China's official voice, the Xinhua News Agency, quickly eliminated the mispronounced word in its publication of the official text. But Xinhua did not stop there—it went one step further by replacing the word with "*jingjin*" (greatly delicate). Make no mistake—the word "*jingjin*" also does not exist in Chinese vocabulary. But at least it looked similar to "*jingzhan*" and made more sense than what Xi pronounced. Such a treatment would probably be the envy of any US president, including Trump. The trend of doubling down when confronted about one's mistake was elevated to a national level in 2020. Despite its initial concealment and mishandling of the Covid-19 public health crisis, the Chinese government quickly started an activity mocked by its own netizens as "wok throwing" (*shuai guo*)—throwing blames to others, particularly the United States, as the real culprit behind the virus's global spread.

Yet, being dominating and being transformative are not synonymous. Signs are mixed on whether Xi has acquired the latter status. Of the three conditions behind a political architect, namely, personality, contextual shocks, and duration of legitimacy, the presence of shocks is most unambiguous. Trump's electoral victory in 2016 stunned the world. Yet, before populism's crowning moment in America, it had already been on the rise in other parts of the world, including Western liberal democracies. If anything, Trump's victory showed that populism's surge had finally engulfed America.

From keeping one's head low to throwing woks, China's diplomatic behaviors have changed greatly under Xi's leadership. Immediately after the 1989 Tian'anmen Massacre, Chinese officials at internal party member meetings would often start with this sentence: "Comrades, communist movement around the globe is now experiencing its low tide."[54] The phrase was meant not only to describe the current situation but also to hint that the tide would rise again—as long as China persevered. Communism may yet to have another high wave. But many would agree that liberal democracies are experiencing their own nadir right now. The stagnating West is meeting the ascending China. As the two collide, sentiments of all kinds are being unleashed. On the Chinese side, many perceive the western decline as a rare opportunity for China to claim global leadership. No one is formally announcing the death of Deng's diplomatic decree. Yet, if not buried in spirit, his wisdom has certainly been buried by practices like Xi's massive spending spree of the One Belt One Road Initiative and military projects like the Great Wall of Sand, huge manmade islands scattered in the South China Sea.

The new leadership has also lifted the gate to allow dissenting voices on Deng's guidance. Confronted with critical voices that China was prematurely taking on America on trade and other issues, China's national news agency denounced such views as the "surrender sect," claiming that those who possess such views should be eliminated like "a mouse wandering in public" (*guojie laoshu*). It proclaimed that China had assumed the world's center stage and that, as a result, confronting America had become China's global responsibility.[55]

To what extent has Xi Jinping's personality contributed to Chinese assertiveness and Western anxiety? He certainly seems more comfortable with his authority than his predecessor, forever nervous Hu Jintao. He has also not refrained from expressing his emotions, usually the disdainful sort, at international appearances. Whether he can transform such personal authority into sustainable policies is a wholly different matter. What is clearer than Xi's possession of charisma is the manufacturing of it—that is, a cult of personality is coming back to China. By eliminating presidential term limits, Xi has pushed Chinese politics closer to the bygone era of the one-man state. This change also attests to the point that being transformative does not equate to being progressive.

As Xi eliminated one political rival after another, a word that frequently appeared in the official denunciation of those disgraced officials is "*guiju*," which can be loosely translated into established standards, norms, or rules. Officials fell because they broke the *guiju*.[56] Yet, *guiju* is a colloquial term that typically has no place in the official media's ritualistic vocabulary. Even more importantly, *guiju* carries the connotation that the rule is often informal and tacit. The term has been traditionally associated with hierarchical families or organized crime groups, where the head of the household or gang would dictate *guiju* for junior members to follow. By constantly using this colloquial term, the media apparently want to create an image of the party and the state as a huge family headed by Xi, whose authority is absolute. The irony, though, is that Xi came to his position by breaking the biggest *guiju* of all—term limits and the regular transfer of power.

In foreign policy, realism remains an instinctive drive in Xi's China. But new wine has been put in an old bottle: China is no longer shy about using the phrase "special relations" to describe China-Russia ties.[57] Although the power dynamism between China and Russia has been reversed in terms of economic influence, Xi still feels the need to forge ties with Vladimir Putin to jointly counter the West. Xi openly calls Putin "my good friend." In June 2018, at a grand ceremony, Xi made his good friend the first recipient of China's Medal of Friendship. But Deng's "never claim leadership" wisdom has not faded out completely, even when Xi shifts alliance. Russia has been taking a more vocal tone, backed up by aggressive actions, on issues ranging from Ukraine to Syria. China, though now stronger, still plays the role of the sidekick. Needless to say, on consolidating personal grips of power and spreading the cult of personality, Putin may also serve as a teacher.

To be sure, Xi has promoted a number of ambitious projects, most notably the One Belt One Road (OBOR) Initiative and the establishment of the Asian Investment and Infrastructure Bank. But as a number of China experts have argued, these projects reflect Chinese frustration rather than ambition, as Beijing is feeling its requests for boosting its presence at the World Bank and International Monetary Fund perennially ignored by the West.[58] There is also the real materialistic motivation. As June Teufel Dreyer points out, critics of the OBOR project felt its acronym should more properly represent China's sole benefit of the Our Belt Our Road initiative, which seeks to help the country export its excess production capacity.[59]

Even Xi's slogan "Chinese Dream" came from the party's playbook. Since Jiang Zemin took realm, it has become customary for Chinese leaders to invent pet slogans. Where they lack legitimacy by tradition, a catchy phrase may fill the hole. Hence, Jiang had the slogan "Three Represents," Hu Jintao had "Harmonious Society," and Xi Jinping used the "Chinese Dream." Wang Huning, a top adviser widely accredited with coining all three slogans, has acquired the online moniker "nation's mentor" (*guoshi*). Wang himself finally became a member of the standing committee of the Politburo in 2013. All of the slogans found their way into the party's and the state's formal documentation. Xi outshone his two predecessors by inserting his name into the party charter. If this trend continues, in time the party's foundational document may eventually become a collection of indecipherable slogans.

The meeting of the Western trajectory and the Chinese one may give reason for Xi to feel ambitious. As China's paramount leader sets to affect the world, one should not forget that Xi would not be the first Chinese leader to trek down this path. It did not end well for Mao's China and for those on the receiving end. Xi is now leading a much stronger country. But eventually he has to go. Will his policies and legacies outlive his tenure? What would happen if the answer is "no"? The rewards would be huge, but so would the failures.

Hu Yaobang, the Accidental Disrupter

> My strength plucked up the hills, My might shadowed the world;
> But the times were against me, and Dapple runs no more;
> When Dapple runs no more, What then can I do?
> Ah, Yu, my princess Yu, What will your fate be?[60]

This lamenting poem, titled "Song of Gaixia," was written by General Xiang Yu on his fateful night in 202 BC. Five years earlier, Xiang, who called himself the "King of Kings" (*bawang*), stormed the Qin capital of Xianyang with his troops four hundred thousand strong, burning down the entire city and forcing the emperor to renounce his throne. Now, however, on the besieged battlefield of Gaixia, the King of Kings was surrounded by only twenty-eight soldiers, his steed Dapple, and his beloved concubine Yu. Turning down a local boatman's offer to help him escape across the Wu River, Xiang made a last charge toward the thousands of Han troops with his men. Seriously injured, Xiang slit his own throat.

The King of Kings wept on the day of his demise, grieving that he was born into the wrong time. For the next two millennia, countless heroes graced Chinese history. Even to this day, though, the phrase "King of Kings" is still reserved for this one man. But the *bawang*'s image is not all positive—more often it pictures a man too impulsive and idealistic to lead, a man whose ambition was poorly supported by his ability, and a man whose end was doomed to be tragic. After all is said and done, the King of Kings was a mere disrupter of his time.

The People's Republic has yet to produce a figure like Xiang Yu, who attempted to overthrow the regime through force. In fact, upon celebrating the People's Liberation Army's takeover of the nationalist government's capital city Nanking in 1949, Mao Zedong warned his troops by bringing up the lesson of Xiang Yu: "With power to spare we must pursue the tottering foe; And not ape the King of Kings seeking idle fame."[61] However, in seeing one's aspiration poorly matched by judgment, and as someone whose ultimate success as an icon happened in death, party general secretary Hu Yaobang came closest to a modern resemblance of the ill-fated King of Kings. For Hu, foreign policy would be his own battle of Gaixia.

Like Xiang Yu, Hu's biggest impact on history happened upon death. In Hu's case, the public's mourning of his sudden passing evolved into a massive pro-democracy movement that ended in a massacre. Although the party could not blame a dead man for writing this violent chapter, Hu's name implicitly turned into a taboo. The party general secretary for much of the

1980s thus lurked as a shadowy figure in the official chronicle. It took twenty-six years before Xi, another party chief, would attend a ceremony dedicated to him, commemorating the one hundredth anniversary of his birthday.[62] Predictably, Xi did not utter a single word on Hu's biggest impact, exerted posthumously on China. There was also nothing in the speech about Hu's forced resignation in 1987.

To China's liberals and to many outside the country, Hu has been fondly remembered as one of the most open-minded leaders the Communist Party has produced. His effort to transform the party was heroic and his fate tragic. Yet his untimely death kindled a pro-democracy spirit that continues to inspire forthcoming generations. In romanticizing and lionizing Hu, however, those on the opposite end of the party's official stance may commit the same mistake as that by his opponents: that is, presenting a one-sided portrayal of a late leader to serve one's current agenda. Both Hu's opponents and his supporters see him as a transformer, not a transactional figure. What Hu really wanted to change, though, was assumed. To what extent was Hu personally accountable for his failure? This question was shunned from scrutiny, especially by his sympathizers.

A closer examination would present a more nuanced picture of a flawed reformer—Hu was indeed remarkably more accommodating of different views than many party elders, including his boss, Deng Xiaoping. Yet, Hu was very much on the same page with other leaders on using a realist lens to examine international politics. For the one area in which Hu really wanted to make a difference—China's relations with Japan—his effort backfired. It turned into the most convenient excuse for his rivals to question his soundness as a leader, that is, his legitimacy. Furthermore, Hu was known for possessing an unrestrained personality. While his supporters would applaud this as open-mindedness, his opponents saw impulsivity and naivety—qualities that made him unfit to lead, if not potentially treasonous. With a garrulous mouth and minimal guard toward strangers, Hu manufactured ample ammunition for his rivals to use on him. He sat on a combustible arsenal that was very much of his own making. No wonder one Politburo member could spend a whole day condemning Hu at the internal meeting that ended his career. In a sense, Hu had prepared for his own demise.

What happened on May 10, 1985, offers a key understanding of Hu's charm and foible, as he put both traits on open display. On this day, Hu Yaobang had a lengthy interview with Lu Keng, a Hong Kong–based journalist. Lu would later express regret for requesting this interview, for the published transcript was later used by the party elders to crush Hu. As described in the party's official document of March 16, 1987, that announced Hu's downfall, one crime that Hu allegedly committed was his disclosure of "confidential information" to Lu and his allowing Lu to "maliciously attack" (*siyi gongji*) two conservative Politburo members in charge of the party propaganda: Hu Qiaomu and Deng Liqun.

The transcript is indeed informative. One surprising element it reveals, despite Hu's reputation as a transformer, is how mainstream his opinions actually were, especially on foreign policy. Hu adamantly believed that Taiwan, just like Hong Kong, is an unalienable part of China. He unambiguously ruled out the possibility of renouncing the use of force to solve this issue. While acknowledging that China simply did not possess the power to take the island, Hu the realist believed that day would come soon—very soon. He further offered a veiled threat to pro-independence forces in Taiwan: "Give us another seven, eight, or ten years, our economy will be stronger, and our national defense folks will know better what to do. The majority of the Taiwanese people want to come back. For those few who are unwilling to return, we will do some little trick to make them obey."[63]

When Lu reminded Hu that most Taiwanese did not want to reunify with Beijing, Hu took one step back and then two steps forward: "That's true, isn't it? But I believe there will be more and more of them [who support reunification]. It'd be an exaggeration to say such people are growing day by day. But I think it's about right to say they are growing year by year." Hu would go on to suggest a blockade of the island, a proposal long favored by military hawks like Wang Zheng, should the Taiwanese authorities resist the inevitable. He also pointed fingers at America, calling it "the biggest obstacle" to Chinese reunification and "very unfriendly" toward China on the Taiwan issue.[64] Clearly, Hu the reformer was not ready to offer his famed understanding and tolerance toward this breakaway island and its security sponsor.

During Hu's reign, the one issue in which he indeed made a difference, however briefly, was China-Japan relations. The first half of the 1980s is commonly perceived as the honeymoon period between these two Asian powers. Hu played no small part in building this affinity. He passionately recommended to party cadres the Japanese conservative architect Yoshida Shigeru's book reflecting on the Meiji Restoration, arguing it could be used as guidance for China's own pursuit of modernization.[65] He also delivered a forward-looking speech at the Japanese Diet with his signature overflowing passion. As one Japanese journalist recalled: "Hu went off script in his speech to the Diet. He is a small man, and his size made his gestures all the more exaggerated. This is very different from the image of Chinese leaders that the Japanese people typically have."[66]

Hu was a rare Chinese leader in developing a genuine friendship with his Japanese counterpart, Prime Minister Nakasone Yasuhiro. Yet, in doing so he misperceived an opening in China-Japan relations that simply was not there. The 1980s, in retrospect, actually marked the beginning of China's use of Japan for domestic mobilization. It was also the decade when a series of disputes surfaced between the two governments, with those disagreements on World War II growing increasingly acrimonious. In the mid-1980s, massive anti-Japan protests broke out in major Chinese cities. As Allen S. Whiting points out, Japan's foreign policy image was pitiful in the eyes of the Chinese public. With minor exceptions, China's popular emotion on Japan tilted toward the negative direction.[67] Even Deng Xiaoping, Hu's mentor whom he held in high esteem, turned increasingly hostile toward Japan. Deng once urged China to learn from Japan, but now he repeatedly shamed the teacher as one who "owes the most to China."[68]

Against this background, Hu's accommodating attitude toward Japan and his brotherly bond with Nakasone boomeranged back to hit him. At his five-day-long dismissal meeting in January 1987, when party elders came up with a list of Hu's crimes, two were about diplomacy. Both were related to Japan: Hu was criticized for inviting Nakasone despite the latter's lack of apology for Japan's wartime sins. Hu was also blamed for causing a "messy situation" by inviting three thousand young Japanese to China.[69]

Even among Hu's supporters and sympathizers, many admitted that his impulsivity worked against him. It made him hard to survive in politics. Hu's interview with Lu proved revealing in this respect as well. During the conversation, Lu brought up the point that both Hu and Wang Zhen, a conservative general, hailed from the same Liuyang area of Hunan Province. Hu answered: "Yes—but he's from the northern county and I am from the south." Lu did not give up: "So, you two can echo each other?" Hu retorted: "Or he can head further northward and I southward."[70] Hu's reply may have sounded like a smart tongue-in-cheek retort, for he was playing on the ancient proverb of "*nanyuan beizhe*"—going south by driving the chariot north—which implies that two parties have nothing in common. But the wit squandered an opportunity that Lu fed him to strike a hometown bond with an influential party elder. Worse yet, it openly exposed his derision toward Wang. Puzzlingly, Hu would go on to say he actually agreed with Wang about the necessity of imposing a blockade on Taiwan. Wang, however, would not show the same light-heartedness toward Hu. He became one of Hu's most vocal critics. Hu may have been right after all—he and Wang were headed for opposite directions. Unbeknownst to Hu, though, among the top party leaders, he was the lone chariot heading south. Though never intending to be a challenger, he ended up sharing the same fate as the King of Kings: an ambitious man poorly matched for his time.

Hu's approach to Japan would receive a belated vindication. In May 2018, after eight years of avoiding Japan, Premier Li Keqiang went to Tokyo on an official visit. At the welcoming banquet, Japanese prime minister Abe hit the audience with an emotional chord: "I have known Premier Li for over thirty years. At the time my father Abe Shintaro was welcoming a youth delegation headed by Mr. Li, I was then my father's secretary. I never thought after so many years we two would stand shoulder to shoulder, meeting the press here. Time has passed, and our appearances have changed. But our hearts of improving Japan-China relations have never dithered." Li responded in emotional terms as well: "I stored this memory in my head, too. Eight years have passed since the last Chinese premier's visit to Japan, and twenty-six years have passed since my own visit. For two immediate countries and global major economies, this was too long."[71]

This conversation may offer a moving exoneration of Hu's "impulsivity" that was blamed for his fostering large-scale youth exchanges. Yet, Hu's name was not mentioned by Li, though the latter was working as a promising star at the Communist Youth League, a branch under Hu's tutelage. Hu's vision may have been vindicated, but the mentioning of his name is as elusive as ever.

A discussion of Hu naturally invites the question, What about Zhao Ziyang, Hu's successor who shared the same fate of political demise? Zhao was sacked for openly expressing sympathy to pro-democracy protestors. He would spend the last sixteen years of his life as a political prisoner. When Zhao died, the US State Department praised him as "a dynamic and forward-looking leader, a champion of reform at a time of momentous change in China."[72]

Such effusive remarks owe much to Zhao's opposition to his own government's violent suppression of the 1989 pro-democracy movement. Zhao paid for this choice by losing his freedom for the last sixteen years of his life. However, it should be noted that Zhao was not always a champion of democracy. During the 1980s while serving as the premier and then the party chief, he was less adventurous than Hu. In fact, almost three years before Hu's downfall, Zhao wrote a letter to Deng Xiaoping, urging him and Chen Yun, another party elder, to continue guiding the country. Given that Hu was at the time the party chief, Hu's allies perceived Zhao as a backstabber.[73] As a corroborative note, one conservative leader, Bo Yibo, would bring up Zhao's letter three years later at the internal meeting where Hu was sacked. Bo used the letter as evidence of Hu's attempt to establish his own authority. Zhao also admitted that he criticized Hu for his "flamboyance" and "unwillingness to obey the party discipline."[74] Like Hu, Zhao may have misperceived an opening and a chance of jolting China onto a different path at the crucial juncture of 1989. Yet, up to that point, Zhao had been a far less radical figure than Hu. He carefully trotted within the parameters set by Deng and other elders. Zhao became a rising star because he aligned himself with the establishment. In other words, he convinced them he was not another Hu Yaobang. The only flamboyance he showed was his love of golf, a rare sport to many Chinese at the time. His promotion of the sport was touted by the party's propaganda machine as exemplifying his "opening" attitude. Later, though, this would become proof of his pro-West crime.

From Burning Candle to Bored Monk

China's governing structure carves out a position specifically for manager-type, transactional leaders: premiership. The party general secretary, also known as the "core" (*hexin*), is the center of legitimacy. He is entrusted with the supreme mission of setting the course for the giant vessel called China. The core, in other words, is supposed to be a visionary. The premier is more like a chief engineer, responsible to the captain through navigation, deck operations, and maintenance of the engine room. While the captain decides where to sail, the chief engineer works on how to get there.

On a superficial level, China's dual-leadership arrangement rolls the division of labor and checks and balances into one. This structure also permeates into almost all governable units. Even for an entering class at an elementary school, one first-grade student would be the political commissar (*zhongdui zhang*) and another first grader the class president (*banzhang*). In this way, Chinese citizens are socialized to be familiar with this governing structure at a very young age. Yet, as one climbs to the upper echelon of government, such division of labor may get increasingly blurred and power could tip toward the political end. In the name of taking care of the "big picture," the political head could interfere in the work of the administrative head. The latter, however, may only offer advice and suggestions to the former. If the structure were likened to a two-headed dragon, authority flows from the political head to the administrative one. Hence, by institutional design, China creates a high office for transactional leaders. A premier is the country's ultimate workhorse.

This design has been further reinforced by historical precedence. A premier's reputation lies in not only competence but also servitude and loyalty.

For officials who have met these expectations, they have been applauded as a "grand chancellor" (*zaixiang*), a brilliant top administrator. The term started as an official title, but it evolved into an acclamation. Every government had its top administrator. But throughout China's long history, only a handful would be remembered as acquiring the "qualities of a grand chancellor" (*zaixiang zhicai*).

One person who became the epitome of *zaixiang* is Zhuge Liang, prime minister of the kingdom of Shu eighteen hundred years ago. Tales about Zhuge Liang have been well known to Chinese throughout millennia. They paint an idealistic picture of a grand chancellor: competent and unconditionally loyal to his master, Liu Bei. One famous story records a conversation between Liu on his deathbed and Zhuge Liang. Knowing his son Liu Shan was not wise enough to lead the kingdom, Liu Bei asked Zhuge Liang to assist the prince. If this arrangement failed, Liu Bei continued, Zhuge Liang could dethrone the young master and make himself the new emperor.

Some would point out that by offering Zhuge Liang this option in front of others, Liu Bei smartly preempted the very possibility he had feared. Whether genuine or manipulative, Liu's gesture sent Zhuge Liang down to his knees. The prime minister wept and vowed he would serve the young master loyally to the end. And he did.

As Andrew Nathan points out, to many Chinese, the People's Republic of China's first premier, Zhou Enlai, is the modern Zhuge Liang.[75] Zhou Enlai became the norm setter of the behavioral code of a premier. Invoking two famous proses from a Song Dynasty poem, party elder Song Renqiong praised Zhou as "a silkworm spins till death, running out of yarn thread; a candle keeps burning, till it becomes ashes."[76] He was the country's premier and top diplomat. But to Mao, Zhou was his secretary, bodyguard, head nurse, and potential rival. Keenly aware of Mao's suspicion, Zhou remained excessively servile and paranoid toward Mao. Seven months before his own life candle burned out, a gravely sick Zhou wrote a reflection of "mistakes and crimes I committed" to Mao. He did not forget to tell Mao's secretary, Zhang Yufeng, to read his confession to Mao "only when the chairman is in good spirit, sleeps well and eats well. Never do so when he is tired. Please. I entrust you."[77]

If the country's first and widely respected premier had to be this timid, one could only expect such timidity to grow further down the line. Among Zhou's six successors, only Zhu Rongji was popularly accorded the title "*zaixiang*." Zhu once proclaimed to the nation that he would prepare one hundred coffins—ninety-nine for corrupt officials and one for himself. Such no-nonsense style and tough words on curbing down corrupt officials earned him the moniker of "Iron and Blood Grand Chancellor" (*tiexue zaixiang*)—the Bismarckian element is hard to miss.

But Zhu was no Bismarck. The Chinese premier may have possessed a charismatic personality, but he showed little desire to challenge the order of things. Indeed, political reform was a minefield he delicately tiptoed around. Zhu's own promotion was controversial, for his reform measures while serving as the mayor of Shanghai earned him the nickname "China's Gorbachev" from his opponents. His political ascendancy only became possible after Deng Xiaoping openly praised him for his knowledge of economics.[78] But the episode left Zhu haunted. In practice, he was more like the bird in a traditional Chinese folklore, which startles each time it hears the mere twang of a bowstring. Zhu remained vigilant to any association of him with political reformers, telling reporters, "I am very unhappy about being called 'China's Gorbachev' and 'economic czar.'"[79] He went on to call on the entire country to be united "under the correct leadership of the Party with Comrade Jiang Zemin as our core."[80]

Zhu was right—he was no "China's Gorbachev." This made his tough words on fighting corruption sound hollow. Faithfully living up to Deng's remarks about him, Zhu devoted almost all of his energy into steering the country's economy. On foreign policy, he treaded the party line carefully. In his first press conference as premier, he vowed to "continue adamantly to execute the foreign policy designed by President Jiang and Premier Li Peng."[81] There were occasions where Zhu made headline news on foreign policy. In 1999, for example, Zhu visited America and attempted in vain to wrap up negotiations with the Clinton administration over China's entry into the World Trade Organization. In 2000, Zhu visited Japan and assured a Japanese audience that he was not trying to force them to apologize. On both occasions, Zhu was showered by harsh criticism from within. His debacle in America was further labeled as "the darkest day" in China-US relations.[82] Zhu grew increasingly mum as he approached the end of his tenure, propelling multiple foreign media outlets to call him a lame-duck premier.[83]

The imbalance of power between the premier and the party chief, coupled with the fact that the country's diplomatic paradigm was already set by Deng Xiaoping, created a new challenge to premiers: now the country had two, not one, managerial leadership slots. As the ship's captain stole the show to justify his own performance, the premier was having an identity crisis about what role he was left to play.

This problem has become apparent under Xi Jinping, who has been busy adding authoritative-sounding titles to his role: president, general secretary, commander in chief, and head of various working groups ranging from Taiwan to finance to internet security. As Xi makes himself the "chairman of everything," a question is emerging: where is Li Keqiang, the premier? On foreign policy, Xi has enhanced his control by assigning loyal lieutenants like Liu He as vice premier and, more importantly, his ally Wang Qishan as vice president. The office of the vice president used to be symbolic and nominal. But clearly Xi has entrusted Wang with new, substantial authority to manage China's relations with major powers, especially with America. This also means that Wang has become a hidden, eighth member of the standing committee of the Politburo, China's highest decision-making organ. Meanwhile, Premier Li's eclipse in the country's diplomacy is accelerating. Li's visit to Japan in May 2018 was barely mentioned in the official media, in sharp contrast to any presidential visit Xi would pay to a country. Indeed, even ceremonially congratulatory letters written by Xi's office to international conferences would be mentioned ahead of the premier's actual appearances on international stages. According to Tony Saich, who tracked Premier Li's 2017 government report, the Chinese equivalent of the American State of the Union speech, Li mentioned the party about thirty times, more than at any time since reforms began in the late 1970s, and Xi himself was mentioned eight times while the "core" was mentioned eleven times.[84]

Li's workload as premier is getting lighter as foreign policy, a traditional highlight of a premier's job, is slipping out of his hands. Even when Li works hard, he finds fewer and fewer outlets to let people know this fact. In July 2020, as both Xi and Li inspected flood disaster areas, two very different photos emerged: Xi was shown in impeccably clean clothes, talking to a smiling woman who was later exposed as a local security officer pretending to be a refugee; Li was trudging flood with muddied boots and pants, frowning and looking concerned. When online comparisons began to emerge, Li's photo disappeared from the Chinese internet, as did Xi's photo of talking to a fake refugee.

The muffling of China's top administrator is unmistakable. Not a single day would pass in China's cyberworld without multiple deferential mentions of Xi. There is even an app called *Xuexi Yulu* that monitors whether party members are logging in daily to learn Xi's sayings. Those who fail to do so may face punishment. In the app's name, "Xuexi" could be interpreted as either "learn" or "learn from Xi"; "Yulu," on the other hand, leaves no room for ambiguity. Literally translated as "sayings," it was associated with only one Chinese leader prior to Xi—Chairman Mao and his Little Red Book. The cult of personality connection cannot be missed.

In a randomly chosen week of August 31 to September 6, 2020, coverage of Xi ranges from diplomacy to protection of the Yellow River, to the construction of a reservoir in Beijing and about the publication of a journal article and to his addressing an international trade convention, as well as other things such as his sending flower baskets to a museum.[85] By contrast, coverage of Li is intermittent at best. There is certainly no equivalent of a column like "Li Keqiang's One Week." In such an environment, Li no longer has to be a burning candle. With Xi renewing his own presidential term into the infinite future while term limits for the premier remain, Li and future Chinese premiers may look increasingly like a bored monk who, in the traditional Chinese saying, "cares nothing but tolling a bell as each day comes." For a top manager who has been shoveled aside (*kaobianzhan*), such a passive attitude would not surprise anyone.

3 • Sheep in Wolf's Clothing

Why Aggression Is the New Obedience for Chinese Diplomats

Even when right, an intellectual always loses when talking to
a soldier.
    —Chinese proverb

China is a big country and other countries are small countries.
And that's just a fact.
    —Yang Jiechi, Chinese foreign minister

"Hottie Wang" and "Tiger Yang": China's Chief Diplomats Learn to Get Tough

Wang Yi is known as a *wanghong* (cyber-star) in China, a title that typically belongs to people who achieve wide, though often short-lived, fame or notoriety on the internet. But Wang has not secured this title through the popular paths. After all, he is neither a contestant in a reality show pulling off staggering stunts nor a prolific blogger chasing controversial issues. Wang is China's foreign minister.

In a land where Facebook, Twitter, and Instagram are banned, the authorities apparently tolerate, if not encourage, Minister Wang's multiple online fan groups. A search of Wang's name coupled with "*fensi tuan*" (fans groups) yielded close to 319,000 results on Baidu in September 2020. This number is all the more remarkable when one considers the country's ever-tightening internet environment. It is an open secret that the party's propaganda apparatus and the internet police have been closely monitoring *wanghong*s, particularly the political sort. But the authorities are still uneasy. In a campaign in May 2019, most political *wanghong*s were wiped out.[1] So far, Wang's social media followers have not been impacted.

To build and sustain one's cyber popularity, having an army of faithful *fensi* is crucial. *Fensi* literally means thin rice noodles, a popular, simple dish in Chinese cuisine. But the word has become an internet slang, playing on its sound mimicking the English word "fans"—an interlinguistic homonym, so to speak. It is not unusual for some cyber-stars, desperate for fame or notoriety, to self-sponsor their own *fensi*. Some bloat or outright fabricate the number of members in their fan groups. This scenario would be unlikely in Wang's case. There is no evidence that Minister Wang has any personal role in creating these fans groups. His followers consist of voluntary members who claim to be genuinely fascinated by him.

So, what has made China's top diplomat an enduring political celebrity immune to being "404ed" by the authorities (that is, to suffer the fate of being removed from the internet)? To start, appearance helps. Many of Minister Wang's fans call him "China's most handsome diplomat since Zhou Enlai,"[2] who was the country's beloved premier and famous diplomatic architect. To many, Wang carries a small but visible resemblance to Zhou. Some fans would go so far as to term Wang a *"guomin nanshen"* (national male hottie), a title that usually goes to movie stars or singers rather than a foreign minister in his mid-sixties.[3] Wang has even more meaningful connections with Zhou: to state the obvious, he got Zhou's job. Wang's wife is the daughter of Qian Jiadong, Zhou's secretary. Hence, on multiple fronts Wang could strike a nostalgic chord among many Chinese, who continue to view Zhou as the most charming statesman the People's Republic has produced.

Wang's popularity also stems from his rhetorical toughness. Yet, this is where Wang differs significantly from Zhou, as the latter is known for soothing tensions and building bonds even with enemies. To the contrary, Wang's speeches and remarks often receive polarizing receptions from domestic and international audiences. To Wang's Chinese fans, he is a staunch defender of China's interest and pride. To foreign audiences, though, Wang represents China's new belligerent, bullying face.

One particular episode crystalizes the contrasting receptions to Wang's diplomatic performance: the date was June 1, 2016; the setting was Ottawa, the Canadian capital; and the occasion was a joint press conference by Wang and his Canadian counterpart, Stéphane Dion. Reporter Amanda Connolly of the online news site IPolitics directed her question to Dion, asking him about the case of Canadian citizen Kevin Garratt, who was detained by China on espionage charges. She then followed up with a second question, still to Dion: "Given these concerns, why is Canada pursuing closer ties with China, how do you plan to use that relationship to improve human rights and security in the region, and did you specifically raise the case of the Garratts during your talks?" Dion offered a diplomatic answer. He said he had an "honest and frank" conversation on human rights with his Chinese colleague. He further added: "We expect that we will not always see eye-to-eye with each other, but we need to make progress."[4]

Had the exchange ended there, it would have been a forgettable component of a mundane press conference. However, Minister Wang felt a need to jump in. What he said next and the way he said it made headlines around the world. In fact, as of September 2020, Wang's unsolicited response to the Canadian reporter has received more than 2.2 million views on YouTube.[5] This would certainly be a personal record for Wang or for any Chinese diplomat.

So, what happened? In short, Wang chose to go ballistic. Through an interpreter he told Connolly: "I have to say that your question is full of prejudice against China and arrogance. . . . I don't know where that comes from. This is totally unacceptable." A visibly irked Wang continued: "Other people don't know better than the Chinese people about the human rights condition in China and it is the Chinese people who are in the best situation, in the best position to have a say about China's human rights situation." And Wang was not done—he went on to berate the Canadian reporter: "Have you been to China? Do you know that China has lifted more than six hundred million people out of poverty? . . . And do you know China has written protection and promotion of human rights into our constitution?"[6]

Wang's defending narrative was not a new approach. When confronted by Western criticism, it is quite common for Chinese officials and even some citizens to resort to nativist responses along the lines of "You just don't understand China" or "Only Chinese people really know China and thus have a right to comment on Chinese human rights." But that Wang would publicly vent his anger to the press in the face of his host—that was something new. Even to Justin Trudeau, the Canadian prime minister known for embodying Canadian sunniness, Wang's lengthy scolding crossed the line. The next day, Trudeau said his government expressed "dissatisfaction" to China over this exchange, adding that "the fact of the matter is freedom of the press is extremely important to me."[7]

To Wang's Chinese fans, though, the episode was a heroic tale. According to China's national Xinhua News Agency, many Canadian journalists "clapped their hands" once the press conference ended.[8] Even if this had been true, it was highly doubtful these journalists were hailing Wang in support of his angry attack on their female colleague. A more plausible explanation would be a mere ceremonial gesture of "Canadian nice." But the Xinhua article, by describing this act, apparently hinted at the former unlikely sce-

nario. The article went on to say that the Chinese press corps were "all supportive of Minister Wang Yi's righteous and moral response." To make the
coverage superficially objective, it cited an allegedly local reader by the name
of Mike Jones, who criticized Connolly for being "very rude."[9]

The reception to Wang's blast was not divided neatly along domestic and
international lines, though. It is fair to assume that inside China he had critics. Even on Baidu, where search results are filtered, at least one critical post,
as of July 2018, had evaded government surveillance, in which the netizen
called Wang's response "shameful."[10] One year later, this lone critical post
had disappeared. On Google, however, which is banned in mainland China,
criticisms of Wang's meltdown appear on every page. Apparently, the overwhelming domestic support for Wang's rebuke was an artificial scene manufactured by the government.

A more revealing point, though, is that Wang has not always been this
boorish. In fact, when he assumed the office, he was seen as "urbane, multi-
lingual, pragmatic, and, when needed, a wily negotiator. In short: he is everything a top diplomat should be."[11] Groomed as a Japan specialist, Wang was
credited as a speech writer for Hu Yaobang. Wang would rise to become the
ambassador to Japan from 2004 to 2007, a time when Sino-Japanese relations deteriorated significantly due to Prime Minister Koizumi Jun'ichiro's
visits to the Yasukuni Shrine and China's massive anti-Japan protests.

Even during this difficult time, Wang showed his flexible and sensible
side. A US cable described Wang telling the US ambassador to Japan, Thomas
Scheiffer, that despite Chinese pressure, China knew it was difficult for Japan
to alter its position on Yasukuni and that Beijing was willing to negotiate a
mutually acceptable "soft landing" of the issue.[12] From 2009 to 2013, Wang
served as the director of the Taiwan Affairs Office. His tenure was smooth.
In 2012, Wang hosted a dinner reception for Frank Hsieh, a pro-independence
former premier of Taiwan. According to Hsieh, the two-hour meeting over
dinner was cordial, and Wang was an attentive listener as Hsieh explained
Taiwan's rejection of the "92 Consensus," a formula that Beijing insists on as
the precondition for cross-strait negotiations.[13]

What this means is that Wang's bold persona as foreign minister was
acquired. Getting tough is not necessarily a sign of influence, however. To
the contrary, China's top diplomat's combative performance could paradoxically reveal a struggling ministry, a diplomatic corps that is getting increasingly nervous enough to heed rather than to advise the top leadership. In
other words, getting tough and growing servile could be two sides of the
same coin.

Indeed, Wang would not be the first foreign minister to stir up international anxiety for belligerent remarks. In 2010, at a security forum sponsored by the Association of Southeast Asian Nations in Hanoi, US secretary of state Hillary Clinton and officials from eleven other nations expressed concerns at China's aggressive policy in the South China Sea. Confronted by this concerted wave of criticism, Foreign Minister Yang Jiechi abruptly left the meeting. Thirty minutes later he returned, telling everyone in a deal-with-it manner that "China is a big country, and other countries are small countries, and that's just a fact."[14] Yang would later be promoted to the position of state councillor, one level above the foreign minister. His admonishing in Hanoi added new credentials to his nickname—"Tiger Yang." Allegedly, the nickname was coined by George H. W. Bush while Yang accompanied the Bush family as an interpreter in the 1970s. The nickname played on the facts that Yang was born in the year of the tiger and that his name "Chi" has the Chinese character "tiger" as a part of its strokes. As Yang rose to prominence, the official media began to present a different story: now Yang was called a fierce tiger because he was not afraid of attacking those who seek to hurt China.[15] When a future president of the United States nicknamed his young Chinese interpreter "tiger" in the 1970s, this meaning was probably not on his mind. A light-hearted joke has now evolved into praise for China's long overdue assertiveness.

Such attitudinal hardening is spilling over to the entire ministry. Chinese diplomats have collectively become more assertive and even uncivil. In January 2020, when confronted by a Swedish reporter's critical report of China, Chinese ambassador Gui Congyou compared the relationship between Swedish reporters and the Chinese government to a 100-pound boxer challenging a 190-pound boxer to a fight. Ambassador Gui continued to say that "out of good will to protect the lightweight boxer," China the heavyweight advised Sweden the lightweight to "mind his own business." But the ambassador complained that the lightweight "refuses to listen." So, "what choice do you expect the heavyweight boxer to have?"[16]

The ministry's once mundane daily press briefing has become a constant battlefield, where its spokespersons clash with the Western press almost on a daily basis. Entering the words "Hua Chunying," the ministry's top spokesperson, and "*nu dui*" (fiercely refute) into Google generated more than 8 million results as of September 2020. Hua is an avid Twitter user and debates frequently with Morgan Ortagus, her American counterpart, on this platform—never mind the irony that Twitter is banned in China. Hua has her own fan groups. Her fans refer to her as "Hua Jie" (Sister Hua) or simply "*nüshen*" (the Goddess) who is leading the foreign ministry's information department, also known as China's "*waijiao diyi tiantuan*" (top diplomatic godlike troupe).[17]

A Voice of America news analysis, by invoking a Confucian saying, tried to make sense of the hardening attitudes among Chinese diplomats.[18] Confucius once said: *"Shangyou suohao; xiabi shenyan"*—when subordinates sense what their superiors want, they will try to serve to the extreme. This saying suggests that there must be leaders still higher on the chain of decision making whose words and actions serve as clear signals to China's diplomats, emboldening the latter to turn uncompromising even at the cost of looking cantankerous in the eyes of foreign audiences. In a sense, Xi Jinping's zing at "well-fed foreigners" in 2011 became foretelling. By turning Xi's colorful rebuke into a constant choir, Chinese diplomats are revealing their increasing sensitivity to the need to hail the leader.

The strategy has worked for Yang and Wang professionally. Both ministers have been promoted to the position of state councillor. In Wang's case, the promotion was particularly significant. Before him, two foreign ministers had been promoted to state councillor: Tang Jiaxuan and Yang Jiechi. But this only happened after their tenure at the foreign ministry had ended. Wang, by contrast, was elevated to state councillor while still serving as the foreign minister. Apparently, Wang's controversial handling of the press conference in Canada did not hurt him back at home. It may even have helped him gain political capital. Wang's promotion could be seen as a personal victory, but even so, Wang is still excluded from the country's core decision-making unit—namely, the executive branch of the Communist Party of China (CCP), the Politburo. Hence, Wang's influence is not comparable to that enjoyed by his Western counterparts like the American secretary of state or the British foreign secretary.

This observation is not to suggest that the Chinese Ministry of Foreign Affairs (MFA) has simply been pushed aside. Rather, it enriches a fuller account of how Chinese diplomats' fight for their influence continues. In 2017, for the first time in twenty years, Yang Jiechi secured a seat at the Politburo. This would be a major career breakthrough for China's top diplomat. In this new capacity, Yang has served as Xi's "personal envoy" on multiple occasions, dispatched to solve contingent issues like the nuclear crisis on the Korean Peninsula, China's border dispute with India, and anxiety about China's Belt and Road Initiative (BRI), among others. In June 2020, at a time when much of the world was in lock down to combat the Covid-19 pandemic, Yang flew to Hawaii to meet with Mike Pompeo, the US secretary of state that the Chinese media just called "the public enemy of mankind."[19] The meeting did not go well but Yang's authority in Chinese foreign policy making left few in doubt.

By looking at Yang's ascendancy, Wang Yi and China's future foreign ministers may see that their true opportunities lie in the post-ministerial phase—that is, they could be settled into a shadowy yet institutionalized role as a senior adviser to the top leadership, a diplomatic consigliere, so to speak. Needless to say, the role has a Chinese-sounding title: director of the Central Foreign Affairs Commission Office. In much the same way as the movie *The Godfather*, where the German Irish Tom Hagen does not have Sicilian blood running in his veins yet gains the ear of two generations of godfathers thanks to his loyalty and knowledge, Chinese diplomats are facing a similar predicament. They may not be able to claim the ideological lineage possessed by those in the military—that is, the *redness*—but their loyalty and expertise still help them, at least the very top few of them, to sail far.

One Ministry, Multiple Battlefronts[20]

Things used to be simpler for Chinese diplomats. When China opened its door in 1978, officials at the foreign ministry were the targets of popular envy. After all, in a country of more than a billion people, diplomats were among the few who had the rare privilege of seeing the world and purchasing sought-after commodities at special stores.

Those years are gone for good. Today, as the world's second biggest economy and the top trading nation, China boasts global connections vast and deep. An ever-growing number of Chinese citizens are headed for destinations from pole to pole—for business and for pleasure. Needless to say, a global power calls for a global diplomacy. However, the MFA is feeling rising duress. Its diplomats are confronting battlefronts from multiple directions. Horizontally, inter-ministerial competition is unfolding to the disadvantage of the MFA. As the country's diplomatic landscape expands, the MFA is meeting more and more domestic contestants vying for influence in foreign policy making. In the game of intragovernmental competition, the MFA's most formidable challenger comes from the military. As an institution, the People's Liberation Army (PLA) claims a superior ideological ground buttressed by its direct lineage tied to the birth of the party. Its demographics are more rural, and its indoctrination more nationalistic. In recent years, the military has been increasingly active in Chinese diplomacy. While doing so, its voices do not always match those preferred by career diplomats.

This is not to suggest that the PLA is winning in the diplomatic turf war. A more accurate account is that the military is gaining momentum as a new player. But it has its own Achilles' heel; lacking combat experience for more than three decades, its capability does not always match its ambition. By contrast, utilizing their on-the-ground knowledge and sensitivity, the Chinese diplomats are the ones who played a key role in crisis management like the withdrawal of citizens from war-torn regions of Yemen and Libya.[21]

The military is but one competitor. Other civilian ministries, due to their expertise in specific functional issue areas, have narrower and better-defined agendas than the MFA. The MFA has undergone a paradoxical transformation: as the organization professionalizes, its authority in foreign policy making is eroding. To use the term of Margaret G. Hermann and Charles F. Hermann, despite the MFA's nominal significance, the ministry has seen its status as a core "legitimate decision unit"—that is, a unit capable of committing the necessary resources and making authoritative decisions—contested.[22] Zheng Yongnian, a prominent China watcher, echoes this view by contending that Chinese diplomats have become technical workers conducting procedural "petty diplomacy" with no long-term strategies. Even executing "petty diplomacy" turns out to be difficult, for the governmental constituents that the MFA serves often have conflicting agendas.[23]

Another battlefront comes from above: the MFA's organizational maturation has created an increasingly professional but docile career bureaucracy. Executing Chinese diplomacy has always been a political process. Yet, until recently, the ministry's heads had been denied a crucial access point to decision making at the core—that is, a seat in the Politburo. Yang Jiechi's post-MFA promotion ended this long drought. Assuming this pattern sustains, the country's current and future foreign ministers may ease into the club of absolute elites by serving as shadowy yet powerful advisers to the political core.

To be sure, there has been much talk about Xi Jinping's effort to crown himself the "chairman of everything."[24] Since 2018, the party's propaganda machine has been intensifying the campaign of "one singular authority decides all" (dingyuyizun). This phrase originally came from China's monumental history book *Record of the Grand Historian*. Author Sima Qian used it to describe the overwhelming authority enjoyed by Qin Shihuang, the first emperor who united China. Almost two thousand years later, the phrase has found a new claimant in Xi Jinping.[25] But as politics goes personalistic, a new role could be carved out for China's senior diplomats—diplomatic confidants for the one man. Serving as this singular authority's "personal envoy" could mean a new spring of career enhancement.

The third battlefront confronting the MFA comes from below: societal pressure. Such pressure takes various forms: one is the popular tendency of blaming the MFA for China's diplomatic woes, thus making the ministry a scapegoat by default. Relatedly, the party leadership's populist message has overstretched the MFA's resources. Freedom of international travel enjoyed by more and more Chinese has also reduced the allure of becoming a diplomat. Wang Yi's status as a celebrity minister could solicit admiring remarks from his fans, but being an internet sensation does not necessarily translate into the ability to fire up troops and lure in young blood. In recent years, brain drain has become a serious problem for the ministry. The fight for maintaining influence on multiple battlefronts is exhausting an overcommitted ministry and testing its people's morale. Minister Wang and his successors may finally see some light at the end of their personal career tunnels. But long-term problems for the MFA's foot soldiers remain.

Where You Sit Determines Where You Stand

Studying Chinese diplomats' role in foreign policy making requires a domestic level of analysis, which treats groups as actors and examines their collective identities and agendas vis-à-vis those of other domestic competitors and/or collaborators. This is a relatively new direction in the study of international relations. A much longer tradition is the statist rational actor model. Realism, both classical and its structuralist variants, treats states as singular, coherent actors. These actors make calculated, rational decisions to maximize their interest in a fundamentally zero-sum world.[26] It would be unfair, though, to single out realism as the sole perspective that treats states as unitary actors. Institutional liberalists like Robert Keohane and Michael Doyle challenge the pessimistic realist perception of seeing the world as a win-lose situation. However, they share the realist assumption of treating the state as a unitary actor with a clear-headed calculation of its interests.[27]

Such statist analysis is particularly influential in the study of Chinese foreign policy. Realism has a markedly receptive audience in China. The theory was among the first to be introduced to the country after it opened up. Henry Kissinger, one of realism's most well-known practitioners, has been courted by generations of Chinese leaders.[28] Many in China may not know Kissinger's official titles during the Nixon and Ford presidencies; still fewer would know how controversial Kissinger remains in his home country. In the presidential campaign season of 2016, Bernie Sanders criticized Hillary Clinton for praising Kissinger on multiple occasions. He called Kissinger "one of the most destructive secretaries of state in the modern history of this country."[29] Such noises do not exist in China. There, Kissinger's most familiar title is "*Zhongguo renmin de laopengyou*"—an old friend of the Chinese people. For a culture that stresses connections, to be granted this title is no small feat.[30]

Meanwhile, numerous works have examined Kissinger and Richard Nixon's joint decision to open relations with China through the realist lens of balance of power.[31]

To be sure, Sanders's repeated bashings of Kissinger sound archaic, given that his base consists largely of young voters who barely know who Kissinger is and what he did. But the theory that Kissinger is associated with remains influential to contemporary policy makers and scholars. This would include the tendency of treating states as rational, unitary actors. For example, there has been much discussion on China's rising aggressiveness in recent years, especially its military buildup and confrontations with Southeast Asia and Japan on maritime disputes. Scholarly analysis and media coverage often see "Beijing," shorthand for the unitary Chinese state, as launching a calculated and coherent offensive to intimidate neighbors, challenge America, and expand its own authority.[32] As a recent example, in August 2019, President Trump's musing of purchasing Greenland from Denmark was made public and received ridicule at home and abroad. Angered by the Danish prime minister Mette Frederiksen's comment that the idea was "absurd," Trump abruptly postponed his trip to Denmark. In defense of the president, Senator Tom Cotton published an op-ed in the *New York Times*, claiming that he was the brain behind the purchasing idea and that if America does not lock in Greenland's security significance and economic benefit, Beijing will. In a Machiavellian applaud of the president, Cotton praised Trump as being "crazy like a fox."[33]

But this line of analysis has problems. First, it is not entirely convincing that the personalized "Beijing" has become consistently aggressive. Alastair Iain Johnston contends that there is really nothing new in China's "new" assertiveness. The Chinese government is still following the same foreign policy preferences and rhetoric laid down in the early 1990s. According to Johnston, recent talks on China's mounting assertiveness are more of a media phenomenon than a high-quality intellectual endeavor.[34] Likewise, Camilla T. N. Sørensen sees Chinese foreign policy not as self-confident and assertive but rather as increasingly inward looking, reactive, and incoherent.[35]

This statist model does not fit Chinese political development either. At the time when China shut its door, diplomacy was an elitist concept. People looked at those able to travel abroad in awe and envy. Diplomats constituted a sizeable portion of such privileged few. A point could be made that, at that time, the MFA was more or less like one ministerial actor monopolizing the execution of Chinese diplomacy. Today, China's reach has penetrated into every corner of the globe. Countless domestic actors—national, local, public, private, collective, individual—are interacting with the world. For the statist rational actor model to hold, one has to assume either that none of these actors would matter in foreign policy or that they have identical policy preferences. Neither assumption is convincing. The diversification of domestic sources of Chinese diplomacy is real. Its impact should be analyzed, not glossed over.

Challenging the state-as-unitary-actor assumption, the theory of bureaucratic politics tries to pry open the black box of policy contestation among domestic actors. As Max Weber points out, "In a modern state the actual ruler is necessarily and unavoidably the bureaucracy, since power is exercised neither through parliamentary speeches nor monarchical enunciations but through the routines of administration."[36] Indeed, a key feature of Chinese modernization has been the rise of bureaucratic politics. By boosting the role of administrators, China has joined the global mainstream of modern governance.

Building on the Weberian tradition, Graham Allison questions the rational actor assumption, termed Model I, by developing two alternative models focusing on bureaucratic politics: Model II, which analyzes organizational process and coordination from the top, and Model III, which studies the diverse conceptualizations of goals of various administrative units.[37] Allison's models are valuable. They call for attention to the dynamics of governmental politics. Nonetheless, they have conceptual caveats: some scholars question whether one can really distinguish between Model II and Model III.[38] The inter-ministerial relations are unlikely to be consistently cooperative (Model II) or confrontational (Model III). Therefore, instead of attempting to clearly demarcate one model from another, one should study how powers of competing ministries wax and wane in the decision-making process and across issue areas. It is through this lens this chapter examines the Chinese Foreign Ministry's changing roles in foreign policy making.

Servile by Design

China's governing structure has accorded the MFA great nominal importance. The State Council, which is synonymous with the central government of China, currently has twenty-six ministerial units under its jurisdiction. If one counts the council's affiliated units whose heads are accorded full minister status, the number swells to more than fifty. On March 24, 2018, a few days after Li Keqiang assumed his second term of premiership, he announced the structure of the new State Council to the nation. The document listed the MFA as the top ministry, followed by the Ministry of

Defense (MOD) and the National Development and Reform Commission (NDRC).[39] Accordingly, Wang Yi, the current foreign minister, is ranked as the top minister in the Li cabinet.

The 2018 ranking was not new. In fact, in ranking the ministries, the premier was simply following a time-honored tradition. These ministries have been ranked in their exact positions since 2003, when the NDRC was formed under Premier Wen Jiabao. Prior to 2003, the archive shows that as early as 1988 the MFA and the MOD were ranked as the top two, followed by the State Planning Commission, the predecessor of the NDRC.[40] At the organizational level, the Chinese government has consistently designated the MFA as the country's most important ministry. With such great prestige comes the ultimate demand on discipline. That the MFA is consistently ranked above the MOD is revealing—being the "elder brother" in the governing hierarchy carries a heavy dose of servility. The MFA's position is indicative of the scrutiny and constraint it receives from the top.

On shaping the MFA's identity, no leader has a more profound impact than Zhou Enlai, the People's Republic of China's first premier and foreign minister. Zhou was not only a competent diplomat but also an effective educator. His diplomatic thoughts and policies have outlived his era. Chinese diplomats today continue to cherish Zhou's teachings as sacred wisdom. In 1954, Zhou issued a sixteen-character statement to his subordinates that remains the cardinal requirements for Chinese diplomats: unswerving loyalty, mastery of policies, professional competency, and observance of discipline (*zhanwen lichang, zhangwo zhengce, shuxi yewu, yanshou jilü*).[41] They are the motto for the Chinese Foreign Affairs University, the MFA's training institution. Today the school's front gate still features Zhou's calligraphy, the only inscription Zhou ever produced for any Chinese higher-learning institution. Mao may be worshiped as the country's founding father, but among the country's diplomats Zhou is the divine figure.

Zhou demanded diplomats to carry out their duties as "plainclothes People's Liberation Army soldiers" (*buchuan junzhuang de jiefangjun zhanshi*).[42] This metaphor created an ingrained image for generations of Chinese diplomats. Just like their uniformed colleagues, Chinese diplomats must place absolute loyalty to the party and complete submission to leaders as their most fundamental principles. Indeed, if there is any difference between the MFA and the military, it is the diplomats' civilian clothes: paradoxically their civilian clothing serves as a reminder for greater self-discipline. Diplomats are held to an even more stringent standard than the military when it comes to self-monitored compliance.

The identity of plainclothes soldiers remains powerful. It is not uncommon for the MFA's top bureaucrats to use military-style rhetoric when addressing junior colleagues. They use "troops" (*duiwu*) to describe China's diplomatic corps and "war front" (*zhanxian*) to depict diplomatic agendas.[43] Such militant vocabulary, once familiar to everyone during the Mao era, has largely disappeared in public life—except in the most politicized units. These combatant-style words apparently remain robust as mobilizing terms inside the MFA. For young people who join the Chinese military, the majority of them will serve for three to four years and then return to civilian life, at which point they will no longer live under stringent codes of conduct. For young college graduates who join the MFA, however, they will remain soldiers throughout their career. Requirements for unquestionable loyalty and complete obedience are lifelong.

Growing Professionalism, Narrowing Career Path

For decades, the paramilitary identity of "plainclothes soldiers" has persisted as a core requirement for Chinese diplomats. However, this norm cannot fully explain the recent trajectory: that is, the MFA's growing servility and marginalization in policy making. To make sense of this trend, one needs to turn to more contemporary reasons. Paradoxically, the MFA's professionalization contributes to its beleaguered situation.

The MFA, like other Chinese governmental agencies, has come to be managed by technocrats. These are trained experts with knowledge in specific functional issue areas. Though anyone with a college degree may apply to the ministry, its entrance examination clearly favors those majoring in foreign languages, political science, and international business.[44] This professionalization, however, has been coupled with the delinking of top MFA officials from the core of the party's decision-making process—until recently.

Wang Yi' promotion to state councillor while still serving as foreign minister rekindled any hope of elevating the MFA's status. Yang Jiechi's entry into the Politburo was even more significant, as it ended the absence of diplomatic bureaucrats in the party's top executive branch since 2002, when Qian Qichen retired from the post of vice premiership. Qian was popularly referred to by the Chinese media as the country's "diplomatic godfather" (*waijiao jiaofu*), an odd metaphor given the mafia connotation that the word "godfather" carries in the West.[45] But the term was certainly indicative of the influence Qian yielded in the diplomatic realm. His most celebrated accomplishment, according to the official narrative, was helping China end its fate of being shunned in the wake of the 1989 Tian'anmen Massacre and achieving this goal by practicing the spirit of "enduring humiliation in order to accomplish something crucial" (*renru fuzhong*).[46]

Sixteen years after Qian departed the stage, Yang eventually secured another diplomatic seat at the Politburo. But he was still one step below the diplomatic godfather's highest achievement—vice premiership. To put it another way, by serving as both a member of the Politburo and a vice premier, Qian Qichen could claim being in the top leadership in both the party *and* the administrative apparatuses. Given that all four current vice premiers are either about the same age or significantly younger than Yang Jiechi and Wang Yi, it would be unlikely that either minister would advance further upward to vice premiership. The personnel distancing from the party core is apparent when one examines the backgrounds of those who have held China's top diplomat position, the foreign minister (table 3.1).

One can make a number of observations from table 3.1. The eleven foreign ministers of the People's Republic can be placed into three generational groups. The first three were professional revolutionaries. All participated in the Communist Revolution as prominent or high-ranking cadres. Zhou Enlai and Chen Yi were among the founding fathers of the military. All three fought wars. Zhou's and Chen's tenures as foreign minister overlapped with higher administrative posts for some years—Zhou as premier and Chen as vice premier and marshal.

The next four foreign ministers belonged to the second generation—the underground activist generation. All secretly joined the CCP as students. In fact, as Qian Qichen recalls in his memoir, at age sixteen he joined the party inside a telephone booth, taking oath to a stranger sent by the organization.[47] To use the CCP's vocabulary, these four ministers jointed the revolution in the "white zone"—areas ruled by Chiang Kai-shek's nationalist government. Most of them had little military experience.

For this generation, their higher administrative positions did not overlap with their foreign minister tenures. But most of them reached vice premiership, the second highest position in the State Council. Wu Xueqian and Qian Qichen were also members of the Politburo. The lone exception was Qiao Guanhua, but even for him the pattern would have applied. As revealed by the *People's Daily's*, during the Cultural Revolution, the Maoist Gang of Four promised Qiao a vice premiership. After the arrest of the four, Qiao maintained a symbolic consulting post at the Chinese People's Friendship Association. The would-be vice premier spent his last six years in humiliation and depression.[48]

From 1998 to the present, China has had four foreign ministers. They constitute the third, technocrat generation. All four received a college education under the People's Republic; all majored in foreign languages, and all were career diplomats. Their post-MFA career achievements were lower than those of their predecessors. Thus far only Yang has been admitted to the Politburo. None of them were promoted to vice premier. Tang Jiaxuan, Yang Jiechi, and Wang Yi became state councillors, a position ranked one level lower than the vice premiership. Li Zhaoxing, a diplomatic firebrand, turned into a self-proclaimed poet and joined the Foreign Affairs Committee of the National People's Congress, China's rubberstamp legislature.

The personnel distancing from the party core hurts the MFA's clout. The

Table 3.1. Backgrounds and Highest Political Positions of Chinese Foreign Ministers

Name	MFA Tenure	Background	Highest Party/ Government/ Military Positions Held	Military Experience
Zhou Enlai	1949–58	Revolutionary	• Premier (1949–76) • Politburo Standing Committee member (1956–76)	Yes
Chen Yi	1958–72	Revolutionary	• Marshal of the PLA (1955–74) • Vice Premier (1965–75) • Politburo member (1956–69)	Yes
Ji Pengfei	1972–73	Revolutionary	• Vice President of the National People's Congress (NPC) (1978–83)	Yes
Qiao Guanhua	1973–76	Underground party activist	• Purged after the Cultural Revolution	No
Huang Hua	1976–82	Underground party activist	• Vice Premier (1976–82) • Vice President of the National People's Congress (NPC) (1983–88)	Yes
Wu Xueqian	1982–88	Underground party activist	• Politburo member (1982–92) • Vice Premier (1988–93)	No
Qian Qichen	1988–98	Underground party activist	• Politburo member (1992–2002) • Vice Premier (1993–2003)	No
Tang Jiaxuan	1998–2003	Career diplomat	• State councillor (2003–8)	No
Li Zhaoxing	2003–7	Career diplomat	• Foreign Affairs Committee of the NPC (2008–13)	No
Yang Jiechi	2007–13	Career diplomat	• State councillor (2013–18) • Politburo member (2018-present)	No
Wang Yi	2013-present	Career diplomat	• State councillor (2018-present)	No

party emphasizes its absolute control of the MFA, in much the same way it imposes control on the PLA. Hence, for the ministry to matter, its chief needs to be institutionally included as a member of the top political branch. After all, under the party's monopoly, a leader's political or military title has always been more important than his ministerial one. Yang's ascendancy to the Politburo is significant. Yet it remains to be seen whether this promotion will become institutionalized. Will the current minister, Wang Yi, be able to walk on Yang's path? Wang is only three years junior to Yang. By the time the next Politburo members are chosen, he will be seventy-two years old. The burden of securing another diplomatic seat at the party core will be heavy on a septuagenarian bureaucrat.

Lost in Exhaustion: The *Zheteng* of Chinese Diplomats

As a country's diplomatic scope broadens, it is natural that more actors will be involved. But Chinese diplomats have greater challenges. Simply put, the MFA has been under bureaucratic stress by serving too many administrative patrons with different agendas: it needs to, as always, serve "up" to leaders; it needs to serve horizontally, offering assistance to lateral ministries; and it needs to serve "down" to the public, providing services to people traveling overseas, whose number has been increasing exponentially. To be sure, these are the responsibilities for all foreign ministries. But Chinese bureaucrats were so used to serving in just one direction—upward—that many are feeling overwhelmed. Furthermore, the MFA is handling growing expectations with shrinking authority. The stretch of its resources has exhausted the ministry.

A multidirectional analysis of the MFA's services starts with the one direction it is most familiar with—serving the leaders. The party has experienced three leadership transitions since the Tian'anmen Massacre of 1989: from Deng Xiaoping to Jiang Zemin in 1992, to Hu Jintao in 2002, and to Xi Jinping in 2012. This is also the era when China ascended from the position of an international pariah to a global powerhouse. How did these three generations of leadership manage their relations with the country's diplomats? One trend is their efforts to synchronize China's domestic and foreign policy agendas into one grand strategy, often framed in zeitgeist-like slogans. But the two components are not equal—its foreign agenda is to serve its domestic counterpart.

As a leader, Jiang Zemin started the habit of using a slogan to justify his legitimacy. For Jiang, though, his "Three Represents" was primarily domestic—it was about transforming the party into a more inclusive, capitalist-friendly political organization. He did not really have an equivalent foreign policy agenda. Instead, he carefully heeded Deng's famous "hide brightness, nourish obscurity" (*taoguang yanghui*) low-profile master plan. Jiang had neither the authority nor the need to come up with his own diplomatic strategy.

Domestic changes that Jiang initiated would later haunt his successors and hurt the MFA particularly badly. To justify the party's legitimacy in the post–Cold War world, Jiang turned to nationalism. One foreign policy consequence was to turn Japan into an enemy. Though anti-Japan sentiment began to creep up in the 1980s, the government then was suspicious toward young protestors denouncing Japan's "economic invasion." Now, desperate for a new pillar to support its legitimacy, it decided to steal the show. Stirring up hatred toward Japan became a government-sponsored mega project.

Japan was the first in the West to approach China after the 1989 Tian'anmen Massacre. For several years in the early 1990s, it was the lone voice in urging its allies to lift sanctions at the G7 summits. In 1992, the Miyazawa Ki'ichi cabinet even sent off the Japanese emperor on an unprecedented royal visit to China—a rare victory for a Chinese government shunned by most Western countries. But as Chinese self-confidence recovered, nationalist education intensified. Meanwhile, the Chinese government conducted consecutive nuclear tests, much to Tokyo's chagrin. Patriotic education led to the rise of nationalistic and chauvinistic sentiments, especially among the young. The so-called angry youth (*fenqing*) generation, frustrated by what they perceived as China's spineless diplomacy, vented their anger to the MFA. As Susan Shirk points out, the Chinese government wanted its people to hate Japan and America enough to support the government's legitimacy—but not too much to rock the boat of trade and investment.[49] To walk on this tightrope is not always possible. For all the problems created by the inconsistency of the leadership's domestic and foreign agendas, the MFA has become the scapegoat by default.

Among the three post-1989 party leaders, Hu Jintao is commonly perceived as the weakest, if not an outright puppet, with the Jiang loyalists known as the "Shanghai Clique" maintaining actual control.[50] However, one should not underestimate Hu's effort of reorienting Chinese diplomacy. Indeed, it was Hu who first tried to synchronize China's domestic and foreign policy agendas into a coherent whole: that is, to establish a "harmonious" and "people-oriented" world (*hexie shijie, yiren weiben*). The agenda encompassed both domestic and international dimensions. Driven by this slogan, Hu and Premier Wen Jiabao, his populist partner, attempted to merge domestic and foreign policies into one grand package.

As Chinese folk wisdom goes, when leaders propagate a value, it is often a concealed way of admitting that the propagated value is where the country is failing the most. Hu's China was a country with rising ambitions and explosive tensions. Corruption and inequality became so rampant that they could implode the Chinese society.[51] Seen from this perspective, Hu was promoting "harmony" and "people first" ideology exactly because China was at risk of being torn by conflicts of all sorts.

Like his predecessors, Hu focused on internal politics. Soon after assuming leadership, Hu told the nation in a very colloquial way that his goal for the country was "*bu zheteng.*" The Chinese audience got the message right away, but the English media were baffled. The MFA translated it as "avoid self-inflicted setbacks." But many media outlets, including the national Xinhua News Agency, rejected this translation, pointing out that the MFA's translation failed to convey the idea of "chaos" and "self-inflicted exhaustion" associated with the word "*zheteng.*" Unable to find a matching English equivalent, many outlets simply chose to use the word "*zheteng*" as if it were an English verb. Hu's speech came to be known as the speech of "no *zheteng,*" often with a lengthy footnote to make sense of the inexplicable word.[52]

For the MFA, however, Hu's "no *zheteng*" created the opposite effect: it overwhelmed the ministry. Its inelegant translation was only the beginning. The ministry was busily heeding Hu's vision by committing to two grand projects: promoting China's soft power to substantiate the "harmonious world" and enhancing services to citizens to satisfy the populist "people-oriented" demand. Structurally, Hu's slogans transformed the ministry into an intragovernmental coordinator, as both the "harmonious world" and the "people-oriented" agendas required mobilizing governmental agencies at all levels. Normatively, Hu's synchronized agenda strengthened the servile attitude of the MFA, making it abundantly clear that the ministry's job was to serve the leaders, to serve sibling ministries, and to serve the public. To quote Ma Zhengang, a senior Chinese diplomat, the MFA staff would need to be "all eyes and ears at all times."[53] In an internal speech, the then foreign minister Yang Jiechi reminded colleagues that the ministry was nothing more than a small piece of a grand chess set called China (*yipanqi*). The term "*yipanqi*" in Chinese political vocabulary carries the unmistakable connotation of self-belittling and self-sacrificing for the common good—the "big picture," so to speak. By invoking this term, Yang implicitly admitted the exhaustion his subordinates are facing. But his message remains upbeat: Chinese diplomats must stop self-pitying in order to better serve the country's overall interest.[54]

Following Hu is the strongest leader China has seen since Deng Xiaoping. One year after Xi Jinping took the helm, he created the National Security Commission. Prior to the founding of this organization, Chinese leaders tended to handle major domestic and international security issues in ad hoc "leading groups." It is widely speculated that the Chinese leaders longed to establish a permanent organization modeled after America's National Security Council.[55] However, there is a crucial structural difference between the American NSC and its Chinese counterpart. The American one has six key members: president, vice president, secretary of state, secretary of defense, secretary of treasury, and national security advisor.[56] The Chinese structure is quite different. At present, it has only three publicized members: Xi as the chairman, Premier Li Keqiang, and the first vice premier as vice chairmen. All three are members of the ultra-elitist standing committee of the Politburo—the core of the core. Xi's aide Ding Xuexiang, director of the party's general office, is also widely believed to be in the committee.

The Chinese NSC is thus party machinery, not a governmental agency. Its composition is political, and its purpose is to consolidate Xi's personal control of China's vast security apparatus.[57] Its focus tips toward domestic security.[58] In stark contrast to America's NSC, which the secretary of state is a key member of, no one from any ministry is a publicly acknowledged member of the Chinese NSC. The foreign ministry is most likely consulted on matters related to Chinese foreign policy, but its presence in the NSC is elusive. Wang Yi, the current Chinese foreign minister, is apparently not a leading member of this crucial decision-making body. So far, Wang has witnessed three US secretaries of state come and go—John Kerry, Rex Tillerson, and Mike Pompeo—but he is no equivalent to any of them.

Under Xi, all authorities point to him—hence, the nationwide propaganda campaign of rekindling the ancient saying *dingyu yizun* (one singular authority decides all). Diplomacy is no exception. This power concentration reveals Xi's perception of security: domestic stability is the core, and the control of the security apparatus needs to be personal. Such concentration of authority does not necessarily mean bad news to China's top diplomats: though lacking any formally assured arrangement, they may serve as the singular authority's diplomatic confidants. Yang's promotion to the Politburo and his consecutive missions in the capacity of Xi's "personal envoy" could mean new opportunities for his future successors.

But the role of close confidants is contested. Vice President Wang Qishan and Vice Premier Liu He are two formidable competitors. Neither of them is a member of the standing committee of the Politburo. But they are widely perceived as Xi's surrogates on managing vital diplomatic issues like relations with America. Another contestant is Wang Huning, a political adviser who has mentored three generations of top leadership, from Jiang to Xi. Wang is a member of the standing committee, though until recently his main responsibility seemed to be ideological control. In July 2019, Wang accompanied Xi in meeting with Chinese ambassadors. His publicized presence signaled that Wang is no longer just the country's ideological tsar. His influence has now spilled into diplomacy. The Chinese premier, Li Keqiang, on the other hand, was absent at this meeting. His non-attendance was peculiar, for it is his government, not the party, to which these ambassadors are institutionally answerable. Now, as the head of the Chinese government has publicly stepped aside on managing diplomacy, his diplomatic lieutenants' feelings of being marginalized should no longer surprise anyone. Maybe to be idolized as an internet sensation is the best a Chinese foreign minister could hope for.

An Enlarged Agenda and More Competitors

Besides dealing with constraints from the top, the MFA is also facing competition from fellow ministries. At the time when China shut its door, its diplomats enjoyed a near monopoly of representing the country on the international stage. This privilege began to erode in the 1980s. The reform and open-door policy empowered those ministries administering trade and commerce, especially the Ministry of Foreign Economic Relations and Trade (MFERT). Two MFERT ministers would rise to the ranks of national leadership: Li Lanqing, a close ally of Jiang Zemin, became a member of the standing committee of the Politburo; Wu Yi, called by *Forbes* "China's most powerful woman" and "the second most powerful woman in the world" in 2004 and 2007, became a vice premier. Only US Secretary of State Condoleezza Rice and German chancellor Angela Merkel overtook Wu on influence in these two years respectively.[59] No one from the MFA has matched either Li's or Wu's post-ministerial influence.

Chinese diplomacy now is a crowded game, with even more players entering the field. Among these players, the one who has made the most assertive entry is the Chinese military.[60] The term "military diplomacy" (*junshi waijiao*) appeared officially in the *Chinese National Defense Whitepaper* for the first time in 1998. Since then the phrase has become a buzzword for Chinese and foreign media outlets.[61] Though a relative newcomer, the military has been boosting its foreign policy influence with swagger. In doing so, it has clashed with its plainclothes counterpart—the MFA. Such tension can be witnessed in at least three realms: the PLA's rapidly growing international exposure, its more conservative and nationalist identity, and its sensational, militant rhetoric to audiences at home and abroad.

Prior to the PLA's recently enhanced influence, though, its power waned significantly in the 1980s. Deng Xiaoping told the troops to make way for economic development. He further downsized the ground forces by 19 percent.[62] The government only began to seriously reinvest in the military after 1991, when the Gulf War demonstrated the decisive power of a high-tech military. America's swift victory stunned the government and those in uniform, many of whom were still believers in Mao's "People's War" strategy with its emphasis on winning through the sheer number of soldiers.

The PLA's entry into diplomacy would occur later. A new agenda during the Hu Jintao years formally transformed the Chinese military into an active diplomatic player. In 2009, Hu announced Beijing's "New Security" concept, proclaiming that China would adopt a much broader definition of security that encompasses both traditional and nontraditional threats. The latter category would include terrorism, separatism, extremism (the "Three Evils" as termed by the Chinese government), environment, energy, drug and human trafficking, pandemics, and so forth.[63]

To combat these threats would require China to mobilize a variety of resources, especially the armed forces. Their role would be crucial in dealing with the "Three Evils" that topped Hu's list of nontraditional threats. In 2002, the PLA conducted its first joint military exercise with Kyrgyzstan. Since then, as table 3.2 shows, the Chinese military has regularized such exercises, with partners expanding to countries in Europe, North America, Oceania, and Africa.

The military's rising profile has created problems for the MFA. Here it is worth revisiting the phrase "plainclothes soldiers"—this identity has created dual challenges to Chinese diplomats. The "soldiers" part demands them to be just as loyal to the party as those in uniform. Yet, the "plainclothes" part raises the demand of self-discipline still higher for diplomats. Furthermore, it is a self-discipline with no perks in return. Mao Zedong famously said: "Political power grows out of the barrel of a gun."[64] Diplomats, however, hold pens, not guns. It is institutionally impossible for them to launch any credible threat to the party. In other words, while the military needs to be tamed, lamblike diplomats are tamed by default.[65] The party leadership has little to fear when it chooses to axe the MFA's power.

The "plainclothes" identity also hints at a value-based clash between the MFA and the PLA: that is, diplomats and military officers tend to perceive the world differently due to their professional backgrounds. As Graham T. Allison puts it in analyzing domestic sources of American foreign policy making, "Where you sit determines where you stand."[66] Such a perceptive difference used to be minor. After all, the party came to power through consecutive wars over nearly three decades. When the People's Republic was founded, almost every ministry had military roots in terms of its personnel. In the 1950s and 1960s, many diplomats were veterans. A lot of them lacked knowledge of dining, sitting, standing, and speaking properly on diplomatic occasions. Premier Zhou had to offer crash courses on basic etiquette to these peasant-soldier ambassadors.[67] Although these officials lacked in style and class, they compensated their mannerism deficit with ideological purity and revolutionary zeal. They heeded not only Zhou's reminder on discipline

Table 3.2. Chinese Military's Joint Exercise Partners (2002–18)

Year	Exercise Partners
2002	Kyrgyzstan
2003	Shanghai-5 (China, Russia, Kyrgyzstan, Kazakhstan, Tajikistan, Uzbekistan), Pakistan, India
2004	France, Britain, Pakistan, India, Australia, Russia
2005	Russia, Pakistan, India, Thailand, Tajikistan
2006	America, Pakistan
2007	Thailand, Shanghai-5, Western Pacific Naval Symposium (*12 countries*), Russia, Britain, Spain, France, India
2008	India
2009	Peace-09 Multinational Joint Drill (*12 countries*), Gabon, Singapore, Mongolia, Russia
2010	Pakistan, Shanghai-5, Thailand, Singapore
2011	Kyrgzstan, Tajikistan, Indonesia, Pakistan
2012	Russia, Thailand, Shanghai-5, Australia, Belarus
2013	Russia, Indonesia, India
2014	Shanghai-5, Russia, India, United States, Australia, RIMPAC 2014 (*22 countries*)
2015	Russia, Thailand, Kazakhstan, Australia, Khaan Quest (*23 countries*)
2016	Russia, Shanghai-5, Germany, Malaysia, UN Peacekeeping Mission Mali, Khaan Quest (*47 countries*), RIMPAC 2016 (*26 countries*)
2017	Russia, Pakistan, Shanghai-5, UN Peacekeeping Mission in Mali, Cobra Gold (*29 countries*)
2018	Russia, Australia, Nepal, Malaysia, Thailand, ASEAN, United States, Belarus, Khaan Quest (*26 countries*), Komodo 2018 (*34 countries*), Kakadu-2018 (*27 countries*), Bangladesh, Spain, Laos, Myanmar
2019	Russia, Pakistan, Thailand, Peace-2019 (9 countries), Khaan Quest (*38 countries*), Cambodia, ASEAN, Germany, Kygyzstan, Singapore, Laos, Australia, Nepal, Egypt, South Africa

Sources: 2002 to 2013 data provided by the Xinhua News Agency, accessed at http://news.xinhuanet.com/zil iao/2009-07/20/content_11737557_4.htm, May 29, 2015; 2014–17 data provided by the *People's Daily,* accessed at http://military.people.com.cn/n/2014/1216/c1011-26212639.html, January 22, 2016; http://mil.sohu.com/s2015/ zgjy2015/; http://www.sohu.com/a/128270575_628598; http://www.xinhuanet.com/mil/2017-12/23/c_12977 3187.htm; 2018–19 data provided by the Ministry of Defense, accessed at http://www.mod.gov.cn/action/ node_46956_2.htm

but also Mao's call for spreading revolution around the world. To use Mao's metaphor, these battle-hardened diplomats were the sparks that could start a prairie fire around the globe.[68]

Since then, the demographic difference between the MFA and the PLA has widened. Few Chinese diplomats today have a military background. Some brief training to learn the goose step and to fold blankets into a shape resembling tofu is probably the only military exposure China's young diplomats get. The revolutionary zeal is long gone. Nowadays the MFA is full of college graduates from China's most selective universities. They are cosmopolitan, urbane, fluent in foreign languages, and well versed in diplomatic protocols. Meanwhile, the PLA demographics continue to be predominantly rural. The epistemic communities the MFA and the PLA belong to are markedly dissimilar.

This difference did not matter when the PLA had little international exposure. However, this has changed, blurring the division of labor between the MFA and the PLA. Armed with guns, populated with people from poorer and more nationalist regions, and proud of its direct lineage with the party bloodline, the military has been voicing its own stance on delicate issues more loudly. It has also gained more and more high-profile venues to make its voices heard: in 2007, the Chinese military sent its first senior delegation to the prestigious Shangri-la Dialogue, headed by Vice Chief of the General Staff Zhang Qinsheng. The top Chinese participant's rank was raised to defense minister in 2011. Since then, whether the Chinese defense minister will show up at the dialogue has become a weathervane used by observers to gauge the turbulence level of the regional security situation. Ministerial presence is a sign that China at least is willing to talk; ministerial absence is a sign that China has decided to snub the occasion.[69] Meanwhile, the military has begun sponsoring its own security dialogue titled the Xiangshan Forum since 2006. The Ministry of Defense's spokesmen have become celebrity faces to Chinese viewers, like their colleagues at the MFA.

Unlike diplomats, who need to carefully weigh every word they intend to say, military officers are blunt. Their rhetoric may sound gravely menacing to foreign observers. Rear Admiral Zhu Chenghu, for example, once told the *Wall Street Journal* that China would use nuclear weapons on America, even when the latter would use conventional weapons on China. In the same interview, Admiral Zhu also stated that China should be prepared "for the destruction of all the cities east of Xi'an," while America should likewise be prepared for the decimation of hundreds of its cities by the Chinese if the two powers fight.[70] Another senior military officer, whose name remains disputed, warned his American counterpart about a Chinese attack on Los Angeles if America intervened in Taiwan.[71] Chinese diplomats have their own frustration with such military-civilian rhetorical clashes. One Chinese diplomat resorted to a Chinese proverb: "Even when right, an intellectual always loses when talking to a soldier" (*xiucai yujian bing, youli shuobuqing*).[72]

This recognition resonates with the theory of bureaucratic politics. As Francis Rourke points out, the law of bureaucratic inertia suggests that "bureaucracies at rest tend to stay at rest, and bureaucracies in motion tend to stay in motion."[73] No doubt the MFA is fighting to maintain its momentum. Despite the military's assertive posture, this is a fight that civilian soldiers from the MFA are not easily giving up. One weapon that could empower the Chinese diplomats, it turns out, is their expertise and experience. After all, the Chinese military has not engaged in any major military combat since the 1980s, when its clash with Vietnam over disputed borders was winding down. Plainly speaking, as a fighting force, the Chinese military lacks professional experience. With a force that has had little exposure to real fighting experience for almost four decades, even some of its own senior members have expressed lack of confidence—they are unsure whether their troops could live up to the task when duty calls.[74]

By contrast, the MFA's institutional maturation has been accompanied by the rise of an increasingly professional staff team with real experience. They not only are conversant in foreign languages but also possess knowledge about international protocols at times of both peace and crisis. They certainly have better local knowledge of the posts they are assigned to. As a result, it was the MFA rather than the military that acted as the chief coordinating force in orchestrating the withdrawal of Chinese citizens from Libya and Yemen. After all, knowledge is power. An internet search for the phrase "withdrawal of Chinese citizens," however, reveals that media coverage offered more space and attention to those in uniform, with search hits invariably showing photos of smiling soldiers welcoming flag-waving Chinese citizens aboard navy ships. Yet, rank-and-file diplomats armed with knowledge were the unsung heroes.

The PLA is not the only competitor to the MFA. For a long time, the Chinese administrative structure has consisted of governing systems or bureaucratic centers called *xitong*. The foreign-oriented bureaucratic center (*duiwai xitong*) used to be dominated by the MFA with a marginal presence of the MFERT. Today, numerous administrative agencies are feeling entitled to join this *xitong*. One only needs to look at the ministerial participants in the party's Central Conference on Working Relating to Foreign Affairs to get a sense of the packed stage of Chinese diplomacy. An incomplete list of participants shows that the International Department of the Central Committee, the NPC Foreign Affairs Committee, the Ministry of Commerce, the Ministry of Culture, the Information Office of the State Council, the General Staff Department of the PLA, the Supreme Court, the General Prosecutor's Office, the foreign affairs offices at the provincial level, and the chief administrators of major banks all participated in this conference.[75] In fact, for the two conferences in 2013 and 2018, the official news stories did not even list the MFA as the top ministerial participant. That title went to the International Liaison Department of the Central Committee of the CCP in 2013 and to the Central Propaganda Department in 2018. Compared with the meeting chaired by Hu Jintao in 2006, the lists of participants in 2013 and 2018 under Xi Jinping continued to grow longer.[76]

The MFA was once the dominating force of the foreign-related *xitong*. Now it is but one in a crowd. It needs to fight with other ministries for the right to be heard. Many competing ministries are sending their own staff to China's overseas missions. Some of them, like the Ministry of Education, are actively conducting their mini-diplomacy through subsidiaries like the Confucius Institute. Other ministries have found their niche markets in diplomacy—for example, the International Liaison Department of the Central Committee has come to play a leading role in managing China's relations with North Korea. Two recent Chinese ambassadors to North Korea have both come from this department, not the MFA. Hence, handling relations with Pyongyang has become this ministry's guarded home turf. In September, the Chinese government announced its new ambassador to Pakistan, the country's close ally in the region. Ambassador Nong Rong hails from Guangxi Zhuang Autonomous Region and was an official of ethnic affairs. His entire career up to this point was confined to Guangxi.[77] This very unconventional choice is indicative of the ever-expanding pool of competitors that the MFA has to confront.

Pressure from Below

Finally, the MFA is facing pressure from below. The Chinese government has been walking a tightrope, trying to maintain both its open-door policy and nationalist fervor among its citizenry.[78] Such a balancing act is not always possible. When the balance is lost, someone needs to take the blame, and the MFA finds itself the scapegoat by default. As a spokesman for the MFA admitted, the ministry has been receiving calcium pills in the mail on a regular basis—a popular choice of insult from a public that sees Chinese diplomats as spineless.[79] Meanwhile, diplomatic phrases like "strongly denounce" or "strongly protest" have entered Chinese netizens' vocabulary to describe their anger at apparently trivial things, thus a derision that the MFA's "strong denouncements" were worthless. Indeed, in the online world, the MFA has gained a new moniker as the "Ministry of Protests."[80]

When the MFA proudly announced its donation of twenty-three school buses to Macedonia in 2011, it inadvertently turned itself into the target of public ire. More than five hundred thousand comments were posted on China's leading web portal Sina.com. People were asking how the Chinese government could donate school buses to a foreign country when many Chinese schools did not have safe means of transportation for students.[81] Less than two weeks prior to the donation, nineteen children and one adult were killed in a school bus collision in northwestern China. The angry public could not help drawing the harsh comparison between devastating Chinese parents wailing over their children's bodies and smiling Macedonian children in front of shiny school buses. Online mockeries of the MFA in songs and dances exploded. The MFA, having just shown off its school bus donation to echo the party leadership's call for a "harmonious world," had to explain that the donation was "per request from the Macedonian government" and "offered in a limited amount."[82] Such climbdown, however, received little public sympathy. People's rage continued for weeks. For leaders in Beijing, this incident was exactly what *zheteng* looked like—self-inflicted exhaustion.

Societal pressure on diplomacy is also taking the form of feet fleeing—that is, young diplomats are quitting the MFA in hordes. In the earlier years of diplomacy, when even domestic travel was beyond most people's reach, the MFA was envied for having the rare privilege of sending people overseas to see the world. Chinese diplomats and their family members could also purchase highly sought-after items like color televisions, refrigerators, and other electronic appliances at discounted prices in special stores. Ordinary folks, on the other hand, had to save for years and then wait for government-issued vouchers to purchase these items at full prices.

Such days are long gone. Beijing Friendship Store, a once prestigious outlet catering specifically to officials and foreign tourists, became a dilapidated historic relic itself, finally closing its door in 2019. International travel has become affordable to millions of Chinese. The Japanese consulate in Shanghai issued a record-setting 870,000 visas in 2014, despite icy relations between the two governments.[83] At one point in 2015, the consulate even exhausted its entire stock of visa stamps due to the explosive number of Chinese applicants.[84] In 2015, the US diplomatic missions also issued more than 2.44 million nonimmigrant visas to Chinese visitors—though by 2019 this number had been more than halved due to the deterioration of bilateral relations.[85] Given the continuing 20 percent annual increase in Chinese passport holders, the decline in US nonimmigrant visas issued to Chinese applicants simply means that Chinese travelers are headed for other destinations.[86]

For those working in the public sector, ministries and governments at all levels may send their staff on international trips. Their travels are often shorter in duration, lighter on workload, and even recreational in nature. Public sector workers outside the MFA also face fewer disciplinary constraints. Indeed, government-funded international travels have become a major target of Xi Jinping's anticorruption campaign. The collision between partly recreational international travels and obedience to the central leadership's policy on frugality can sometimes produce comical results. In 2013, for example, the Confucius Institute held its North American convention in Bowling Green, Kentucky. Its general director complained to hundreds of attendants, including her Kentuckian hosts, that the original venue had been Honolulu. However, one person wrote a secret report to the higher authorities, claiming that the institute was blatantly violating Xi's anticorruption campaign by hosting the convention at such an expensive location. Fearing that the convention site could attract anger from the top, the institute decided to shift to a low-key place, hence, a small town in western Kentucky. The director went on to complain that all the legal fees and fines the institute had to pay to hosts and hotels in Honolulu for its sudden cancellation, plus bus rental for transporting hundreds of attendees from the Nashville airport to Bowling Green, ended up costing far more than its original budget. She ended her speech by wishing all the convention participants good luck in having nothing to do but drink bourbon in their hotel rooms. The director's candid speech was interrupted by rounds of laughter and applause. And the convention hotel thoughtfully placed free bourbon sample bottles in every room for their Chinese guests. Paradoxically, Xi's crackdown and the Confucius Institute general director's confession reveal the prevalence of such overseas splurges.

The MFA, with its long overseas tenure, underpaid staff, adamant emphasis on discipline, and steep climb to top positions, is losing its lure. Responding to a compliment that the MFA is "fertile ground for talents," a young diplomat quickly quipped: "Thanks to excessive manure like me."[87] Official data show that from 1998 to 2002, 164 people quit their job at the MFA, with 80 percent of them under the age of thirty-five. The trend apparently continues, as one insider revealed that the ministry had to "borrow" personnel from other ministries on multiple occasions.[88] A spokesperson for the Ministry of Personnel admitted that the foreign-oriented *xitong*, especially the MFA and the MFERT, was hit the hardest by such brain drain.[89] To be sure, joining the MFA is still competitive. However, government statistics show that getting into some other foreign-oriented *xitong* units, for example, the Customs Bureau, is much harder. In 2018, sixteen vacant positions at the Shanghai Customs Bureau attracted 975 applicants—a selection ratio of 60.9 applicants per position. Meanwhile, forty-seven vacant positions at the MFA attracted 1,268 applicants. The selection ratio was 27 applicants per position. The MFA was indeed among the top ten most competitive public sector examinations. But it was ranked tenth.[90]

Sidestepped from the top, challenged by lateral ministries, and mocked from below, the MFA, no wonder, is feeling embattled. The ministry's problem is an open secret. In fact, China's official English media, the *China Daily*, published a stinging criticism of the ministry's low morale and excessive bureaucratism. The post was swiftly taken down after just a few hours.[91]

Diplomats as Daughters-in-Law

With ever-deepening integration and technological advancements, connections among nation-states at all levels are growing rapidly. Deepening integration has also led to increasingly specific divisions of labor. Against this background, it is inevitable that more and more actors—public, private, state, and society—will meet, argue, cooperate, and compromise. The days of such acts reserved mostly for diplomats are gone.

The majority of Chinese diplomats, like their colleagues around the world, graduated from college with degrees in foreign languages and international studies. While this may have equipped them with an internationalist perspective, they seldom have expert-level knowledge in functional issue areas. However, more and more international actions are becoming functional. To conduct diplomacy, diplomats can no longer rely on just familiarity with protocol and proficiency in foreign languages. In this sense, ministries of foreign affairs around the globe are reorienting their mission: it is no longer about having *one* ministry handle "affairs" with foreign countries. Rather, it is about having the foreign ministry offer services to leaders, fellow ministries, and the public, as these actors interact with the world. As international interactions become diffusive, diplomacy is becoming dispersive. As functional issues become a major component of international relations, the authority of those well versed in procedure will need to team up with those well versed in substance. Increasingly, the procedure- and language-based, generalist-type diplomats need to serve substance-driven, expert-type technocrats. Diplomats around the world are all dealing with the transition from conducting relations to offering services. Chinese diplomats are no exception to this pattern.

Common challenges notwithstanding, issues confronting the Chinese MFA are particularly worrisome. First, being a Chinese diplomat has always been more political than administrative. The notion of "plainclothes soldiers" speaks volumes about the core values of diplomatic service in China: unswerving loyalty to the party and unconditional submission to discipline. However, these ultimate values attempt to survive at a time when Chinese diplomats' political access has been atrophying—until recently. Even with Yang Jiechi's promotion to the Politburo and Wang Yi's promotion to state councillor, their status is still not equal to the institutionalized roles reserved for their Western counterparts, not to mention that Yang and Wang have internal competitors in the game of earning the party core's attention. Consequences are not just domestic—the MFA's relatively marginalized position in policy making is no secret. To have the ear of the Chinese foreign minister is often not enough, since this person is not a member of the decision-making core. Hence, for foreign governments that seek to strike deals with Beijing, they need to talk *over*, rather than *through*, the MFA.

From Jiang Zemin to Xi Jinping, Chinese leadership has transitioned every ten years, and each generation of leadership aspires to create a pet slogan to boost its own legacy. The MFA has attempted to conduct diplomacy to heed these pet slogans. Such generational jolts have stretched the MFA's resources and enhanced its servility. In 2018, Xi disrupted this pattern by eliminating presidential term limits, thus openly allowing himself to remain China's paramount leader at least for another decade, if not indefinitely. Known as the "chairman of everything," Xi greatly boosted his personal control of the party and the government. A key measure was the founding of the NSC, which consolidated the party's, especially Xi's, control of security affairs. This new development does not necessarily mean bad news to the beleaguered MFA, as a new possibility of serving as the chairman's diplomatic confidant is beginning to emerge. However, it should be noted that the foreign minister is not a statutory member, and the MFA is but one among many ministries to be consulted with. According to the CCP central committee, the NSC's core mission is to "complete and improve the construction of national security institution and national security strategy," an area outside the administrative scope of any single ministry.[92] If anything, the NSC has solidified Xi's personal control at the cost of making China's administrative apparatus auxiliary.

Other ministries are competing with the MFA for access to the top.

Among its challengers, the PLA is the most powerful one due to its privileged access to the political center, self-proclaimed ideological purity, possession of violent means, more nationalist demographics, and sheer number of memberships. Upon the sudden death of Wu Jianmin, a former high-ranking MFA official known for his internationalist and accommodating stance, some high-ranking military officers continued to mock him as "ignorant," "grumpy," and "like a pet dog to foreigners."[93] The PLA seldom, if ever, inform their civilian counterparts of any military act even when such acts could have major diplomatic impact. In fact, during the Hu Jintao years, the military even showed signs of ignoring the party leadership, let alone diplomats. Then US secretary of defense Robert Gates recalls in his memoir that in January 2011, the Chinese military web portal posted photos of the test flights of its secretive J-20 stealth fighter hours before Gates's meeting with Hu. When Gates brought up the issue, Hu seemed taken aback by the test. The party chief later assured his American guest that the test "had absolutely nothing to do" with his visit.[94] But the episode underscored Gates's concern that the PLA could run amok, acting independently of the country's civilian leadership. If they did not bother to check with Hu, they certainly would not bother consulting with their plainclothes, pen-holding civilian soldiers, also known as diplomats. In addition, the PLA is but one of the MFA's many competitors, though probably the most formidable one. Multiple ministries and governments at lower levels are beginning to carry out their own diplomatic activities in parallel to those of the MFA. In this competition, the MFA, shouldered by a staid bureaucratic culture, is fighting to maintain momentum.

Finally, the ministry is under pressure from below—Chinese society. As millions of Chinese head for overseas destinations, the demand for consular services is rising rapidly. The following chapter will examine in detail the challenges this change has brought to Chinese diplomacy. Insofar as the MFA is concerned, the increase has created much administrative stress. In the meantime, two decades of patriotic education has begun to bear fruit. The MFA has often found itself a vulnerable target for public wrath and ridicule. It has become a foreign policy scapegoat by default, at a time when its actual influence in foreign policy making is being contested. The MFA is also struggling to keep talents—it can no longer claim the privilege of offering people international trips or imported merchandises, since numerous ordinary Chinese can just do that, discipline free.

In an interview, a Chinese diplomat likened his ministry to being a "daughter-in-law."[95] The metaphor carries an unmistakably bitter connotation: in a traditional Chinese family, a daughter-in-law sits at the bottom of the hierarchy. She needs to be hardworking, dutiful, loyal, obedient, and willing to take blame for others' mistakes. This diplomat further complained that the MFA has too many mothers-in-law. His grievances would certainly be echoed by some of his colleagues. Yet, to see the MFA as in a hopeless decline would be misleading. By gaining new access points to the top leadership, utilizing policy expertise and on-ground knowledge to offer better services to citizens, and fostering a celebrity-like status of its top officials, the MFA is fighting back. It turns out that even an obedient daughter-in-law has her own ways to persist, rebel, and reclaim her pride in a huge family.

4 • Riding on Dragon's Back

Celebrities, Masses, and Foreign Policy

We have a very large territory and a big population. Atomic
bombs could not kill all of us. What if they killed 300 million of
us? We would still have many people left.
  —Mao Zedong

I use one foot to kick America, and the other to go to America.
  —Joke among Chinese college students

Chinese Hawk or Admiral Seaweed

In an article titled "China's Hawks in Command," the *Wall Street Journal*
journalist William Lam reported on the rising assertiveness expressed by
China's top brass military officers. Lam identified in particular a certain
Major Admiral Zhang Zhaozhong and his McCarthyist attack with Chinese characteristics. In a TV interview, Admiral Zhang claimed that there
are "more than one million traitors" in China and that "some of our scholars are trained by the Americans." He later elaborated in another online
interview: "They read American books, accepted American ideals and they
are now helping the U.S. to fool the Chinese."[1]

Admiral Zhang is indeed a famous man in China. Before retiring in 2015,
he was a professor at the People's Liberation Army National Defense University. While in uniform and now as a civilian, Zhang has been a regular commentator for China Central Television (CCTV) and other media outlets for
nearly two decades. His hosts invariably refer to him as "China's renowned
military theorist" and "famous military commentator."[2] Given his celebrity status, one should not fault an American reporter for citing his words as evidence
of China's rising assertiveness toward enemies from within and without.

People in China, though, have a quite different impression of Admiral Zhang. There he is known by the nickname "Ju Zuo"—a Chinese acronym for "Director of Strategic Fool-You Agency" (*Zhanlve huyouju juzhang*). Netizens jokingly refer to the made-up agency as China's "most secretive administrative unit."[3] Not many people are aware of the admiral's proposed hunting crusade for Chinese traitors. In fact, this comment would fall out of line with Zhang's dismissive attitude toward America, as he frequently resorts to Chairman Mao's metaphor of "paper tiger" when describing the US military.[4]

Described as a scholar in uniform, Zhang has added his derision of America with a pseudoscientific flavor. He once claimed on a CCTV program that China's infamous, cancer-inducing smog is the country's top defense mechanism against American laser weapons: "Smog with PM2.5 readings of 500–600 is virtually impenetrable to lasers. In clear weather, laser weapons have a range of 10 kilometers, but smog can reduce this to less than one kilometer," explained Zhang to the audience.[5] If the admiral's purpose was to attract ridicule, he succeeded—numerous people weighed in online, expressing their amusement. As one commentator put it, "I never knew our government is this thoughtful and caring. It is trying to protect us from American laser weapons almost every day."[6]

This is not the only occasion when Zhang proudly announced China's possession of one-of-a-kind weapons. In a Beijing Television interview, the admiral ensured viewers that they should have no fear of American nuclear submarines: "Our fisherman at the Yellow Sea placed a lot of fishing nets to farm seaweed. Those nets and the plants would entangle and trap the American submarines."[7] This comment earned him a new moniker—"Admiral Seaweed" (*haidai jiangjun*).[8] A cartoon titled "Seaweed War" depicts the admiral in seaweed-donned camouflage, aiming at the enemy with his microphone.[9]

Admiral Zhang has a cult-like following in China. Many fans do not see him as a Chinese hawk; rather, they see him as a comedian in a navy uniform, hence the somewhat affectionate nickname "Juzuo," or "Director of Strategic Fool-You Agency." Even China's own English-language media admit Zhang's notoriety, calling him the "butt of jokes."[10] To many people, tuning in to him adds humor to an otherwise stressful or boring day. Zhang has a self-deprecating persona: though fully aware of the mocking connotation of "Ju Zuo," he has gladly embraced this title. As an editor of a popular Phoenix TV talk show put it: "Young people don't like experts with condescending attitudes. They like people who can be their friends. For example, Zhang encourages playing video games, saying it's a good way to acquire military knowledge. Young people can relate to this, and it makes them feel that Zhang is from their world."[11] In other words, Zhang's appeal to the digital generation lies not in the quality of his comments but in his manner as a down-to-earth, harmless uncle who has turned international security and foreign policy, traditionally dull topics, into something entertaining. The admiral is a comical legend.

To scholars, Zhang's popularity can offer more food for thought than just being a pleasurable snack. It is indicative of the new ways that foreign policy is being connected to the Chinese masses. What Zhang highlights is the economic dimension of foreign policy: glorifying China and trashing America means good business. Admiral Zhang is not really a military theorist. He is an entrepreneur shrewdly cultivating a market of public opinions. For the media who are chasing Zhang, many are doing it not because they want to get serious analysis. To the contrary, they know there is a good chance Zhang will say something hilariously absurd. To them, covering foreign policy through Zhang's mouth could lead to good ratings and bigger circulation numbers. Needless to say, as the author of several best-selling books, Admiral Zhang has profited from his own celebrity status as an expert of war and peace. He is frequently sighted on promotional tours throughout the country, signing piles of his books and shaking hands with fans.

Through Zhang and similar media performers, foreign policy coverage has been commercialized for the public's recreational consumption. This economic process has major political implications. First, it invites the question of what constitutes the concept "public" as one discusses its impact on Chinese foreign policy making. Before China went to a market-based economy, the answer was simple: except for those working for the foreign-oriented system (*duiwai xitong*), foreign policy was largely irrelevant. It was an elitist arena reserved for leaders and officials at the MFA or Ministry of Foreign Economic Relations and Trade. The public, though large in number, was singular in mission—a tool for mass mobilization.

This is no longer true. With the country's rapidly growing international connections, the concept "public" is now a noun with plural form. One often needs to ask which "public" one is examining in state-public interactions over foreign policy. Insofar as this study is concerned, the Chinese public can be categorized into three groups: the publicity hunters like Admiral Zhang, the popular mass as consumers, and the media in the middle, with economic logic linking all three intra-public groups. Furthermore, this economic logic is colliding with the political logic that emphasizes the state's absolute control. The collision is producing mixed results to all players involved.

Common wisdom used to have a simpler and rosier perception of such interactions. In the late 1990s, hopes were high that the internet would render it impossible for authoritarian regimes to maintain their blockage on the public's access to information. As Bill Clinton famously hailed, a new era would dawn on China because controlling the internet would be like "nailing Jell-O to a wall."[12] I may have personally benefited from such optimism—in 1999, when I applied for my first visa to the United States, rejection by the visa officer was the norm; approval was extremely lucky. My own visa interview lasted for about less than a minute. It swiftly ended when I told the visa officer I was going to America to study how the internet could help China become more democratic. No more words were needed. I got my visa. Afterward other applicants surrounded me, eager to know what magical sentences I had used to be so lucky so quickly. Alas, those were the days of great expectations.

The mood could not be more different today. Recently, academics and policy makers have shifted to ask how the Chinese state has managed to nail Jell-O to the wall after all. Some insightful scholarship has been generated on how authoritarian regimes could adapt to a market economy by launching economic propaganda. As Anne-Marie Brady points out, a new generation of Chinese propaganda officials who are knowledgeable about modern methods of mass persuasion, public relations, and political communications is on the rise. They have skillfully transplanted such methods commonly utilized in Western democratic societies onto Chinese soil.[13] The party also has issued broad guidance like "no bad news during holiday/ sensitive dates" or "talk up the economy" to restrict the information flow.[14] Furthermore, a marketized media in compliance with the state's political control, as Daniela Stockmann contends, could even benefit the authoritarian rule because such media brand themselves as trustworthy representatives of ordinary citizens.[15] Finally, Xi Jinping assumed the leadership of the Central Internet Safety and Information Small Group (*zhongyang wangluo anquan he xinxihua xiaozu*). Willy Wo-Lap Lam points out in his study of Xi that the "chairman of everything" repeatedly emphasizes control of the internet as "a matter of life and death for the party." Under his leadership, the government has begun using legal action against netizens who spread "rumors" on microblogs that are reposted more than five hundred times or seen by more than five thousand people.[16] One consensus is emerging from these research findings: the balance tips decisively toward the Chinese government even in the age of the internet.

My own assessment on state-public interactions is in the dynamic middle—it certainly rejects the earlier optimism that saw media in the internet age as tolling the death bell for authoritarian regimes; on the other hand, I am not ready to call the game for the Chinese authorities. In a technology-driven economy, speed with which information is transmitted has become a factor in itself. In a sense, the political logic is always chasing the economic one, even when superficially the former is trying to regulate the latter. As the public enjoys more access points to alternative sources of information with greater speed, people are always playing a "catch me if you can" game with the government. In this game, commercialized media are not a natural ally to the state. They could always first chase the economic logic before they succumb to the political one, utilizing the gap between the two to make profits. Scholars like Stockmann and Carl Minzner suggest that the Chinese government is also using social media as bottom-up "input institutions"—that is, as a mechanism for obtaining societal feedback about their policies.[17] In practice, this means some social space has to be tolerated for citizens to air their sentiments. As the government attempts to close one space, another is opened. There is always a mole to be wacked.

The implications do not stop here. The role of consumer is not the only one that the Chinese public has acquired in influencing foreign policy. Never in China's history has its people been this intricately connected with the rest of the world—both in materialistic and emotive terms. Long gone are the days when watching foreigners was a spectator sport. In 2017, China was the fourth most visited country in the world—following France, Spain, and America but leading Italy. In the same year, people from China made 145 million international trips, an increase of 1,380 percent from the number at the beginning of the new millennium.[18] The average amount of money they spent overseas reached US$2,611 per trip, more than doubling the average spending power of Americans per trip at US$1,236. The potential is even more enticing—in 2017 only 7 percent of Chinese citizens had passports, compared with 42 percent of Americans and 76 percent of British.[19] Figure 4.1 offers a trajectory-based comparison of five selected major outbound tourism markets over a period of twenty-four years. While the other four markets have been stable in the past two decades, China's rise to the top position has been meteoric.

What this means to the world is that China has become the most alluring outbound tourism market. What this means to China is that its people have truly gone global. Interacting with the world is no longer a privilege for leaders and diplomats. As a child growing up in Beijing, I used to perceive my only connection with the world as the occasional summoning to the Tian'anmen Square to jump and wave flags at visiting foreign dignitaries. Chinese people today have far more meaningful and regular contacts with the world.

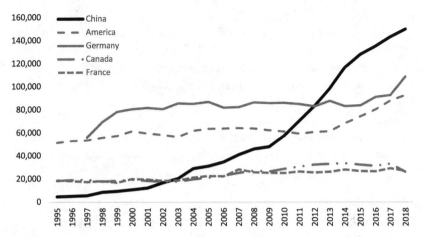

Fig. 4.1. Trajectory-based comparison of selected major outbound tourism markets measured by international arrivals (1995–2018) (*Note:* The number is in thousands. *Data source:* The United Nations World Tourism Organization, https://www.e-un wto.or/doi/suppl/10.5555/unwtotfb0000290019952018202001)

Besides being consumers and constituents, the public could also become disrupters to foreign policy. Unlike disrupters at the leadership level, who invariably end up seeing their own careers ruined and personal freedom stripped, disrupters from the masses have an advantage in their numbers. A new trend is on the rise: people genuinely believe they are defending China's honor, sometimes heroically, on foreign soils by getting combative with local hosts. In practice, though, they act as patriotic vigilantes and create headaches for the Chinese government. This is not to deny that the government is not using popular sentiment to serve its own agendas. The "People's War" tactic remains a mobilization heirloom passed on from one generation of leadership to the next. Yet, as China's propaganda machine keeps drumbeating national pride, the public may voluntarily subcontract the work of boosting ultranationalism and chauvinism. In this process, it may embarrass rather than help leaders and officials. Apparently for one reporter from CCTV, defending national honor meant practically screaming in Birmingham at a British journalist just expelled from Hong Kong for being "anti-China" and then slapping a volunteer in the face who tried to calm the situation.[20] To some other Chinese, honoring China could mean to get hysterical in the streets of Stockholm for being refused the ability to check into a hotel they had booked for one day later and to manhandle a female student from Hong Kong on the campus of the University of Auckland for her support for the pro-democracy movement unfolding in Hong Kong.[21] In all these cases, the government was forced to stand up to protect these acts and portray the Western responses as "racist," "imperialist," and "arrogant." Meanwhile, its swift crackdown on social media's viral reportage on these incidents revealed the other side: the government treated them as headaches rather than glorious moments. Its public display of support was involuntary and even self-defeating. What do all these changes imply? Relations between the Chinese public and the government over foreign policy are getting dynamic. The Chinese government was so used to being on the controlling end. But now the tail can often wag the dog, and the tail is getting very big.

Mass Public and Foreign Policy: How Much Do People Matter?

The study of international relations started with a human touch—though the touch was on the shoulders of leaders. Greek philosopher Plato contended that a "perfect state" was one governed by rulers who were superior in the ways of philosophy and war. He called such ideal rulers "philosopher-kings."[22] As realism began to take root, scholars in this tradition continued their focus on leaders and high-ranking diplomats, in other words, foreign policy elites. In recent decades a new perspective has been on the rise in studying powerful private individuals—retired leaders and former high-ranking officials in particular and their impact on foreign policy. Such prominent individuals' diplomatic maneuvers are sometimes alluded to as "track-two diplomacy," since they exert influence typically in nonofficial capacities. One example would be former US president Jimmy Carter's or former New Mexico governor Bill Richardson's instrumental role in arranging the release of Americans jailed by North Korea.[23]

Inquiries have also been made on influential entrepreneurs like Bill Gates of Microsoft, Mark Zuckerberg of Facebook, or Jack Ma of China's Alibaba. Some have examined the political impact of Hollywood celebrities.[24] These individuals, due to their tremendous wealth, the global presence of their business operations, and their worldwide name recognition, may shape international politics in ways unavailable to governments. As an example, billionaire Jack Ma was the first Chinese guest whom president-elect Donald Trump met. Ma emerged from Trump Tower promising to create one million jobs in America;[25] however, more than one year later, with a trade war looming, Ma warned he would back away from this promise.[26] Besides examining retired leaders and other prominent political and economic dignitaries, this line of inquiries also studies "bad" or "menacing" private individuals like leaders of terrorist groups. One case in point is the examination of the Pakistani nuclear scientist Abdul Qadeer Khan and his secretive transfer of nuclear technology to Iran, Libya, and North Korea, a violation that he admitted on TV in 2004.[27]

This perspective on private individuals offers useful supplements to the traditional approach preoccupied with statist actors. Yet, it does not change the top-down perspective. Its interest remains in studying the elites, given its focus on retired presidents, business tycoons, movie and sports stars, and the fictional Dr. Evil in real life. Furthermore, such track-two diplomacy carried out in individual capacities often invites questions from both the governments involved and the media about these individuals' purposes and utilities of such acts. For instance, then Democratic presidential candidate Jesse Jackson's trip to Damascus in 1984 to free an American pilot was portrayed by *Time* magazine as "dubious"[28] and by the *Washington Post* as "a dash of ginger in American politics—a spice, not a nutriment."[29] President Ronald Reagan emphasized the private nature of Jackson's trip, calling it "a personal mission of mercy," thus rendering Jackson's promises to Syrian president Hafez Al Assad on opening up relations hollow.[30] Some alleged track-two diplomacies were plainly bizarre. They were more like celebrity publicity stunts to fan up fame or notoriety. As former basketball player Dennis Rodman traveled to Pyongyang and sang "Happy Birthday" to the country's young dictator, Kim Jung Un, the Obama administration denounced his visit and declared it would not consult with him after his return.[31] Such reservation was warranted—after all, Rodman apparently mixed up North Korea with its southern neighbor, expressing his hope of running into rapper Psy on his trip to the north, forcing the "Gangnam Style" singer to teach Rodman by tweeting, "I am from the south, man!"[32]

Is the study of international relations thus devoid of approaches that highlight the importance of the masses? There are indeed bottom-up perspectives, most notably Marxism and its contemporary successor, the dependency theory. However, focusing on the masses is not the logical equivalent of seeing people as important. To Marxists and their modern followers, the masses could become agents of revolution only because of their class identities. Yet, as the Chinese experience shows, assigning class labels to people was a subjective, arbitrary, and messy process. It was the culprit for countless human tragedies. The class identity was not only fixed but also hereditary. For those assigned to reactionary classes, no amount of personal effort or sacrifice may soften the party's heart. An allegedly scientific and progressive approach in essence transformed Chinese society into a caste system. Despite the superficial importance that Marxism accorded to the masses, at best the theory was overly deterministic as it focused on one subjective indicator. At worst, and as it happened in China, it offered opportunities for those more equal than others to mislead, delude, and persecute the masses they were singing high praises for.

Masses vis-à-vis Foreign Policy: Hypocrites or Shrewd Consumers?

So, how do we explore the impact that the masses exert on Chinese foreign policy? This question cannot be answered by exclusively relying on a particular perspective. The impact that the Chinese people have on the country's foreign policy has varied. The roles they have played are not fixed. The top-down approach is right in pointing out ample cases by which the Chinese government and its leaders manufactured national sentiments for domestic purposes. Yet, China's global connections have experienced explosive growth in number and complexity. The speed, scope, and substance of such expansion is beyond the control of any government. Since the start of the new millennium, the skyrocketing number of international trips attests to the Chinese public's ever-increasing presence in constituting China's global presence. Never in any country's history has such a massive number of people become constituents of its foreign policy in such a short period of time. People have been creators of the Chinese power. Now they are ready to become its consumers. And as consumers everywhere, their decisions are driven by two main factors: calculation and passion.

These two forces do not always act in tandem. Sometimes people have to cave in to one at the cost of abandoning the other. In this regard, the story of a student named Ma Nan from Peking University (Beida) is revealing. During President Bill Clinton's visit to her university in 1998, Ma stood up during the Q&A session and offered a stinging criticism of America's human rights record. After listing America's human rights abuses, Ma asked Clinton on what grounds America felt it had the moral superiority to criticize China on human rights. In effect, Ma's question was a speech denouncing America as a hypocrite, and, as a speech, it did not need an answer.

The episode earned Ma transient fame: she became known as the "anti-America girl from Beida." But it was quickly buried by the next news cycle. A few years later, though, the story resurfaced as people found out Ma went to America and married an American. The anti-America girl decided to call the country she had denounced her adopted home. To Ma's critics, she became the epitome of a hypocrite.

Such criticism on Ma, though, would be unfair. Q&A sessions on such occasions are almost always staged. As a student at Fudan University in 1995, I had the experience of "asking" questions to the Indian vice president K. R. Narayanan and South Korean politician Kim Dae-jung during their visits to my school. Both would later become presidents of their respective countries. But their importance was clearly one level below that of a sitting American president. Even for these two lesser important guests, I, along with a dozen Fudan students, underwent a weeklong training of reciting questions we were to "ask." From the podium, Narayanan and Kim would see hands raised from every corner of the auditorium, a sign of widespread curiosity. But the truth is that all the hands were planted. They would come from me and other trainees who by then had memorized our questions and knew how to deliver them. Everyone else who was not chosen knew very well it would be wise to remain silent.

If this was the arrangement for an Indian vice president and a South Korean politician, one could only imagine the training that Ma and her chosen peers had to undergo before Clinton's visit. Ma's question most certainly was one she had been made to ask. Her intention of going to America and calling the country home, on the other hand, was probably not imposed by the government. And Ma was not alone—in the wake of NATO's bombing of the Chinese embassy in Belgrade in May 1999, numerous students protested angrily in front of the American embassy. Many of them were from top-ranked schools like Peking University and Tsinghua University, among others. Given their schools' Chinese nickname, "prep-school for American universities" (*liumei yubeixiao*), it would not be a wild guess that some of the protesting students were applying for opportunities to study at American universities. In fact, there was the self-deprecating joke among student protestors at the time: "I use one foot to kick America, and the other to go to America."[33]

Many students took to the street to protest because they were genuinely furious toward "American bullying." Few in China accepted the explanation offered by the Clinton administration that the bombing was an accident. Student protestors felt the old wound of China's "Century of Humiliation" torn open again by the American bombing. They were upset that Chinese lives had been lost and China's national dignity had been compromised. However, just like Ma Nan, when it came to designing their own future, they thought strategically and let their American Dream prevail over their Chinese patriotism. By doing so, students were not being hypocrites. They were simply being human. In this regard, Ma became a scapegoat for taking a path chosen by many, including her critics. Later, public mockery would turn to a more famous figure—Sima Nan, who was popularly known as China's "No.

1 anti-America warrior" (*diyi fanmei doushi*).[34] In 2015, after publishing another anti-America tirade, Sima Nan got on a flight bound for America to spend the Chinese New Year with his wife and child, who had emigrated to the country. Sima's itinerary became exposed when he was injured by an airport elevator after he landed. The Chinese public responded to his injury not with sympathy but with mockery or even celebration. Sima Nan allegedly replied to such popular sentiments with no sense of hypocrisy: "Opposing America is my job. Staying in America is my life."[35] The sentence became instantly notorious. To this day it has remained unmistakably associated with him—China's "Mr. Anti-America." People know Sima was not alone—in recent years, exposing "patriotic" celebrities' foreign citizenship, permanent residency, or foreign spouses and children has almost become an industry, reinforcing an atmosphere of hypocrisy and resentment.

Ma Nan's and Sima Nan's stories have another implication: people's relations with their country's foreign policy are often incoherent and discursive. We should study how the public's role has evolved in relation to the country's foreign policy and how the noun "role" changed from a singular to plural form as the country opened up. We may want to ask to what extent the government is behind the manufacturing of certain roles to serve its agenda. We may also want to ask how the public may disagree with, resist, or even challenge the government's script. Furthermore, it is worth examining how the multiple roles the public carries may collide with one other as a result of people balancing collective passion with personal interest.

To answer these questions, this chapter will look at three grand processes: the diversification of the public's roles in Chinese foreign policy from Mao to the present; the government's effort to manufacture public sentiment and how such sentiment has inadvertently empowered the public to become disrupters of the government's foreign policy agendas; and the economic dimension in the production of the popular perception of foreign countries. Using anti-Japan education as an example, the chapter shows how this phenomenon started as a government campaign but has evolved into a lucrative business.

"Many Hands Make Our Job Easy"

Mao and his comrades had an unmistakably top-down perspective on their relations with the masses. But they arrived at the same conclusion via different paths. Many of China's first-generation communists studied and worked in Europe or Japan. Such Western exposure often played a key role in instilling communism into their young minds. This was certainly true for Zhou Enlai, Deng Xiaoping, and Zhu De, among others. Some continued traveling to their ideological mecca—the Soviet Union—to finish their transformation into professional revolutionaries. Home-based communists had an even more elitist background. Chen Duxiu, the party's first general secretary, was a professor at Peking University. The other CCP cofounder, Li Dazhao, was a graduate of Japan's Waseda University and served as the head of Peking University's library system and as a professor of economics there.

Mao Zedong was an outlier. The elite Peking University likes to remind its students of the school's connection with Mao.[36] But in a conversation with American journalist Edgar Snow, the chairman himself dismissed his experience as a Beida library assistant working at its reading room: "My office was so low that people avoided me. One of my tasks was to register the names of people who came to read newspapers, but to most of them I didn't exist as a human being. Among those who came to read I recognized the names of famous leaders of the renaissance movement, men like Fu Ssu-nien, Lo Chai-lung, and others, in whom I was intensely interested. I tried to begin conversations with them on political and cultural subjects, but they were very busy men. They had no time to listen to an assistant librarian speaking a southern dialect."[37]

Frustrated, Mao ended his seven-month northern exposure. In March 1919, he returned to his home province of Hunan to take "a more direct role in politics."[38] Despite his growing influence in the countryside, or exactly because of it, Mao's opponents continued to mock him as a "dirt communist" (*tugong*).[39] Mao would later use his rural background as a weapon to attack his more internationalist and urbane colleagues, implanting a sense of original sin that would haunt many, including Premier Zhou, throughout their careers. Yet, it would be misleading to go to the other extreme by casting Mao as lacking basic interest in acquiring foreign knowledge. In fact, one reason for Mao's trip to Peking was to raise funds to support fellow Hunan students to go to France. On one occasion he bid a poetic farewell to Luo Zhanglong, a fellow Hunan countryman, before Luo's departure for Japan. In the poem, Mao urged Luo to "learn truth" in Japan and return to establish a fame that would last five hundred years. Mao's encouraging words seemed to match Luo's ambition. In the poem, Mao referred to Luo by using his Japanese-looking name, Zongyu Yilang, meaning "the eldest son who would traverse the Universe."[40]

Though supportive of others' foreign adventures, Mao perceived his own priority differently, as he confessed to Snow years later: "I did not want to go to Europe. I felt that I did not know enough about my own country, and that my time could be more profitably spent in China."[41] He was content with being a keen observer of the world from home. Mao's lack of passion for venturing outside China would continue even after the founding of the People's Republic. The Soviet Union would be the only foreign country the chairman ever set foot on.

Mao's "dirt communist" label made him a more convincing spokesman for the ordinary. And what an eloquent spokesman Mao was. He offered effusive praise for the power of the masses: "The people, and the people alone, are the motive force in the making of world history."[42] On another occasion, Mao lauded the masses as "the real heroes, while we ourselves are often childish and ignorant."[43] In practice, though, Mao seemed to reverse his and the masses' positions on the maturity-to-ignorance spectrum, as he made himself the great helmsman of the nation. The importance of the masses lay in their potential to be mobilized. What really mattered was not their "boundless creative power," as Mao exclaimed. Rather, it was their sheer number. To use Mao's own words, "Many hands make our job easy" (*renduo hao banshi*).[44] "Many hands" would be essential in helping Mao implement his own agendas, creative or destructive.

As chapter 2 contends in its discussion of leadership, Mao's foreign policy paradigm consisted of two conflictual dimensions: a highly interventionist policy driven by ideological fanaticism and a high sensitivity to foreign interventions. Mao's use of the masses as countless foot soldiers was prevalent in both dimensions. Paradoxically, the masses had a bigger, though superficial, presence in China's foreign policy during his reign than in the 1980s when Deng opened the country. But their role was singular—to carry out the chairman's mission.

The masses were regularly mobilized to serve purely ceremonial purposes. Foreign guests visiting Beijing during Mao's era were often greeted by tens of thousands of people pouring onto Chang'an Avenue, the city's thoroughfare, jumping up and down and waving flags. The masses could also be used as first-responder reserves—the city government of Beijing mobilized eight hundred thousand people to sweep snow from downtown all the way to the Great Wall in preparation for Richard Nixon's trip.[45] In this regard, many hands could indeed make a job easier. But mishaps did occur. When asked by American journalists about the children they saw in colorful yet thin clothes playing outside in chilly temperatures, Zhou Enlai admitted the scene was staged for Nixon's motorcade.[46] This confession should not surprise anyone in China. It was a time when public display of any emotion—enmity or hostility—was manufactured by the government. The same eight hundred thousand Beijingers who swept the whole city overnight for the American president might well have participated in massive anti-America protests earlier.

Serving the chairman did not stop at the ceremonial level. China sent not only money but also personnel in the tens of thousands to Africa, Southeast Asia, and Latin America, fulfilling Mao's call of aiding the Third World's struggle against both American and Soviet evil forces. The number of Chinese headed overseas could reach more than three hundred thousand for one mission.[47] Their tasks ranged from combat to infrastructure—fighting Americans in Vietnam and building railroads in Africa. But their missions served the same purpose: to use Mao's metaphor, they were the sparkles to start prairie fires around the globe.[48]

On the other dimension of Mao's foreign policy paradigm, namely, resisting foreign interventions, the masses were also used primarily for their immense numbers. This is where the boundaries between domestic and international issues blurred. In the name of achieving self-sufficiency and self-reliance, Mao employed the human wave strategy to launch consecutive mass mobilization movements. Some were economic, others political; some were bizarre like the one aimed at killing sparrows, others cruel as they aimed at killing people. What is unambiguous, though, was the result: domestically, never-ending mass movements pushed the economy to the edge of collapse; internationally, fanatical Maoist crusaders eager to spread the chairman's glory contributed to a local distrust so deep that it would take China's future leaders decades to dispel it. Meanwhile, overseas spinoffs like Pol Pot of Cambodia and the Sendoro Luminoso (Shining Path) of Peru sealed Maoism's "negative soft power," to borrow William Callahan's term, as a militant ideology associated with genocide and terrorism.[49] The Chinese government was clearly aware of Maoism's bad name and disowned the term. When asked by a foreign reporter whether China felt "uncomfortable" at Nepal's guerrilla forces calling themselves "Maoist" forces, spokesman Kong Quan answered: "This question was raised to me last year and the year before last. At the time I made it very clear that this sector had nothing to do with China. We feel strongly indignant that they stole the name of the Chinese people's great leader Mao Zedong."[50]

In his Little Red Books, Mao was quoted as hailing the masses as history's real creators. However, some other comments he made on the masses, nowhere to be found in his book, exposed other calculations. In meeting with a Yugoslav delegation, Mao dismissed the atomic bomb as a paper tiger: "We have a very large territory and a big population. Atomic bombs could not kill all of us. What if they killed 300 million of us? We would still have many people left."[51] In the chairman's eyes, its size was what made the masses important. Its size was also what made each member of the masses petty.

The World Is So Close; the World Is So Far

Mao's eventual successor, Deng Xiaoping, abandoned Mao's revolutionary fanaticism for cool-headed pragmatism. Deng also replaced Mao's pursuit of self-sufficiency and self-reliance, which in practice led to delinking China from the global economy, with reform and open-door policies. As China rejoined the global community, Chinese citizens had their first taste of making contact with the world without the state looking over their shoulders. Families with overseas connections began to step out of the shadow. During Mao's years, many families cut off or denied such connections for fear of being accused by the revolutionary masses as spies and traitors. Now they became targets of popular envy and resentment, as their foreign relatives and friends came back to visit and brought gifts many had never seen.

Despite such thawing, the Chinese public experienced a shrinking presence in the country's foreign policy. Family-based reunions were sporadic and mostly confined to coastal provinces. The majority of Chinese families did not have any foreign relatives. As Deng opened the country, exposure to the outside world became a more elitist privilege. Several reasons contributed to this paradox. First, as China opened up, its diplomatic priority shifted from the Third World to the First World. As a result, its own identity changed from being a teacher to becoming a student. In the 1970s, for just one megaproject in Africa, namely, the Tazara Railway, which linked Tanzania with Zambia, China would pour in financial resources totaling US$455 million and fifty thousand workers. In 1973, foreign aid consumed 6.92 percent of China's fiscal expenditure. Such generosity would disappear in post-Mao's China. Now, Deng and fellow Chinese leaders were telling Africa and other Third World countries that China was poor and its focus would be on developing itself before it could afford to help others.[52] In the early 1980s, China's trade with the entire African continent hovered around US$1 billion. During the same period, China's trade with Japan alone reached US$10 billion.[53] Africa was but one example—now devoid of revolutionary missions and vibrant trade connections, China determined that building ties with the underdeveloped world was to take a back seat.[54]

The 1980s was a period full of contradictions. As China opened its door, its people realized their country was no human paradise. The experience was eye-opening and humbling at the same time. Deng warned his people that if they did not catch up, China's membership on the globe would be stripped (*kaichu qiuji*).[55] As the entire nation's vision turned outward, its effort turned inward. The era's zeitgeist became one of "revitalizing China by doing my own work well, starting from now" (*zhenxing zhonghua, congwo zuoqi, cong xianzai zuoqi*). Schools of all levels would display banners claiming "March to Science" (*xiang kexue jinjun*) and "Study diligently to serve the country" (*fafendushu/tuqiang lizhichengcai*).[56] Amid a sense of crisis arose a national zeal for catching up.

This veering toward domestic, internal development at both the macro- and microlevels offered foreign policy elites a shielded arena. As one Beijing police officer recalled, a passport was such a rare document that few had seen a real one.[57] Private trips to foreign countries were nonexistent before 1982. Even in 1985, three years after the government lifted the ban on self-funded study abroad trips, only about ten thousand people could afford to embark upon such journeys.[58] Government-funded students would face a bureaucratic behemoth as they secured one approval after another. They would also undergo intensive political training before their departures. One former student recalled that male students were in particular warned not to talk to young Taiwanese women—for the latter could be femme fatales ready to use romance as a weapon to recruit Chinese young men.[59] Most Chinese who could travel internationally were either diplomats or officials in the "foreign-oriented system." Others were intellectuals on government-sponsored trips. Their destinations were almost always countries in the First World. For the non-elite majority, they were no longer needed for fighting or building in the Third World. The opening brought the world beyond China visually closer but substantively more distant.

Accesses to materialistic privileges also contributed to the elitism associated with having foreign contacts. Special stores stocked with hard-to-acquire commodities, household electronic appliances in particular, were only available to "foreign-bound personnel" (*chuguo renyuan*). In practice, officials in the foreign-oriented system would be their core consumers. Meanwhile, a special currency in the form of a Bank of China Foreign Exchange Certificate (*waihuiquan*) was only available to foreigners in China. The special currency would allow these privileged customers to purchase commodities denied to ordinary Chinese. Needless to say, black markets flourished. Constantly dogged by potential buyers, some foreigners were compelled to wear T-shirts with the Chinese sentence "*wo meiyou waihuiquan*" (I have no foreign exchange certificate). In their own way, corruption and crime proved how closely guarded the playing field of China's foreign-oriented system was. Officials occupying these positions became the choke points for controlling a vast country's limited connections with the world. Some did not hesitate to profit from being in the right place at the right time.

China's opening was thus full of contrasts. Contacts were established but heavily restricted. The government's restrictions made the process of accessing to the world elitist and prone to corruption. All the constraints, both political and monetary, created an envious aura to those who were allowed "into" the game of talking and traveling the world on behalf of China. For the overwhelming majority, though, the door to this game was shut. As television programs, movies, and songs brought lives in America, Europe, and Japan closer to ordinary Chinese, it also added a sense of remoteness: to most people, the prospect that one day they could travel internationally for personal pleasure was beyond their wildest dream.

Old Habits Die Hard

Mass mobilization for international publicity has not gone into extinction. However, the scene of a whole city turning out to welcome foreign guests is gone. Now, manpower is to serve more specific functions—to name one example, high school students and retirees are mobilized to pick up trash and monitor neighborhood safety during major international sporting events and conferences. The world also got a glimpse of China's human wave strategy by watching the opening ceremony of the Beijing Olympics in 2008, when tens of thousands of performers, mostly soldiers, beat LED-lit drums in perfect synchronization. The ceremony was supposedly a celebration of peace and friendship. But Western reception was disappointing to the Chinese government. As a *USA Today* reviewer described it, the ceremony was "sort of Albert Speer meets Star Wars. As memorable and impressive as that opening, pounding, screaming drum corps may have been, it was also the least welcoming 'welcome' ever recorded—and having the drummers smile during it just made it seem odder and a bit chilling."[60]

USA Today was not alone in voicing such a scary sentiment. The animated series *South Park* tells a story of how the ceremony terrorizes Eric Cartman, a main figure known for being psychopathic and aggressive. After watching the show, Cartman is plagued by nightmares about the Chinese and believes they will invade America soon.[61] Few Chinese had heard of *South Park* then. But critical voices on the Beijing Olympics opening ceremony should not have entirely surprised them. One Chinese media scholar conducted a content analysis of the coverage of the Beijing Olympics by the Associated Press, L'Agence France-Presse (AFP), and Deutsche Presse-Agentur. She found that all three presses made frequent reference to the same political issues: Tibet, Taiwan, and human rights. In the case of AFP, coverage of Tibet far outweighed that of the ceremony per se. The scholar concluded that such politicized coverage was proof that the "western countries led by America try to protect their national interests and maintain their global hegemon" and that the "international public opinion environment is still hostile to China."[62]

As for *South Park*, the show gained its overdue notoriety in China more than a decade later, when it aired an episode of Randy Marsh going to China to expand his marijuana business, only to be detained and sent to a labor camp, where he witnesses summary executions and tortures. Soon after the show's airing, it joined the Chinese government's ever-growing list of companies that produce "China-shaming" (*ruhua*) products. It disappeared from all online venues in the country.

Occasionally, Beijing's old habit of using human waves could put on a new face—mass immobilization. This practice even gave birth to a new phrase: "APEC Blue." Before China hosted the APEC summit in 2014, the government delivered a strong dose of immobilization to sedate the entire city. Measures included temporarily shutting down factories and keeping vehicles and people off the road. Even restaurants were told to refrain from offering barbeque dishes. Thanks to cooperative weather, the result was impressive: an azure sky graced Beijing for the duration of the summit. Smog quickly returned as Obama's Air Force One departed. Beijing residents woke up to their old normal. The official *China Daily* lamented that Beijing residents "will no doubt feel uneasy when the city is again smothered in smog after the APEC meeting, but they will get used to it as they did before," leading the comedian Jon Stewart to quip that "Welcome to Beijing—you will get used to it as you did before" may be the worst city slogan ever.[63]

Xi Jinping framed China's mass campaign traditions metaphorically: "As everyone collects firewood, the flame will go higher and higher."[64] The APEC experience, though, revealed that sometimes the government would need its people to put out the fire—literally. In either scenario, Chinese leaders have a dilemma on their hands: the public's passion does not always blow in the direction the authorities are fanning. The flame of the masses' emotions, once stirred up, could lick back at the government.

Beyond Droplets

The Chinese masses have played roles other than as droplets in human waves. Since the turn of the new century, China has seen several rounds of xenophobic protests. Some were peaceful, but many were not. The one in

2012 was particularly violent. In the city of Xi'an, mobs besieged hotels and demanded the police to hand over the Japanese guests staying inside. They also looted stores that carried Japanese products and attacked people driving Japanese cars, resulting in at least one driver suffering a severe head injury and becoming permanently disabled.

Such popular movements shared some common characteristics: they were predominantly urban, and Japan was the most popular target. The Western media, particularly those from Japan, criticized the Chinese government for fanning such violent anti-Japan nationalism.[65] In their view, the government and its propaganda machine were primarily responsible for the protestors' warmongering battle cries on Japan.

A brief historical review may add nuances to this view. The government was not omnipotent, and the public was not entirely passive. People could either catch the government off-guard, or their support for the government could quickly turn sour if it failed to respond in a way the public desired. A third scenario arose when the government, perennially paranoid toward any unofficial mass movement, instinctively attempted to quench it but ended up intensifying the situation. In the power game among the government, foreign countries, and the public, the possibilities for alliance abounded.

Looking back, a number of incidents in the 1980s were precursors to their larger successor movements in the 1990s and the new century. The People's Republic's first major anti-foreign protest with no official sponsorship occurred in 1985. In September, Japanese prime minister Nakasone Yasuhiro, a personal friend of party general secretary Hu Yaobang, visited the Yasukuni Shrine. Tensions had already been building—three years earlier, Japan's *Asahi Shimbun* reported that the Japanese Ministry of Education had requested that a textbook change a description of the Japanese military from "invaded" North China to "advanced on." Though the accuracy of the story was disputed, it quickly elevated into a diplomatic crisis. The Chinese government protested, and the Japanese government apologized. One year later, construction of the Memorial Hall of the Victims in the Nanjing Massacre began. "Grand architect" Deng Xiaoping would handwrite the name of the museum to be later engraved on its front gate. Deng used to be an eager student of Japan. But by now, he had grown increasingly disgruntled at the teacher, mentioning Japan for public shaming on multiple occasions. During his meeting with the visiting Clean Government Party delegation from Japan, Deng bluntly reminded his guests that "in the entire world, Japan is the country that owes the most to China."[66]

Amid grievances voiced by the top and the Chinese media's bombardment of the textbook issue, Nakasone's visit to the controversial shrine became the last straw. After all, the shintoist institution was worshipping not only Japan's ordinary military casualties but also 14 convicted Class-A war criminals. Nakasone's visit ended the so-called honeymoon phase in Japan-China relations. Students from Peking University and other colleges began posting protest messages on school billboards criticizing the trade imbalance between Japan and China. What was more unsettling to the authorities, though, was student criticism that turned inward, with messages like "opposing invasion from outside and toppling corrupt officials from inside" (*waifan qinlve, neifan tanguan*). The Peking University president tried to calm the situation by holding dialogues with students. Meanwhile, police sealed the campus. Yet, students managed to march to Tian'anmen Square. They were chanting slogans like "It is not a crime to be patriotic!" and "Down with the revival of Japanese militarism!" Protestors also laid wreaths at the Monument to the People's Heroes. Similar protests took place in other cities. In Xi'an, for example, mobs lit up stores selling Japanese cameras.[67]

Not every clash between the public and the government was political, however. Mishaps would happen as China opened to the world. Even when no diplomatic agenda was looming, the government would suppress such problems with shock-and-awe tactics. These tactics would become preshow glimpses of its management of massive anti-foreign movements in later decades. In 1986, a student protest rocked Shanghai. But unlike the one in Beijing with its clear anti-Japan message, the one in Shanghai was triggered by an accident. In November, an American band came to the city to perform. Toward the end of their concert, the band began singing the song "We Are the World" and invited those who knew it to join them. Two students from Shanghai Jiaotong University jumped onstage, only to be manhandled by the security staff. The police sent the students to jail and allegedly beat them.

The jailed students' peers began demanding justice. Jiang Zemin, then mayor of Shanghai and an alumnus of Jiaotong University, came to soothe tensions. Yet, the mayor lost his temper during his meeting with the students. As one student participant recalled, angered by a question, the future leader of China interrogatingly asked the student who raised the question: "Who are you? Which department are you from?"[68] Jiang also ordered the person who called the American consulate to make his or her presence known. He reprimanded the young protestors: "Don't bluff—what kind of situation have I not seen?"[69]

Governments at all levels would later habitually utilize the package of preempting protests, holding dialogues, and then issuing stern warnings and harsh punishments as they handled mass protests, particularly those with a foreign component. In December 1988, students of Hehai University in

Nanjing protested against African students on campus. The exact cause was murky. According to the school's announcement afterward, two African students had tried to bring two young Chinese women onto campus but refused to register their names. A skirmish ensued, leading to injuries and property damage. Chinese students besieged the building where foreign students were living. Many chanted patriotic songs. Some hurled racial slurs. Unsatisfied with the government's protection of foreign students, the Chinese students marched to the street the next two days, shouting "Down with police bandits" and "Down with traitor government."[70] Some were also protesting against preferential welfare treatments meted out to foreign students. The government always feared that a nonpolitical mass movement could easily escalate into a political one; this concern was not unfounded. The three African students were expelled. Meanwhile, a curfew was imposed on campus until tensions quieted down.

Though sporadic, student protests in the 1980s reveal that relations between the public and the government were already tense. Such tensions were more easily crystalized on incidents with foreign components, due to the high sensitivity all Chinese actors accorded to issues of this nature. This may also explain why, in the wake of the 1989 Tian'anmen Massacre, the government intensified nationalist education: the patriotic sentiment had always been there. But now the government decided to steal the show from students by projecting itself as the most passionate, unapologetic defender of the nation. The oppressor became the leading protestor. What the statist protestor could not foresee, though, was that the explosive growth of wealth, coupled with technological advancement, had intensified old tensions and created new complexities in the relations between the people and the state.

Three mass protests targeting foreign countries have occurred in this new era, namely, the 1999 anti-America protest and the two waves of anti-Japan protests in 2005 and 2012. Scholars and media pundits have offered much discussion on the Chinese government's role behind them, but one should not dismiss the genuine, emotive outburst of the masses. Their love of country is sincere, their support for the government is not unconditional, and the border between support and revolt can be blurry. As China gets stronger, its public confidence is soaring, which has presented two faces to the authorities: supportive and disruptive. The government is clearly aware of the disruptive side. One day after NATO's bombing of the Chinese embassy in Belgrade, then vice president Hu Jintao addressed the nation. In his televised speech, Hu predictably offered strong condemnation of the bombing. But then, he offered the following words: "We believe that our people will definitely keep our country's fundamental interest in their hearts, conscientiously protect the big picture, and make sure that such [protesting] activities are to be carried out orderly. We must guard against extremist behaviors and stay vigilant to those who want to utilize this opportunity to disrupt normal social order. We must resolutely maintain social stability."[71]

Hu's address to the nation was made at a time when protests were only beginning. But the speech was already full of code words expressing the government's desire to control the flame. Judging by the later trajectory of the protests, the leadership's concern was justified, but its preempting effort was not successful. Likewise, in the midst of the 2005 and 2012 anti-Japan protests, the *People's Daily* published editorials to urge protestors to "transform patriotism to activities of doing everyone's own work well, and protect the big picture of reform, development, and stability."[72] The slogan "sensible patriotism" (*lixing aiguo*) appeared frequently in the state media.

Out of instinct for survival, the Chinese government has been adding fuel to the flame of patriotism. But the rounds of mass protests and the government's largely unsuccessful responses revealed the dangerous nature of this game: how to make people hate foreign countries in order to strengthen their support for the regime, but not too much to rock the ship of regime stability. Susan Shirk points out in her 2007 book that this dilemma made China a fragile superpower.[73] More than a decade later, this dilemma remains unaddressed. In fact, with China's superpower dimension continuing to grow, so too does the regime's paranoia toward its fragility. Spontaneous mass movements targeting foreign countries more often reveal tension rather than cooperation between the people and the state.

Ignorant Officials, Informed Citizens

Challenges keep emerging to complicate relations between the people and the state. On the one hand, more and more Chinese citizens have become connected with the world through all kinds of possibilities. On the other hand, Chinese officials continue to dwell on a top-down mentality of the masses, viewing them not so much as constituents to be served but rather as resources to be utilized and troubles to be tamed. While the public expects officials to provide services, officials' self-identification does not have the word "servant" in it. When different expectations meet, conflicts are bound to happen. Insightful scholarship has been generated by scholars like Anne-Marie Brady and Daniela Stockmann on how China's authoritarian government, by coercing media as an accomplice, has managed to maintain its tight control over information dissemination—to nail Jell-O to the wall, so to speak.[74] However, there is another possibility: armed with knowledge and assisted by the speed with which information is disseminated over social media, the public could fight back. State-citizen tensions take the form of not only the government suppressing the information flow but also citizens exposing policy blunders and forcing the government to retract decisions. Purely administrative issues could be turned into a political circus, with the authorities becoming the clown.

A latest example attesting to this point is the Shanghai municipal government's flip-flop on revoking *hukou*, or household registration, for Shanghai-based Chinese citizens with permanent residency overseas. China does not recognize dual citizenship. But for a long time, some Chinese emigrants who changed citizenship have continued to hold onto their *hukou*, for household registration is tied to access to social welfare and local schools. Apparently in an attempt to crack down on these hidden dual citizens, the Shanghai police authorities announced on March 8, 2018, that all Shanghai-based Chinese citizens who have "settled down abroad or obtained other nationalities" needed to report to the police and have their household registration revoked. The authorities also encouraged people to report on those they knew who maintained their *hukou* despite permanent residency in other countries. The authorities further warned those who refused to comply that their *hukou* would be forcibly terminated.

There was only one problem—Shanghai is allegedly mainland China's most internationalist city, yet its public security authorities were apparently unaware of the difference between foreign permanent residency and foreign citizenship. While it is legally sound to crack down on dual citizenships, to strip *hukou* of Chinese citizens with foreign permanent residency is a wholly different matter. China did not recognize the use of a Chinese passport inside the country. By stripping Chinese citizens of their *hukou* and annulling their Chinese identification cards, the Shanghai municipal government would effectively make these people citizens of nowhere.

Predictably, the proposal was met with waves of criticism. Many people questioned the grounds on which a municipal government could take away one's Chinese citizenship. The authorities doubled down. On March 22, it issued a statement insisting the policy was not new, only that this time the government was serious about implementing it. Then, four days later, just as abruptly, the city government made a U-turn by posting a midnight announcement stating it would not revoke residents' *hukou* after all. The announcement made an unusual mea culpa. The government admitted it had no legal definition of "settling down abroad" and was thus unable to implement the policy it had announced.[75] Shanghai citizens won.

Policy blunders like this are not just embarrassing but also revealing. Policy makers are so detached from reality that they are clueless about the conundrums their policies would create for ordinary people. As one Chinese netizen commented on a popular online forum, policies are often made by leaders "tapping their heads" (*paipai naodai*)—a Chinese slang for impulsive policy making. As a result, they are sporadic, confusing, self-conflicting, and inconsiderate of long-term consequences. Fortunately, in the Shanghai case, the more knowledgeable public offered a legal lesson to the government. When, on March 8, the government publicized a policy to whip those it thought were cheating the system, it was unaware of all the complexities associated with the global flow of its population. It did not take long for the whip to swing back and slap the whipper's face.

Wag the Dog: The Rise of Patriotic Vigilantes

If the Shanghai *hukou* incident was a result of officials' top-down perspective hitting the wall of reality, the public-state interplay on the Taiwan issue would present another kind of power dynamism: wagging the dog. Letting the public run the show of anti-Taiwan independence could add a popular, nonofficial narrative to the government's agenda. However, once the masses have a role to play, they could become emboldened to run on their own scripts; that is, mass actors could end up manipulating the director. The media, an official ally of the state, shrewdly use the gap between disseminating sensational information for commercial gains and later shifting to the government narratives for political correctness.

Mainlanders' popular attitude toward Taiwan has undergone several waves of change. During Mao's era, the Taiwanese were portrayed as compatriots in poverty and agony, hungry for the dawn of liberation to shine on them. Even after Mao died, the opening toward Taiwan was markedly later than China's opening to other countries. Up until the mid-1980s, during the Chinese New Year, school students in Beijing were still asked to use their meager pocket money to purchase candies and other gifts later to be balloon lifted and dropped to starving children on the other side of the Taiwan Strait—or so they were told.

Chinese leaders knew better about who should be dropping candies to whom. The Taiwanese authorities were also confident in their island's superiority over the mainland. In fact, this gap in perception was one reason why then Taiwanese president Chiang Ching-kuo allowed family visits to the mainland starting in 1987. As Wu Po-hsiung, then minister of the interior, recalls, Chiang envisioned that this resuming of contact with the mainland would add pressure to the communists and allow the mainlanders to realize who led a better life—them or the Taiwanese they were supposed to save.[76] Singapore's paramount leader Lee Kuan Yew went through a similar calculation. After visiting China in 1976, Lee returned to Singapore feeling relieved. One accompanying official reported that Lee was "happy" to see how backward China was and decided to encourage Singaporean youth to visit and see for themselves the real China.[77] In Lee's eyes, China was a convincing negative example that could help Singaporeans better value their own country's path. Chiang Ching-kuo would probably agree—after all, it was Chiang who encouraged Lee, a personal friend, to go and visit mainland China.[78]

As people-to-people exchanges commenced, mainlanders came to realize that the saviors had been left far behind by those they were supposed to save. Meanwhile, Taiwanese popular culture began to permeate China's young minds. Songs, movies, and TV dramas enjoyed an ever-growing army of clandestine followers—one reason that led the party elders to launch a campaign to crack down on "spiritual pollutions."

Mainlanders' admiring and even envious attitude toward the Taiwanese began to change as the Chinese economy took off after 1992. In Shanghai, the derogatory term *taibazi* (hicks from Taiwan) has become a popular reference to the Taiwanese. Beijingers have their own crude name for the Taiwanese: *Taiwan tubie* (a ground beetle from Taiwan). For many urban mainlanders, it did not take long before they reclaimed cultural superiority over the Taiwanese, viewing them as their hillbilly cousins. Meanwhile, calls for boycotting allegedly pro-independence Taiwanese celebrities are also on the rise.

Shifts in popular attitude and spontaneous boycotting offer new clues to leaders in Beijing. Taiwan is the new Japan—a target to be constantly harassed, humiliated, and mocked. The Chinese government can use popular opinion as a cloak to shield its own agenda of punishing the island. One latest example is the campaign of using popular pressure to force foreign companies to comply with Beijing's "One China" policy. The *Global Times*, a subsidiary of the *People's Daily* known for its chauvinist tones, summed up the calculation well:

> In order to make multinational corporations refer to Taiwan, Hong Kong, and Macau in ways acceptable to China, as a tactic, we should let the societal forces take charge. The government could assist them if necessary. This is because whatever the society may demand, no one can blame such outcries as excessive. In addition, such popular opinions send a strong message of whom the Chinese market welcomes and whom it rejects. As a result, it is particularly intimidating.[79]

This tactic seems to draw its inspiration from Mao's argument on guerrilla warfare, though now the warriors are Chinese consumers. In early April 2018, a Chinese student in South Korea protested the airline Jeju Air for listing Hong Kong and Taiwan along with China, Japan, and Vietnam as destinations on their travel posters. She viewed the poster as an insult to Chinese unity and told the company representative that "Hong Kong people and Taiwanese are all Chinese." In her eyes, these places did not deserve being listed as equals next to China. She also notified the Chinese embassy in Seoul of this "violation" and threatened to tear down the poster on her campus. The airline's first response was to fight back, stating that the poster was nonpolitical and that it was quite natural for South Koreans to use terms like "Hong Kong people" and "Taiwanese." The company also warned the student that it would report her to the school authorities if she damaged even one poster. The student retorted, "As a Chinese, it is my responsibility to protect China."[80]

A storm in a teacup was thus born. Before long, Chinese netizens began calling for a boycott of Jeju Air. On April 20, the company representative issued an apology, admitting it had made a "grave error" (*zhongda cuowu*) and that it had corrected the problem to address the student's concern.[81] By doing so, Jeju Air joined an ever-growing list of multinational corporations like Gap, Zara, and Marriott, among others, that had to apologize to Chinese consumers for violating the "One China" policy. Likewise was the case for Mercedes Benz, which had quoted the Dalai Lama in its commercial poster— "Look at situations from all angles, and you will become more open," the Tibetan spiritual leader allegedly said. Mercedes would later apologize for "hurting the feelings" of the people of China for its zen-style commercial. Among the foreign enterprises that China's patriotic vigilantes terrorized, the German luxury automaker sounded particularly contrite, announcing that the poster "published extremely incorrect information, for this we are sincerely sorry. . . . We have immediately taken meaningful actions to deepen our understanding of Chinese culture and values, including among our colleagues abroad, and in this way regulate our behavior."[82]

Anti-Taiwan online guerrilla warfare jumped to a new level in May 2018, when China's aviation bureau, citing "public complaints," demanded thirty-six foreign air carriers to remove references on their websites or in other materials that listed Taiwan, Hong Kong, and Macau as places independent of China.[83] The list of violators would later be expanded to forty-four. Although the Trump administration denounced Beijing's threat as "Orwellian nonsense," eighteen of the forty-four air carriers chose to comply by May 25, with the remaining twenty-six pledging to fix the problem by July 25. Of course, this could become a game of whack-a-mole for China: there is always a violator out there waiting to be smashed. On the day its media announced victoriously the compliance of foreign airliners, Tesla came to ruin the party. It used "Taiwan time" in an online post to Taiwanese owners about a possible signal outage at noon, with a warning that they should keep their car keys with them. Chinese patriots complained that Taiwan does not deserve to have its own time. There is only "Beijing Time."[84]

Beijing's "catch them if you can" battle cry to the masses could exhaust itself. Various bureaucratic units are getting busier and busier policing the "One China" policy in the commercial world. But an informant society could create unintended, embarrassing consequences to the government. Some companies and individuals see an opportunity to use this name-and-shame tactic to drive out competitors or achieve personal vendettas. In December 2017, a Taiwanese TV drama titled *My Boy*, starring celebrity actress Ruby Lin, was taken off the screen in China. The reason? Two netizens notified the broadcasting bureau that the drama received funding from Taiwan's Ministry of Culture. Such a depth of knowledge of a specific TV drama's production was curious—the Taiwanese media later revealed that other TV dramas receiving similar funding had no problem of entering the mainland market. The union leader of the Taiwanese TV Drama Production Federation suspected that a commercial dispute between Ruby Lin and investors was at play, which led to the latter's blackmailing of Lin by utilizing Beijing's sensitivity to Taiwanese independence. In other words, a commercial infight among the Taiwanese spilled over into China. One side decided to use politics to punish the other.[85] In an effort at damage control, Lin chose to overcompensate: she stated not only that she always saw herself as Chinese but also that she supported China's sovereignty over the entire South China Sea. Eighteen days later, the TV drama returned to the screen.

A more extreme example lies in the case of Michael Huang (Chinese name Huang An), a Taiwanese singer in his sixties who now resides mostly in Beijing. Huang's heyday was in the early 1990s. In recent years, though, he has rekindled his name recognition by becoming "the most hated man in Taiwan," as one foreign correspondent put it.[86] Huang took great pride in becoming an open informant for the Chinese government on reporting allegedly pro-independence Taiwanese entertainers. His most publicized, though many would say notorious, case happened in January 2016, when Huang took on the sixteen-year-old celebrity Chou Tsu-yu. Huang accused the young Taiwanese pop star of advocating for Taiwan independence because she was seen holding a Taiwanese national flag on a South Korean TV program. Soon after Huang announced his accusation, Chou's performances in China were cancelled. On January 15, JYP Entertainment, a Korean company Chou was affiliated with, released a video of Chou visibly shaken. She bowed and tearfully apologized: "There is only one China. The cross-straits territories are one in the same, and I am proud to consider myself thoroughly Chinese.... As a Chinese, when performing in a foreign country, I hurt my company and the feelings of netizens on both sides of the Strait by my erroneous words and actions. I am very, very sorry."[87]

Chou ended her speech with another deep bow. To many, watching the video was a distressing experience. If anything, the teen pop star's apology, delivered the night before the election day, drove younger Taiwanese voters in hordes to Tsai Ing-wen, the candidate from the pro-independence Democratic Progressive Party (DPP).[88] Huang also sealed his reputation among many in Taiwan as a pro-China bullying thug, though many in the DPP may have thanked him secretly for being the party's most effective campaign manager.

The infamy that Huang received in Taiwan did not necessarily help him on the mainland. Huang's never-ending reporting on pro-independence activities rendered the Taiwan Affairs Office his personal tool for achieving petty vengeances. The Chou incident became the breaking point—the Taiwan Affairs Office issued a statement, warning people to "stay highly vigilant" to "some Taiwanese political forces that attempt to instigate confrontations between people on both sides of the Strait by manipulating individual incidents."[89] Shortly thereafter, netizens found videos of Huang himself waving the Taiwanese national flag on TV programs. Two months after the Chou incident, Huang flew back from China to Taiwan in a private jet to receive medical treatment. Pictures of Huang lying on a gurney, covering himself with sunglasses, a surgical face mask, and a blanket, received little public sympathy. Huang's second spring of fame was transient. However, with the Chinese government subcontracting the job of policing the "One China" policy to the masses, similar figures will keep popping up. Similar dramas will continue to create personal agonies for the individuals involved, causing embarrassment to Beijing while at the same time distancing the relations between Taiwan and China.

In these incidents, many Chinese media outlets chose to join the brief online fiestas, competing with one another for how fast and sensationally they could get the words out before government censors moved in to "unify the tones" (tongyi koujing). The media were behind not only the eventual disappearance of these stories but also their virulence in the first place. While they need to comply with the government eventually, media professionals utilize every crack in the government censorship structure to gain attention. After all, to commercialized media everywhere, attention means money.

The Crotch-Bomb Actress and the Economics of Hating Japan

Incidents surrounding Michael Huang and Ruby Lin suggest a new kind of power relations between political and nonpolitical issues. In both cases, political agendas were no longer the ends. Rather, related actors were using politics to achieve nonpolitical goals: to regain fame for a washed-up star, to expose an economic dispute between investors and producers, and to boost viewership and readership by carrying these stories in sensational tones. Economics is the motive while politics becomes the means.

Nowhere is the economic dimension of foreign issues more pronounced than in the flood of so-called *kangri shenju* (farcical anti-Japan TV series) in China. One notorious example of the *kangri shenju* stars an actress named Ge Tian. In the TV series *Together We Fight the Devils*, a TV drama about resisting Japanese invaders, Ge plays Sister Yin, the lover of an imprisoned communist. Ge visits her hero in his jail cell, where he is seen bruised and bloodied, apparently due to torture by his Japanese captors. Ge puts her lover's hand inside her red cloth and lets him fondle her breasts. The two begin kissing each other as a Japanese military officer and his Chinese interpreter stand by. A very sexually suggestive conversation ensues. Among many crude lines, Ge tells her lover: "Earlier, the little Japanese wanted to touch my groin. How can I let them? That place only belongs to you. Come—touch it!" The jailed communist pulls his hand from underneath her dress and is shown holding a grenade. He shouts: "Let's have another great time!" and then detonates the grenade, killing everyone in the cell.[90]

The TV series was broadcast by Sichuan TV in 2015, at a time when the marital status of Ge and Liu Xiang, the country's celebrated hurdler, was the talk of the nation. Many viewers were stunned to see the wife of China's national sports hero in such a scene. Comments on social media were overwhelmingly negative. One user wrote, "The outlandish drama is horrifying. The authorities have banned foreign shows—only to let us see this?" Others felt it bizarre and lewd.[91] The TV series was quickly taken off the network, and the remaining episodes were never shown.

As outlandish as the plot is, it probably would not have attracted intensive public opinions had the female character not been played by Ge Tian— allegedly China's most famous divorcée at the time. Without her celebrity face, *Together We Fight the Devils* was simply one of numerous similar war dramas that inundated all TV channels. Screenwriters seemed to be competing with one another to see who could conjure up a more ridiculous feat— tearing a Japanese soldier in half with bare hands, shaking a pistol while firing to make the bullet path curve, attacking enemy trains with fire crackers, bombing Japanese motorcades with popcorn, or letting a Japanese officer charge by riding a pig? This is a league where the crotch-bomb heroine would meet ample superhuman matches. Had this role been played by someone lesser known than the famous athlete's ex-wife, it would have been buried for its mediocre creativity.

It is true that the Chinese government has intensified nationalistic education since the 1989 Tian'anmen Massacre. It is also true that nationalism is all about a "we-they" feeling and that in Chinese collective memory, Japan has been the easiest target as the "bad guy." Since then, however, hating Japan and, increasingly, cursing America have become an institution that has acquired a life of its own. It is no longer purely a government campaign. Rather, it has earned its own economic logic and evolved into a billion-yuan patriotic industry that the Chinese comically refer to as *huyou* (fool you). The deluging *kangri shenju* simply constituted a pillar of this lucrative industry. To borrow a quote from *The Godfather*—there's nothing personal about hating Japan or cursing America. It's only business.

So, who are fishing for fame and money in this flourishing business? One can identify publicity profiteers at all levels. At the individual level, there are the patriotic talking heads—pro-government celebrity intellectuals and top brass military officers. We have already met one in Rear Admiral Zhang Zhaozhong at the beginning of this chapter. Two other admirals known for their hawkish remarks are Luo Yuan and Zhu Chenghu. Admiral Luo openly questioned whether Okinawa should be a part of Japan. In his speeches, he invariably used the island's ancient name, "Liuqiu" (Ryukyu), and claimed that 75 percent of the islanders wanted to restore their relations with China. As Admiral Luo saw it, China should not be satisfied with demanding the Diaoyu/Senkaku Islands. China needs to ask for bigger: ownership of Okinawa entirely.[92] Admiral Zhu once warned that China would not abide by its pledge of not using nuclear weapons first in a case of self-defense and that the country is ready to sacrifice all major cities east of Xi'an in a nuclear showdown with America—a remark hauntingly similar to Mao's casual prediction of an atomic bomb wiping out 300 million Chinese. Indeed, Zhu's remarks led China's most famous political dissident and Nobel Peace Prize laureate Liu Xiaobo to quip about Zhu being a miniature Mao.[93]

On the civilian side, there are intellectuals like Professor Jin Canrong of Chinese Renmin University and Professor Zhang Weiwei of Fudan University. They make frequent media appearances, both domestic and international, and use their professorial rhetoric to deliver strictly pro-government messages. This is not to deny their popularity—their public lectures are often standing-room only. But a reading of Professor Jin's speeches on Chinese diplomacy over the past four years, for example, reveals a high degree of rhetorical consistency: Chinese diplomacy has been invariably described by him as "stable" (*wending*) and other parts of the world as "unstable." In 2018, Jin went so far as to argue that the entire world is unstable "except China."[94] The key evidence the professor cited of China's success was, in his words, "a significant increase in political stability," a euphemism for Xi's tightening political control. In May 2020, when America, Australia, and western European countries were pushing for an independent inquiry into the coronavirus outbreak, Professor Jin accused the West of basing their criticism on racism and cultural superiority. He further mocked that by questioning China over its handling of the Covid-19 crisis, the West was showing signs of "not just menopause, but perhaps dementia."[95]

Professor Zhang, on the other hand, has been actively promoting his "unique China" argument. He contends that China has "unique language, unique politics, unique society, and unique economy." His tautological conclusion, then, is that "Chinese politics is unique and the country can only govern by using its own method." Professor Zhang further proclaims that the Chinese Dream is more "enduringly amazing" (*chixu jingcai*) than the American Dream.[96]

These publicity hunters, the media, and the masses together form a commercial ecosystem. Exactly because their messages are uniformly pro-government, patriotic public intellectuals and military top brass have paradoxically gained a higher degree of immunity from governmental monitoring. The media, both domestic and international, love reaching out to them, particularly those in uniform, because they know there is a good chance they will say something jaw-dropping. Their ranks further offer a facade justification of their representing China. However, big-mouthed Chinese military officers tend to share similar institutional affiliations—Zhang Zhaozhong, Luo Yuan, Zhu Chenghu, and Jin Yinan were all "theorists" working at military academies. None of them are from the PLA's core units, whose personnel tend to keep a much lower public profile. Their marginal position in the military's hierarchy offers them more rhetorical freedom as armchair strategists. One institute, the PLA Military Academy, is known as not only a base of talkative admirals but also a nursing home of princelings. Rear Admiral Mao Xinyu, the grandson of Chairman Mao, is constantly mocked by Chinese netizens for his girth, his intellect, his handwriting (contrasting his grandfather's famous calligraphy), and his career.[97]

To media practitioners and people in the entertainment industry, to be patriotic simply means good business. In 2012, for instance, the government approved 303 new TV shows. More than half had a "revolutionary" theme, and of those the vast majority depicted the anti-Japanese war.[98] For producers, any show about fighting the Japanese would be bulletproof in the license application process. Production was also fast and cheap—Japanese, after all, is an Asian race. Directors could simply hire an army of Chinese temporary actors to pretend to be Japanese, most of whom were from rural areas lured by a salary of seven dollars per day.[99] To be fair, though, there was at least one incident of a black actor playing a Japanese soldier, which created a déjà vu of racial diversity meeting the imperial army.

Whether the Chinese peasant actors could deliver a convincing performance as Japanese soldiers would be of little importance. Almost none of the Japanese military officers speak any Japanese in these war dramas. Instead, they speak flawless Chinese. Minowa Yasufumi, a Japanese actor, reported the experience of playing a Japanese military officer in one such TV drama. He wanted to add a dose of authenticity. The director simply told Minowa to say whatever he wanted to say when the camera started rolling—because "nobody cares." Minowa was disappointed and turned it down because he wanted to play a convincing "Japanese devil."[100]

Many such shows are broadcast during the daytime. It is thus reasonable to assume that a key group of viewers they want to attract are retirees or those in rural areas. As corroborative evidence, such shows are often sponsored by companies selling herbal medicines or promoting alternative therapies. Such shows are also visual fast food: in one episode, viewers could see martial arts, weapons, explosions, high-speed chases, an astronomical amount of blood, and a China win. With these many striking images and a guaranteed victory, who cares about the plot? Even more disturbingly, as China's own media pointed out, is that many stories feature females who are sexually assaulted or, in the case of Ge Tian, sexually seductive. They thus have a luring effect on male viewers.[101] In this new economy of hating Japan, even pornography becomes patriotic.

Local governments are one more group benefiting from this booming patriotic "fool you" industry. Hengdian, a small town in Dongyang City, Zhejiang Province, has become a giant television studio, generating 28 billion yuan of tourism revenue in 2019.[102] The town advertises itself as the "Oriental Hollywood." As one journalist reported, during the Chinese New Year break in 2013, staff members were still working overtime in town to produce nineteen TV shows, ten of which were about fighting the Japanese.[103] On an annual basis, studios in Hengdian alone would churn out close to fifty TV shows featuring the war against Japan. Shi Zhongpeng, one of the many temporary actors, told a reporter that on his busiest day on set he reported to eight different shows featuring the war—and he died eight times that day as a Japanese devil.[104]

Patriotic Chinese Are Irritable Chinese

On shaping China's interactions with the world, the delicate dance between the state and society continues to evolve: Who is leading whom? The process remains dynamic. What Professor Jin Canrong touted as China's biggest success—namely, the country's tilt toward one-man rule—looks like political retrogression to many others. Among Chinese intellectuals, there is a growing fear that political taboos are becoming institutionalized. In 2013, multiple Chinese scholars revealed to foreign media a new regulation from the "top." The regulation was termed "seven do-not-talks" (*qibujiang*), as it dictated that college teachers not talk about seven issues in their teaching:

1. Do not talk about universal values.
2. Do not talk about press freedom.
3. Do not talk about civil society.
4. Do not talk about citizen rights.
5. Do not talk about past mistakes of the Communist Party.
6. Do not talk about privileged capitalist class.
7. Do not talk about judicial independence.

The "seven do-not-talks" would be accompanied by a "sixteen clause" (*shiliu tiao*) to offer more detailed guidelines on controlling "young college faculty members"—traditional troublemakers to party authority.[105] Both documents were elaborations of an earlier, shorter list of "five do-not-adopts" (*wubugao*) laid out by then National People's Congress speaker Wu Bangguo. In 2011, Wu stated in his report that China would not adopt the following five concepts: a multiparty alternation system, diversity in leading theory, three branches of government and a bicameral legislature, federation, and privatization.[106]

Wu's "five do-not-adopts" was a public speech. The "seven do-not-talks," by contrast, was shrouded in secrecy. A search of the term in Chinese on the search engine Baidu in May 2020 generated only ten results, almost none of them related to the seven demands listed on overseas sites. The only entry that touched upon it was from an article for the *People's Daily*. Even there, the reference was transient and murky. It neither admitted nor denied the existence of these seven do-not-talks, only endorsing the government's effort of banning "wrongful intellectual trends" (*cuowu sichao*).[107]

My own conversations with multiple China-based scholars, though, show that all of them were aware of the seven do-not-talks policy. An identical search on Google generated results in the tens of thousands. Though the contrast was by no means scientific, there is no doubt that the lone relevant entry on China's top search engine was artificially low. Space for voicing alternative thoughts is definitely shrinking in China. When so many topics have been disallowed, what is left to be allowed? All that remain are only aggressive talks from armchair admirals that pass as entertaining jokes and propagandist lectures from establishment intellectuals that pass as scholarship.

Chinese scholars and students traveling overseas have also become emboldened at organizing themselves. Setting up an overseas Communist Party branch is nothing new—state-owned Chinese companies have been doing this for decades. What is different this time, though, is the voluntary organization by private Chinese citizens in foreign countries. In November 2017, several Chinese visiting scholars at the University of California-Davis stirred up a controversy by establishing a Communist Party cell on campus. A few days later, the cell was dissolved as the leader learned the organization did not comply with the US Foreign Agents Registration Act, which requires all individuals and groups acting under the direction or control of a foreign government or political party to register with the Department of Justice in advance and regularly report their activities.[108]

Similar requests have also been made by Chinese students and scholars at the University of Illinois and at Chiba University in Japan.[109] Local media viewed these stories alarmingly. They took it as evidence of China's aggressive exportation of its values. However, such proposals were invariably raised by short-term Chinese visitors. There has been no report of permanent residents of Chinese origin attempting to establish party cells. Noting this difference is important—for those who will return to China, the experience of setting up and participating in party cell activities even when overseas can add loyalty perks to their portfolios. After all, the University of California-Davis Communist Party cell only became known because its leader notified his Chinese home institution, which gladly announced it on its website. Compared with the assumption that they were trying to spread communism, it is more reasonable to assume that the cell leader and other participants were simply trying to impress their bosses at home. Preaching communism to Americans and Japanese was not their priority.

In the world of commercial cultivation of patriotism, farcical anti-Japan TV shows were receding. The notoriety of the crotch-bomb heroine contributed to the genre's demise. Even the party mouthpiece opined that depicting the Japanese as idiots was a cruel act of belittling the Chinese people who underwent all the atrocities and sacrifices during the war.[110] If the Japanese invasion was round 1 of hurting the Chinese, now more people are wondering if these shows are round 2 of hurting them—only this time the Chinese are doing it to the generations of their grandparents and great-grandparents.

War-related stories with patriotic themes remain popular. In fact, the trend is now turning to big-budget, big-screen productions. In 2017, the Chinese action movie *Wolf Warrior 2* broke numerous box office records—it yielded the biggest single-day gross for a Chinese movie at US$874 million, becoming the second-highest-grossing movie of all time in a single market behind only *Star Wars: The Force Awakens*.[111] The story features Leng Feng, a Chinese veteran who travels around the globe and punishes those who offend China. Its movie poster makes this point very clear, as it displays the sentence: "No matter how far away, whoever offends China shall be wiped out" (*fanwozhonghuazhe, suiyuanbizhu*). In the movie, the story ends with a shot of the cover of a Chinese passport and an accompanying message: "Citizens of the People's Republic of China—when you encounter danger in a foreign land, do not give up! Please remember: at your back stands a strong motherland."[112]

The massive commercial success of a story about a Chinese Rambo shows the lucrative potential of commercializing patriotism. In 2018, another patriotic big production *Operation Red Sea* grossed US$579 million, becoming the second-highest-grossing movie in China only behind its even more successful predecessor, *Wolf Warrior 2*. Without the disruption caused by the Covid-19 crisis, *Wolf Warrior 3* would have played at nearly every Chinese cinema during the 2020 Chinese New Year. Unlike cheap anti-Japan TV shows, these movies are of significantly higher quality in every aspect: from acting to cinematography, from costume design to original score, from screenplay to visual effects. Another noticeable change is thematic. Both *Wolf Warrior 2* and *Operation Red Sea* are no longer about a historical China during its so-called Century of Humiliation. They are about China today and China in an imagined future. The message is no longer about grievance. It is about taking revenge.

An unintended consequence has ensued as a result of the success of such patriotic blockbusters: citizens have invited drama into reality. At airports and seaports in Tehran, Bangkok, Tokyo, and Nagasaki, among other places, people have witnessed odd scenes of angry Chinese passengers singing the Chinese national anthem and clashing with local police. They were not protesting against foreign violation of the "One China" policy or China's sovereign claim over the South China Sea. Rather, they were stranded tourists facing flight and cruise delays. Thanks to movies like *Wolf Warrior 2* and its heart-warming ending message, many Chinese tourists now see any experience of inconvenience as an offense to their national pride. In one case, a single Chinese family, by resorting to patriotism, held a powerful government hostage: in September 2018, this Chinese family was removed from a Swedish hostel after failing to check in fifteen hours prior to their booking. After throwing a fit on the street, the family took to social media and claimed mistreatment. The nationalist *Global Times* picked up the story and framed it as "China shaming" (*ruhua*), a call surely to attract attention. From there the dispute escalated into a diplomatic incident. Unable to get an official apology from the Swedish government, the Chinese Foreign Ministry issued a travel warning to its citizens, alerting them not to go to Sweden. As diplomats of the two countries were quarreling, the family moved on and posted happy travel pictures.

Once locked in by patriotic adrenaline, China's officials had to make a hawkish stand. But behind the scenes they might think differently. By quoting Chinese diplomats from multiple embassies, China's official media issued a reprimand on its meltdown-prone travelers: "By putting on a 'Wolf Warrior' style of patriotism improperly and shouting 'China!' whenever you feel like it, you won't gain sympathy from either staff at foreign airports or your domestic compatriots," a Xinhua News Agency commentary said.[113]

That is the conundrum China has created for itself—one Wolf Warrior is good. Millions of Wolf Warriors bring national disgrace. With the Covid-19 crisis greatly disrupting international travel, Chinese visitors stranded overseas also came to a painful realization: their Chinese passports were no guarantee of a swift return, contrary to the aspiring ending message of the movie. Neither flag-waving Chinese soldiers nor hordes of Chinese planes appeared. Instead, desperate Chinese visitors had to fight for whatever few flight tickets became available, sending the price of returning home into six figures in yuan and even in dollar. One Chinese student begged on Weibo, the Chinese equivalent of Twitter, "Wolf Warrior—please take us home!" It did not take long for censors to take down this plea.

5 • One World, Many Dreamers

China and Beyond

Aodaliya renmin zhanqilai! (Australian people have stood up)
   —Malcolm Turnbull, Australian prime minister

Three Asians want to cross a river. The Japanese will build a
bridge, test the bridge, and then cross the bridge; the Korean will
build a bridge and cross the bridge; the Chinese will cross the
river, with or without a bridge.
   —Niwa Uichiro, Japanese ambassador to China

"No Three Hundred Ounces of Silver Buried Here"

Ever since Jiang Zemin, each party chief has created his own pet slogan. For
Jiang, it was "Three Represents"—meaning that the Chinese Communist
Party should represent advanced social productive forces; advanced cul-
ture, and the fundamental interest of the Chinese people. Jiang's successor,
Hu Jintao, was associated with the "Harmonious Society" and "Scientific
Development" slogans. When Xi Jinping took charge, he began to promote
the "Chinese Dream."

   Coining a national ethos for each generation of leadership is a relatively
new phenomenon in Chinese politics. Neither Mao Zedong nor Deng
Xiaoping attempted to beat a one-sentence summary of their times into people's minds. Both leaders excelled at using metaphors. Some have even
entered the conventional vocabularies of non-Chinese languages—for example, Mao's dismissal of reactionaries as "paper tigers," his proclamation of
women as "half the sky," or Deng's "black cat, white cat" analogy. It does not
matter whether a cat is black or white. If it catches mice, it is a good cat. The
cat metaphor encapsulated Deng's extreme pragmatism. Yet, popular adop-

tion of these metaphorical catchphrases was largely spontaneous. It did not demand party cadres at all levels to hold frequent meetings, where officials elaborated how Deng's cat or Mao's paper tiger should guide people's lives. Their adoptions beyond China further attest to the universal values embedded in them; after all, presidential candidate Hillary Clinton launched her "Half the Sky" movement to address the empowerment of women. Needless to say, she never mentioned the phrase's authorship.

People in China remember what Mao and Deng did without having to recite a nationally imposed catchword. These two leaders were comfortable with their authority. They did not feel the need to remind people who was in charge and what he accomplished. Thus, it was no coincidence that the promotion of an official motto started with Jiang Zemin, Deng's third chosen heir. Before him, both Hu Yaobang and Zhao Ziyang had gone down in flames. It was a high-risk job.

All three mottos were coined while the leaders were in office. In fact, for Hu and Xi, the state-run media started to publicize their slogans almost from day 1 of their leadership. Thus, these grand slogans are not summaries of their legacies. Instead, they served as coronation announcements with Chinese characteristics.

These mottos do not stem from day-to-day language. Hu's double slogans of "Harmonious Society" and "Scientific Development" sound dull, much like his public image. Jiang's "Three Represents" would not make any sense to a reader who encountered it. These slogans' genesis was artificial. Deciphering their real messages requires a reader's ability to read between the lines. Fortunately, this is an ability many adult readers in China possess. To find out what Jiang's and Hu's mottos really meant, all people had to do was to look around. Despite these slogans' seemingly positive overtone, they offered clues to the most daunting problems that the leaders needed to tackle: Could the party still credibly claim to represent the masses? Was the country's development sustainable? What about the rising tensions that were rocking social stability?

Most Chinese are familiar with the folktale of a man stealing some silver and burying it in a field. To add another layer of security, the man puts a sign that reads: "No three hundred ounces of silver buried here." There is some thematic connection between the story and China's new habit of inventing national mottos, though some comical twists are required. For the man in the story, he needs to put up a sign of denial to hide something that *is* there; for contemporary leaders, they need to put up an aspiring slogan to promote something that is *not* there. In both scenarios, it would not be very difficult for others to figure out the truth.

Chinese Dream? Which Chinese Dream?

Xi Jinping's Chinese Dream is different. Jiang's and Hu's slogans focused on internal politics and were problem-oriented mottos. Xi's Chinese Dream departed from both: it is future oriented and outward looking in search of China's greatness in the world. There is no longer the hint of the three hundred ounces of silver buried underground. Instead, Xi proclaimed to the world he has a treasure trove known as the Chinese Dream. Unlike the slogans under Jiang and Hu, the dream motto is vague. Xi promoted it as a pursuit of "the great rejuvenation of the Chinese nation."[1] But other than this grandiose vision, there is no authoritative clarification of what would constitute this great rejuvenation, how China will get there, and what the Chinese pursuit for greatness means to the rest of the world. As a result, to interpret Xi's dream has become a booming industry in itself. As Willy Wo-Lap Lam argues, the vagueness of Xi's Chinese Dream allows different political actors to interpret it in a self-serving fashion.[2]

These actors' efforts could be placed on a spectrum ranging from assertive to accommodating. On the assertive end, interpretations of the Chinese Dream are unapologetically Sino-centric, chauvinistic, and racially nativist. One representing voice is that of Liu Mingfu, another armchair strategist from the National Defense University. In his book titled *The China Dream: Great Power Thinking and Strategic Posture in the Post-American Era*, Colonel Liu proclaims that the time has come for China to replace America as the world's top military power. By using Japan as an example, he warns Asian countries that the only way to get along with China is to know their place—they are living next to a gigantic neighbor, the strongest country in the world that keeps getting stronger. Hence, they need to get used to seeing their influence dwindle.[3] Liu's voice is extreme; even Luo Yuan, another Chinese military hawk, commented that Liu's view that China is already leading the world is not a fact but reflects "the gap between a promising ideal and reality."[4] Of course, to China's suspicious neighbors, Liu's view represents what a nightmare could look like.

On the opposing end of the interpretive spectrum lies a Chinese Dream more attune with tradition. It is based on a selectively benign elucidation of the Confucian concept of "Tian Xia"—all under heaven. Xu Jilin, a history professor from East China Normal University, is a leading voice in this camp. Professor Xu contends that the Chinese Dream should embody a decentered, nonhierarchical new universalism. He envisions the Chinese Dream as open and tolerant. By rejecting both Sino- and European centrism, this benevolent Chinese Dream opposes the creation of any civilizational hegemony on the basis of an axial civilization. Instead, Xu supports the future scenario of "huddled masses" from all countries under an open sky, with China being one in a crowd but taking pride in being the creator of this new, accommodating *Tianxia*.[5]

Where would one place China's official understanding on this spectrum? Over the years Xi and the state-run media have been adding components to this dream, ranging from the goals the PRC seeks to achieve by its one hundredth anniversary to current policies like the One Belt One Road Initiative, sustainable development, and anti-corruption campaigns, among others. Various efforts are made to bend and weld the two ends of the interpretive spectrum: Sino-centrism in substance but packaged in open, benevolent rhetoric. In a paper titled "What Does General Secretary Xi Jinping Dream About?" Tony Saich covers the ever-expanding and conflictual components of Xi's dream—promoting nationalism, strengthening party control, coupled with launching a new round of opening to the world.[6] Sino-centrism in foreign policy has been promoted with a new buzzword—*dandang*, which can be translated as the courage to take charge. This would be the opposite of Deng's low-profile diplomacy. Xi defended free trade at the World Economic Forum. Without naming the Trump administration, he likened those pursuing protectionism to "locking oneself in a dark room."[7] The speech earned him the moniker the "New Davos Man"—a rich, powerful and pro-trade global ultra-elite, who also happens to be a communist. Foreign Minister Wang Yi also called for an Asian Community of Common Destiny. Both Xi's and Wang's acts could be framed as examples of *dandang*—as America is showing signs of retrenching and retreating, it is China's turn to assume leadership on the world stage.

This recognition reveals another layer of Xi's dream—a grand geopolitical showdown wrapped up as a competition between two dreams, one from China and the other from America. The connection between the Chinese Dream and the American Dream is hard to miss. Indeed, during the calmer days of China-US relations, the Chinese government loved knotting the two dreams together. When Xi met Obama in 2013, he told the press that the Chinese Dream "is connected to the American Dream and the beautiful dreams people in other countries may have."[8] Obama stayed clear from mentioning any dreamlike connection. America did not even acknowledge the Chinese concept, let alone endorse it.

Fast-forward to today, and any facade of friendly bonding of the two dreams is gone. The lone connecting factor is a desire to amass power, as one Chinese scholar stated that only great powers like China and American "dare to have national dreams."[9] In the summer of 2019, Chinese viewers noticed that in the country's definitively dull prime-time news program *Xinwen Lianbo* (News Simulcast), hosts began to use slangs to mockingly berate America, calling the country's policies "absurd enough to make people spit meal," claiming that America was "a stick swirling shit," "a liar so despicable that he does not even blush when lying," and that the famed American Dream is the "American Nightmare."[10] Such attacks have become further intensified, even personal, as China and America have entered into an increasingly bitter dispute over each other's handling of the Covid-19 crisis. China's state broadcaster CCTV denounced the US secretary of state Mike Pompeo as an "enemy of mankind" for his vocal criticism of the Chinese government. In the same denouncement, Pompeo also collected titles like "stumbling block," "accomplice," and someone "whose name shall be condemned for thousands of years."[11] The program's America bashing has become so regular that netizens have begun to refer to it as "CCTV's Daily Curse" (*Yangshi Meiriyima*). They are certainly entertained when the CCTV's hosts describe American politicians as "lotus spitting" and "tornado gulping"—all slangs to describe someone who talks impressively but acts little.[12]

According to the Chinese media, people are applauding their national TV hosts' ballistic outbursts on America, calling such acts "*nu dui*" and "*da lian*"—internet memes for "furiously refuting" and "slapping in face," respectively. The real picture of the public responses to this propaganda trend is hard to gauge, though, as the official media framing is most certainly selective.

A World of Dreamers

The shaming of its more famous American cousin notwithstanding, the Chinese Dream may embed a dose of universal truth—though probably not in the way China is selling it. The truth is not about global acceptance of Chinese greatness. Rather, the truth lies in the word "dream." If we define it as a country's grand pursuit of a deserving place in the community of nation-states, then we live in a world of dreamers. Obama may have shunned the term, but his chief diplomat John Kerry delivered his "I have a dream" speech in Tokyo to counter the Chinese Dream. Kerry called it the "Pacific Dream" and explained it as having four components, all centered on growth: growth needs to be strong, fair, smart, and just.[13] Kerry's "Pacific Dream" campaign experienced a short shelf life. Three days after Trump became president, he announced America's withdrawal from the Trans-

Pacific Partnership (TPP), the foundation supporting Kerry's "Pacific Dream." This should not surprise anyone, for Trump repeatedly called the TPP a nightmare.

Two propelling forces have turned the word "dream" into a powerful rallying cry. One is emotion. A dream as a political slogan is always about something aspiring. It represents an impassioned future worth fighting for. The other force, though, is the ability to convincingly answer the question of how to get there. This pillar is non-emotive. It is primarily about acquiring capabilities and making accurate assessments, without which a dream would be no different than a fantasy.

Every country's pursuit of greatness consists of these two forces. Yet, the two do not necessarily act in tandem. When they do not, the imagination of a national role on the world stage becomes incoherent. It is also a contested process, as domestic actors may have different understandings of or priorities for the grand goals worth striving for. Furthermore, one nation's dream making interacts with that of another, creating all kinds of merging and colliding possibilities.

Australia is one dreamer torn by contesting pursuits. The two forces, emotive and interest based, are pulling the country in opposite directions. On achieving prosperity, no country is as important to Australia as China. In 2019, China was not only Australia's biggest trading partner, but the total trade volume between the two would be greater than the trade volume Australia achieved with its next nine biggest trading partners combined.[14] On export, China alone consumed 28 percent of Australia's total exports—the total value would be equivalent to the sum of Australia's exports to Japan, America, South Korea, and Britain combined. China's insatiable appetite for iron ore, coal, and other minerals led to the mushrooming of boomtowns in Australia.

In 2019, 1.43 million Chinese travelers visited Australia. This made China the top source of international visitors to Australia, surpassing New Zealand, Australia's nearest neighbor, where people can travel to Australia visa free.[15] America was the third biggest country to send visitors to Australia. Yet, Chinese tourists outnumbered American tourists by more than 600,000. Even more importantly, Chinese tourists were lavish: they spent significantly more than visitors from other countries. For twelve months ending in March 2019, New Zealand sent 1.39 million visitors and China sent 1.43 million visitors to Australia. New Zealanders spent US$2.6 billion; in contrast, Chinese visitors splurged with US$12 billion.[16] China has also become Australia's most important source of educational revenue. As of March 2020, more than 620,000 foreign students were studying in Australia. Approximately one in every four were from China.[17]

It would not be an exaggeration to say, then, that China is the most important country to the economic health of Australia. While the Chinese connections have brought in riches, they have also stirred up Australian anxieties. The Australian uneasiness has come from more than one source, and some of them conflict with each other. Given the tremendous weight that China carries in Australia's trade, particularly export, an economic slowdown in China is significant for the world but potentially devastating to Australia. In May 2020, leaked meeting minutes from Australia's central bank showed that its board members saw the Covid-19 pandemic as bringing an "unprecedented" economic hit to the country, with the baseline case for gross domestic products to fall by 10 percent in the first half and 6 percent for the entire year.[18] In an earlier report, the same organization calculated that for every 5 percent drop in Chinese economic growth, it would depress Australian economic growth by up to 2.5 percent. The bank called China's economic slowdown "a key uncertainty for Australia's economic outlook."[19]

But even when the Chinese economy was doing well and, as a result, Australian exports were booming, such seemingly positive developments could also set off Australian angst. China's rapidly expanding influence over the Australian economy has eroded Australia's traditional dependence on America and other Western allies. For years, political forces on the extreme right have been complaining about Australia becoming more Asian than European. One prominent politician promoting this racially nativist view is Pauline Hanson, leader of the One Nation Party. As early as 1996, the newly elected Senator Hanson warned in her maiden speech that Australia was "in danger of being swamped by Asians," who "have their own culture and religion, form ghettos and do not assimilate." Hanson also declared that she wanted to see "multiculturalism abolished."[20]

However, Hanson's view was marginal, and one may argue that such xenophobic sentiment targeted the vaguely defined "Asian" countries, not just China. Nowadays, however, negative sentiment toward China is growing and entering mainstream politics—because the fear is not racial but geopolitical. Even for politicians who support cultural plurality and immigration, or exactly because of their support for such goals, they are growing increasingly concerned about Chinese influence and meddling in Australia's internal affairs. Chinese interventions, some covert and others explicit, penetrate into the parliament, business communities, and universities. As the economic force pulls Australia closer and closer to the Chinese orbit, the other force that supports the Australian dream, namely, the emotive, value-based one, is trying to strengthen Australia's bond with its Western allies. Balancing these two opposing forces is no easy feat, especially in an era when the American president could choose to hang up on the Australian prime minister.[21]

Here is Australia's dilemma: on the one side, Beijing is enriching, court-ing, meddling in, and menacing Australia through its ever-widening connec-tions; on the other side, Australia feels emotively closer to an America that is showing signs of retrenching and retreating. Though Australia may not want to choose a side, the absence of a middle ground between these two opposing forces means a side has to be chosen. Leaders from the country's both center-left Australian Labour Party (ALP) and central-right Liberal Party of Austra-lia (LPA) have chosen to highlight and enhance Australia's ties with tradi-tional allies. The country has been a particularly vocal critic of China's assertive policies in the South China Sea, even sending warships to the hotly contested waters. As the Covid-19 virus pandemic spreads globally, Australia has also been a leading voice in calling for an independent investigation into the virus origin.

Prior to the Covid-19 spat, China was resorting to its traditional punish-ing tactics of refusing to hold conversations with the Australian government, allegedly denying visas to cabinet ministers, or cold-shouldering them when they visited China. When Australia's trade minister, Steve Ciobo, went to Shanghai in May 2018, the highest-level official he could meet with was a vice mayor, with whom he attended an Australian Football League match. Despite his desire, Ciobo was not invited to go to the capital to meet with his Chinese counterpart. Meanwhile, China's customs began holding up prod-uct exports from Australia.[22] Its state-run media further warned Chinese tourists to shun the country. In a widely published opinion piece, a Chinese military commentator referred to the Australian challenge to China's sover-eign claim over the South China Sea as evidence of a country "not knowing its place."[23] In talking about Australia, both the media and popular rhetoric have employed terms like "anxious deputy" (*jixianfeng*) and "second-tiered country" (*erliu guojia*) to mock Australia's importance.[24]

The Australian government's hardline policy toward China had ample domestic critics. Kevin Rudd, a former prime minister and a fluent Manda-rin speaker, bashed Prime Minister Turnbull for derailing Australia's rela-tionship with Beijing and punching China in the face publicly.[25] But Austra-lia's political hardening toward China is continuing under the current Prime Minister Scott Morrison. The country has been a leader in calling for a global inquiry into the origins of the Covid-19 pandemic. The World Health Orga-nization's resolution in support of the inquiry was a diplomatic victory to the Morrison administration, though Beijing dismissed the Australian effort as "nothing but a joke." Australia has also been vocal critic of China's expansion in the South China Sea, its breach of "One Country Two Systems" promise in Hong Kong, and its human rights abuses in Xinjiang.[26]

Amid such an all-out diplomatic confrontation, Australian businesses, big and small, have become increasingly nervous about the prospect of political disagreement damaging trade and investment with a country so crucial to the Australian economy.[27] One new change that the Covid-19 crisis has brought is the increasingly brazenness of Chinese threats to Australia. In an interview with the *Australian Financial Review*, Ambassador Cheng Jingye had this to say when asked about the economic consequence of Australia's push for an independent investigation of the coronavirus pandemic:

> The Chinese public is frustrated, dismayed and disappointed with what you [Australian government] are doing now. In the long term, for example, I think if the mood is going from bad to worse, people would think why we should go to such a country while it's not so friendly to China. The tourists may have second thoughts. Maybe the parents of the students would also think whether this place, which they find is not so friendly, even hostile, is the best place to send their kids to. So, it's up to the public, the people to decide. And also, maybe the ordinary people will think why they should drink Australian wine or eat Australian beef. Why couldn't we do it differently?[28]

Ambassador Cheng's veiled threat was followed by actions. Starting in May 2020, the Chinese government began to launch multiple investigations into Australian beef and barley. In August of the same year, China announced it would start an anti-dumping investigation of Australian wines. Other industries expressed economic anxiety due to their exposure to the Chinese threat.

But if not economic anxiety, then political anxiety would announce its presence—and the political one was most vividly put on show in a TV interview then Prime Minister Turnbull gave in December 2017. When asked about whether he felt intimidated by the Chinese meddling in Australian politics, the Australian prime minister replied: "I will tell you this—modern China was founded in 1949 with these words: Zhongguo renmin zhanqilai. The Chinese people have stood up. It was an assertion of sovereignty. It was an assertion of pride. And we stand up, and so we say, Aodaliyarenmin zhanqilai. The Australian people stand up."[29]

In recent years Australia has produced two leaders who have spoken Mandarin in public. Kevin Rudd delivered speeches and accepted interviews in Mandarin. His fluency in the language could rival that of a native speaker. Turnbull's story is different. He is not known as a Mandarin speaker, and the two sentences he uttered during that TV interview were not beginner sentences. Turnbull apparently choreographed his answer as a publicity stunt: an Australian leader standing up to the Chinese and warning them in their language to back off. Kevin Rudd was not impressed. He called this moment "extraordinarily ridiculous."[30] China's official response was to urge "some people in Australia to stop words and actions that hurt their own image and Sino-Australian relations."[31]

The fact is that Australian people have stood up for a long time. Now, an Australian leader felt the need to wrestle with his own tongue to tell China in Chinese that Australian people stand up against their country. The problem, though, is that the "stand up" framing is one that the Chinese masses associate with their country's one hundred years of foreign aggression and occupation. Turnbull's usage was perplexing to them. In fact, popular responses acquired a more entertaining nature, as many saw Turnbull's Mandarin proclamation as bizarre, even comical. Some nicknamed Turnbull "China basher-in-chief."[32] Turnbull certainly did not deliver his answer as a joke, but that is how it was perceived by many in China, as online ridicule of this moment sprouted. Numerous news portals carried the story titled "Here Is a Joke—Australian People Stand Up!" to describe an artificially inspired slogan that came out of nowhere.[33] Some went even further, seeing the Turnbull answer as revealing Australian weakness and anxiety: it turns out that China is not the only country with three hundred ounces of silver to hide.[34]

Beyond China: Yoshida Shigeru and the Art of Being a "Good Loser"

The previous chapters have examined how three actors—namely, leaders, bureaucrats, and the masses—perform different roles in Chinese foreign policy making. Chinese foreign policy is a result of the cooperation, cooptation, and contestation among the three. Such a tripartite analytical framework applies to other countries as well, though contextual shocks, norms, and domestic institutional arrangements may lead to quite different foreign policy scripts. I will now turn to Japan, China's neighbor to the east, to briefly examine how the three actors jointly shape the dynamic process of Japanese foreign policy making.

I should clarify at the onset, however, the purpose of this discussion: it is not to make Japan a comparative case with the same analytical weight that China carries in this book. I have less ambitious goals: this book is primarily about China. The country's importance and complexity have warranted a book-length study in which I focus on the interactive grid formed by their leaders, bureaucracy, and society and examine how the nodes on this interactive grid generate policies. But China is only one case after all. Researchers have a scholarly obligation to go beyond their particular case selections and demonstrate the wider implications of their findings. By identifying the same tripartite actors in Japan and pointing to the major trajectories of their interactions, my purpose here is to be indicative and generalizable. Every country has its own interactive grid of foreign policy making. When one actor's agendas meet with those of another, the power flow becomes observable. This mechanism applies to China and beyond.

For leadership roles, factors responsible for leadership diversity in China also apply to Japan: contextual shocks, leaders' individual personalities, and the duration of their legitimacy. The biggest shock to Japan was its defeat in World War II. In the wake of its failed endeavor, the country was transformed into a democracy with a pacifist constitution and became a junior partner in a security alliance with America. Hence, postwar Japan started from a very different situation than that confronting China. There was no civil war or communist revolution. As a country conquered and occupied, Japan abandoned its geopolitical ambition and settled into its new role focusing on recovery and development.

Japan as a democracy and a junior partner to America—these two factors created different openings and constraints on what types of leaders Japan is more likely to produce. Transformative leaders are always scarce. But China has produced at least two, Mao Zedong and Deng Xiaoping, with Xi Jinping striving to become a third one. The closest equivalent of an architect-type leader that Japan has seen is Yoshida Shigeru.

Yoshida's tenure as Japanese prime minister was long: a total of 2,614 days divided into two stints, the first from May 1946 to May 1947 and the second from October 1948 to December 1954. But duration of his leadership alone was not what made Yoshida a political architect. Abe Shinzo, the prime minister who resigned in September 2020 for health reasons, is the record holder on the length of tenure: he was in office for a total of 3,186 days. Tenure length is a necessary but insufficient factor for creating a political architect. If a leader's tenure is too short, it is hard for this person to make far-reaching, sustaining changes, but time alone is not enough. What made Yoshida an architect was a package: the institutional arrangement he helped to create, the personality and philosophy that guided his political strategizing, and the longevity of the path he set for Japan.

One question that many may ask is this: Given that Japan was a defeated country under American occupation, is it even sensible to identify a Japanese leader as an architect? It was America that sponsored Japan's security and defined its diplomatic scope. How could the leader of a defeated nation under occupation shape its future? Yoshida provided his own answer to this question—his wisdom was to transform Japan into a "good loser." In Yoshida's own words, "Being a good loser does not mean saying yes to everything the other Party says; still less does it mean saying yes and going back on one's word later."[35] By constantly cultivating the internal schism within the occupational authorities, Yoshida successfully created a watered-down version of America's original plan of democratizing and demilitarizing the country. Self-proclaimed as the "last Meiji Man," Yoshida perceived Japan's war endeavor as an unfortunate detour and believed that Japan should, with the assistance of America, return to the Meiji path of achieving autonomy through modernization.

Yoshida's goal, as a leader serving under America's watchful eyes, was to help Japan regain ownership of its policy making. He saw the American occupation not as a decisive factor but rather as merely a constraint. It could even become an opportunity to be utilized. The winner was actually the student, and the loser was the mentor—the Japanese version of wagging the dog. As Yoshida put it, he perceived his job as one of informing and teaching the Americans how to be good occupiers:

> It was obviously important to cooperate with the occupation authorities to the best of one's power. But it seemed to me that where the men within GHQ [General Headquarters] were mistaken, through their ignorance of the actual facts concerned with my country, it was my duty to explain matters to them; and should their decision nevertheless be carried through, to abide by it until they themselves came to see that they had made a mistake. My policy, in other words, was to say whatever I felt needed saying, and to accept what transpired.[36]

In practice, Yoshida utilized the ideological division among the American occupiers. He dismissed American civilian administrators as "idealists" while expressing his admiration of General Douglas MacArthur and other personnel with military backgrounds. Yoshida further explained that his job was about forging an alliance with "soldiers" to suppress the "willy-nilly" American civilian administrators.[37]

Yoshida's perception of America was tinged with a sense of cultural superiority. Never mind that America won—it lacked basic knowledge of Japan's complexities. Thus, Yoshida, the "good loser," would nurture America, the bad winner. Japanese obedience warped into a facade of tolerance—that is, allowing the ignorant, insensitive Americans to make mistakes and giving them time to come to their own senses. Then Japan would feel vindicated after all. This mentality and its resultant quiet resistance would become a crucial component of Japan's mode of interaction with America. On foreign policy, for example, Yoshida never perceived Mao's China as a communist country like the Soviet Union. He admitted that he was torn between the pressure exerted by then US secretary of state John Foster Dulles to isolate China and his personal desire to recognize the country. Yoshida also admitted that he tried to persuade Dulles to allow Japan to engage China through trade activities and wean the Chinese government from the Soviet bloc. Even when realizing that Japan had to accept the boundaries set by America, Yoshida continued to believe in the need to reach out to China. When greeting young Japanese diplomats in a workshop, where only one diplomat was assigned to the China desk, Yoshida declared that China was the country that "I would like all you folks to study the most."[38]

To win by accepting defeat and to disagree by first nodding his head— such were Yoshida's ways of manipulating American occupation to restore Japan's autonomy, the essence of the Meiji era. The "Yoshida Doctrine," the course he set for Japan that bore his name, has remained the country's orientation. Its two pillars—alliance with America and a mercantilist focus on economy—remain pivotal in shaping Japanese foreign policy.

On domestic politics, though, Yoshida was no architect. In his memoir, he was all fire and fury whenever he discussed left-leaning forces in Japan, especially the communists. Yoshida also had little tolerance for political debate, calling it "bickering and back-biting" and the "curse of the Japanese political world."[39] Though born and raised in the Tokyo area, Yoshida decided to run as a candidate representing Kochi, the ancestral home of his father and a region with which he had little connection. The choice was made as a matter of convenience, as Yoshida later announced to the chagrin of some visiting constituents: "I represent Japan, not Kochi."[40] Such an elitist view of political office would place Yoshida firmly on the extension of the Meiji oligarchs, who saw politics as a vehicle for bolstering authority and railroading national visions rather than for serving constituent interests. Postwar Japanese democracy took root not because of Yoshida and like-minded politicians. Democracy happened and stayed in Japan despite politicians like Yoshida.

Occasional Disrupters and Faithful Managers

The US-Japan alliance remains the bedrock of Japan's foreign policy. Forces to the extreme left and the extreme right have forged an unexpected consensus: both see America as stripping Japan of its independence, and both have campaigned for terminating the alliance. Despite such fringe voices, though, no Japanese leader has attempted to end Japan's special relations with America. Even the socialist prime minister Murayama Tomiichi vowed to protect the alliance. In 1995, his administration revised Japan's National Defense Program Guidelines for the first time after their adoption in 1976, confirming the importance of the US-Japan alliance to regional peace and stability.

However, on Japan's foreign policy grid, when the external factor of America as Japan's security sponsor meets with the internal factor of Japan as an electoral democracy, sparks can fly. Japan has a greater possibility of generating disrupter-type leaders, as their yearning for an independent foreign policy collides with various constraints. Being a democracy also means that for Japanese disrupters, the cost they pay for their adventurous ideas is lower than that for their Chinese counterparts. Compared with Hu Yaobang's ordeal of being shamed at the party's internal meetings for five days, resigning or simply indicating not to run for office again seems a much more acceptable outcome for Japanese disrupters.

Leadership disruptions in Japan happen in two ways: one is policy driven and the other is personality driven. Two recent examples that fit the two categories are the premierships of Hatoyama Yukio and Koizumi Jun'ichiro. Hatoyama came to office in 2009 by riding on a wave of popular discontent toward the conservative Liberal Democratic Party (LDP). As the leader of the central-left Democratic Party of Japan, Hatoyama misconceived an opening when it was just not there—the establishment of an East Asian Community comparable to that of the European Union. Critics warned about ample obstacles—America's absence, different regime types, bitter historical and territorial disputes, the exclusion of Taiwan, and the inclusion of North Korea, among others. Although Beijing had raised the community idea even earlier than Tokyo, it quickly became alert upon knowing Hatoyama's desire to include Australia and India.[41]

Despite lip service paid by China and South Korea, Hatoyama's East Asian Community dream never took off. On the other hand, his effort to create closer ties with China and South Korea drew suspicion from Washington. American opposition killed one core campaign pledge Hatoyama had made—relocating the US military base in Okinawa. As a result, Hatoyama had his own "read my lips" moment like the one that killed George H. W. Bush's reelection bid in 1992. Bush at least claimed some foreign policy credits: liberating Kuwait and announcing victoriously the end of the Cold War. It was his mismanagement of domestic politics that dashed his hopes for winning a second term. Hatoyama, in contrast, had no foreign policy muscle to show off. There was little sympathy from either Washington or local Okinawans on his flip-flop. Meanwhile, his domestic politics were dogged by financial scandals, particularly the revelation that his immensely rich mother had financed his campaigns. Engulfed by self-inflicted crises at home and abroad, Hatoyama abruptly resigned after only eight months in office. As a result of misconceiving a dream of a united Asia and of making an unrealistic campaign promise, coupled with a personality many perceived as "timid," Hatoyama's fate as a transient disrupter was all but sealed from the beginning of his premiership.[42]

Another recent disrupter, Koizumi Jun'ichiro, was the exact opposite of Hatoyama on personality and policy. Timidity was not a characteristic associated with this bachelor Japanese prime minister with a Beethoven-style hairdo. Koizumi was no flip-flopper. In fact, the upheaval he unleashed on Japanese foreign policy was because of his intransigence. Koizumi's disruption to Japanese foreign policy happened in managing Japan's relations with two immediate neighbors, China and South Korea. During his six years in office, he would pay annual homage trips to the controversial Yasukuni Shrine, where fourteen Class-A war criminals were worshiped along with more than two million Japanese war dead since the Meiji era. Unlike Hatoyama, Koizumi was a man of his words. He was determined to carry out his campaign pledge of visiting the shrine no matter what. While his visits fueled anger from China and South Korea, their protests only seemed to fire him up, strengthening his determination to continue to poke them in the eye. My own conversations with Japanese diplomats and scholars on exploring the "why" question behind Koizumi's rigidity turned out unsatisfactory. A common response from them was a Japanese sentence—"*Shoh ga nai na*," which can be translated as "What can I say?" or "Nothing can be done." The analysis was disappointingly tautological: provoking China and South Korea by going to the shrine every year does not make sense. But, Koizumi did this because he was Koizumi. He did not care.

I left these conversations feeling underfed, as they told me very little about what Koizumi wanted to achieve through such shrine visits. Knowing the damages his annual homage trips were destined to incur, Koizumi must have wanted to gain something through such defiant acts. One reason, offered by non-Japanese media, was that he wanted to create the "round the flag" effect. He used such visits to mobilize domestic support. However, domestic mobilization could not explain why Koizumi chose to go there each and every year, when poll numbers were showing that public opinion was divided.[43] Such a realization made me somewhat sympathetic toward the Japanese "What can I say?" view.

This line of reasoning has gained some international currency lately, particularly in America. When a group of psychiatrists speculated openly about the mental fitness of President Donald Trump, Jeffrey A. Lieberman, a past president of the American Psychiatric Association, warned in a *New York Times* op-ed that such speculations are unprofessional and should be stopped. Lieberman listed two reasons for his opposition to such backseat observation: first, unless Trump is properly evaluated, doctors do not have "real" evidence to know with certainty if he has a mental disorder, and second, it assumes that Trump's behavior is involuntary and that his "shockingly 'unpresidential'" behavior is a symptom of mental illness. Lieberman goes on to write: "This kind of thinking contributes to the stigmatization of mental illness. It's entirely possible that he simply has certain personal qualities we don't find ideal in a leader, like being a narcissistic bully who lacks basic civility and common courtesies. That he is, in a word, a jerk. But that alone does not make him mentally unfit to serve."[44]

In retrospect, almost a decade before this top American psychiatrist issued a warning of over-analysis with a dearth of verifiable evidence, diplomats and scholars in Japan had already reached a similar conclusion about their leader, with Japanese-style politeness. Such analysis is certainly underwhelming, but in a way it is honest: it admits the disruptive nature of the leader's conduct and just leaves it there.

For the vast majority of Japan's thirty-four postwar prime ministers, whose average time in office is a little over two years, they performed as the nation's top transactional manager. Both domestic and international reasons contribute to this workhorse role. Inside Japan, the LDP has become the country's ruling party by default since its creation in 1955. The LDP is a party of factions with markedly different backgrounds and constituent interests. As either a factional leader or a prominent member of the party, the LDP prime ministers need to spend much time doing the political acrobatics of balancing competing factional interests. Externally, Japan's fundamental diplomatic course has been set in the form of the US-Japan alliance. The alliance has become an institution with both organizational structures and the norms and values attached to it. Metaphorically speaking, once the US-Japan alliance became a giant building, the job of the Japanese prime minister became that of a building manager. There are always some maintenance and repair jobs to be done. But becoming a human wrecking ball is not an option, for the building must stand.

Major foreign policy renovations are still possible. Two such examples are Prime Minister Tanaka Kakuei's decision to normalize relations with China and Prime Minister Fukuda Takeo's "Fukuda Doctrine," which remains a foundational document guiding Japan–Southeast Asia relations. But both policy changes were made under the overarching framework of the US-Japan alliance, and neither attempted to change the alliance's centrality. In addition, both policies were envisioned by the postwar architect Yoshida Shigeru. Though staunchly anti-communist, Yoshida firmly believed that normalizing relations with China was only a matter of time—that is, the Americans would eventually come to their senses and offer Japan the green light. While Japan was waiting, the country could explore the economic and geopolitical potential of Southeast Asia to compensate for the loss of the Chinese market.

The managerial orientation also applies to the most recent prime minister, Abe Shinzo. To Japan's wary neighbors, China and South Korea in particular, Abe seemed like a conspiratorially transformative architect attempting to dial the clock back to militarist time. Such a view also has a Japanese audience. Many saw him as harboring an authoritarian streak by approving the sweeping State Secrecy Law, as they fear the law could be abused for wiretapping and other invasive monitoring activities by the state. Abe made no secret of his desire to abandon article 9 of Japan's pacifist constitution, which banned Japanese ownership of a military. To his foreign and domestic opponents, it would make him a fascist.[45] However, for Japanese conservatives, dismantling Japan's postwar constitution has been the cause célèbre for decades. The ban on owning a military has long been buried in practice. Most importantly, Abe spearheaded the prioritization of the US-Japan alliance. On foreign policy, he sought to strengthen, not weaken, this foundational piece of Japan's foreign policy. Abe was thus one more diligent manager rather than a transformative architect. Suga Yoshihide, Abe's right-hand man and successor, vowed to continue Abe's policies in his first press conference. At onset, he is aiming for a managerial role.

In chapter 2, I discussed the rise of monk-like Chinese premiers—they carry out their jobs with small autonomy and an even smaller ambition. There is almost a tendency to simply warm their seats and do their jobs minimally during their tenure—similar to a reluctant monk who has to toll the bell every day. It turns out there are monk-like Japanese prime ministers as well. Their relatively short tenure has not always been a result of scandals or crises. Sometimes they have chosen to quit because they felt burned out by the never-ending acts of balancing factional interests or pushing the diplomatic constraints. One latest example in this leadership genre is Fukuda Yasuo, the son of Fukuda Takeo. On September 1, 2008, after a full day of fulfilling various prime ministerial duties, Fukuda came back to his office and called for a fifteen-minute press conference at 9:30 p.m. Then and there, he stunned the nation by announcing that he would resign because he was no longer confident about the next election. Despite an avalanche of criticism that such an act was irresponsible, Fukuda abruptly walked away after serving in office for 364 days, just one day shy of an anniversary. Twelve years later, Abe Shinzo would also resign abruptly due to ill health. Fukuda and Abe should feel thankful for the country they were serving—as a democracy, Japan offers its worn out leaders a safe passage to bow out. Their Chinese counterparts may have similar moments of exhaustion and down-heartedness, but they have to serve out their entire tenure. For them, there is no option of out, only that of down. There is no zen-style relief, only that of an abyss.

Wandering Leaders, Shepherding Diplomats

The three roles that Chinese leaders play in foreign policy making can all find their Japanese adaptations. The same thing cannot be said about diplomats. Bureaucrats in charge of Japanese foreign policy have a group identity quite different from that of the plainclothes soldier. Japanese diplomats have traditionally enjoyed greater autonomy and authority in executing their country's diplomacy.

A number of reasons explain the more privileged position of the Japanese diplomatic corps. First, Japanese diplomats have an even more elitist background. As chapter 3 discussed, many of the PRC's first diplomats had a revolutionary background. Crash courses had to be offered to train these peasant soldiers in basic diplomatic etiquette. Even today, while China's diplomatic corps are all college educated, they tend to be drawn from students majoring in foreign languages. This applies to all five foreign ministers in the past two decades, starting with Tang Jiaxuan in 1998: Tang majored in Japanese and English, current minister Wang Yi in Japanese, and the other three all in English. In addition, a sizeable number of China's future diplomats come from the College of Foreign Affairs, a school directly affiliated with the Chinese Foreign Ministry and known almost singularly for its foreign language program.

By contrast, Japanese diplomats tend to be drawn from its prestigious national universities, with degrees in public policy and law. Graduates from these majors join the ministry through the Category I civil service entrance exam, which is the most esteemed and difficult category. Table 5.1 offers a summary of the educational backgrounds of the freshmen diplomats the foreign ministry recruited in 2014.

Category I sends "generalists" (*sogoshoku*) to the ministry. These are the people who will be charged with the formulation and execution of foreign policy. In 2014, there was even one recruit from medical school. The Category II path sends "specialists" (*senmon shoku*) to the ministry. This is the category into which students majoring in foreign languages have a better chance of being accepted.[46] But as data from the Japanese Ministry of Foreign Affairs (MOFA) shows, diplomats admitted through the path of the generalist have a much stronger chance of being promoted to directorial, ambassadorial, and other higher-ranking positions in the ministry.[47] In 2020, of the top six officials listed on the MOFA's homepage, all of them graduated from top-ranked universities in Japan and the United States, majoring in public policy, economics, management, national security, and law. None majored in foreign languages.

Graduates majoring in social sciences have clear dominance in the generalist path of the MOFA. While they may need to perfect their foreign language skills, they are trained young technocrats of law, economics, public policy, and public administration from day 1. This is the reverse path of young Chinese diplomats, where promising foreign language graduates are sent to the Central Party School, the National College of Administration, or even administrative posts at provincial levels to accumulate administrative cre-

Table 5.1. Educational Backgrounds of Applicants Admitted to MOFA Through Category I Exam (2014)

School Name	Major	Applicants Admitted
University of Tokyo	Public Policy	2
University of Tokyo	Law	6
University of Tokyo	Economics	1
University of Tokyo	College of Arts and Sciences	1
University of Tokyo	Graduate School of Frontier Sciences	1
Hitotsubashi University	Law	2
Hitotsubashi University	Economics	1
University of Kyoto	Law	2
University of Kyoto	Public Policy	1
University of Kyoto	Human and Environmental Studies	1
Keio University	Medical School	1
Keio University	Economics	1
Keio University	School of Policy Management	1
Keio University	Law	1

Source: Data from Japanese Ministry of Foreign Affairs, accessed at https://www.mofa.go.jp/mofaj/files/000025838.pdf

dentials. It should be pointed out that the Chinese pattern also applies to other foreign-related units. Many of the country's foreign correspondents at the Xinhua News Agency and other news outlets major in foreign languages. They have to learn journalistic concepts and skills on the job.

Japan is a democracy. As such, Japanese diplomats are not obligated to be civilian soldiers to any particular party. They unapologetically owe their loyalty to the state rather than to a political party. Since 1955, the LDP has had a near monopoly on the country's politics. The LDP's dominance in the context of electoral democracy, however, has given Japanese diplomats even more leverage. In his seminal work on the Japanese economic miracle, Chalmers Johnson termed Japan a country reigned by LDP politicians but ruled by its bureaucracy. Under this arrangement, politicians can offer a high degree of autonomy to bureaucrats. They may even take some heat from society so that shielded bureaucrats can formulate and execute policies with no concern over political backlash. In exchange, when such policies yield positive results, bureaucrats can offer credit to the politicians, which could enable them to win the next election.[48]

Although Johnson's case was Japan's Ministry of International Trade and Industry, the argument would apply to the MOFA as well. As political scientist Gerald Curtis points out, Japanese politicians do not have the same staff support that American lawmakers have. Parties do not have the same staff support that other parliamentary democracies like Britain and Germany have. As a result, legislation is mostly written by bureaucrats and submitted to the Diet by the cabinet. Judicial committees do very little in the way of legislation.[49] Unlike Chinese diplomats, who are mere infantries carrying out what they are told by the party, Japanese diplomats are the core force in the country's foreign policy-making process, hence the institutional preference for social sciences majors over foreign language majors. Foreign policy making often starts as ideas exchanged among top bureaucrats and politicians over Japanese sake at *izakaya* bars, is verbalized at the ministry's desks, travels to judicial committees for almost guaranteed approval, and comes back to the ministry for execution.

This mini-ecosystem worked well when both the political and administrative ends delivered. It contributed to not only MOFA's sense of prestige but also its sensitivity to political interference. The ministry and its career bureaucrats have come to see and defend foreign policy making as their home turf. This problem is not unique to Japan. Margaret Thatcher's favorite TV political satire *Yes Minister* vividly captured the same problem in Britain. In the sitcom, Minister Jim Hacker, a party politician, attempted to launch sweeping changes to the ministry. It did not take long for him to realize that all his efforts were frustrated and defeated by the civil service branch of the ministry, led by the career bureaucrat Permanent Secretary Humphrey Appleby.

What exacerbated the problem in Japan was the high turnover rate of prime ministers. From 1945 to 2020, postwar Britain had fifteen prime ministers leading seventeen cabinets. Japan, on the other hand, saw thirty-six prime ministers leading thirty-eight cabinets. In 2009, Brazilian president Luiz Inacio Lula da Silva, after stumbling over Prime Minister Hatoyama Yukio's name, joked that in Japan "you say 'good morning' to one prime minister and 'good afternoon' to a different one."[50] The revolving door of the prime minister's office moves fast indeed. This further contributes to Japanese diplomats' sense of taking charge. Politicians with their pet agendas come and go. Diplomats need to stay and think about the "big picture."[51]

So, how do Japanese diplomats exert their influence? The mechanism by default is attempting to shepherd politicians from behind. But this traditional mechanism has been met with rising resistance from politicians as they fight to gain the commanding height in foreign policy making. One example that exposes the MOFA's obstructionist role is the stalemate between Japan and Russia.[52] On the surface level, the one issue that has blocked the improvement of relations between the two countries is the territorial dispute over the Kuril Islands (the Japanese name is the Northern Territories). The real puzzle, though, is that consecutive polls in Japan have revealed low public interest. A 2008 MOFA-sponsored survey shows that close to 60 percent of respondents stated they had little interest in participating in activities that demanded the return of the islands; 33 percent said they would participate "if opportunity permits." Only 3.2 percent identified themselves as potential activists. These numbers mirrored those of an earlier survey in 2008, which also found that close to half of the respondents (48.8 percent) were either "unaware" or "somewhat unaware" of the content of Japan's official demand. Meanwhile, a similar poll in Russia showed that only 1 percent of Russians supported a Japanese sovereign takeover of the islands. Russian president Vladimir Putin, right before a summit with Abe in 2016, flatly denied the "existence" of any territorial dispute.[53] Hence, the real question becomes this: If the hope of getting all the islands back is imaginary and public interest to do so is low, why would the Japanese government insist on setting the unachievable goal of demanding the return of all the islands as a precondition for normalizing relations?

A key reason is the MOFA's obstruction. One tactic it employs is to exaggerate or even manufacture American pressure to warn politicians to stay on the fundamental course of the US-Japan alliance. According to Kimie Hara, it was the MOFA that originally proposed an "all or nothing" claim—that is, the Soviet Union must return all four islands as a way to extract a compromise offer of "two islands." However, the four-islands proposal was later solidified, and it acquired a life of its own.[54] Japanese diplomats' concern was twofold: maintaining American trust and guarding their monopoly on foreign policy making.[55] The first reason could be employed as a decoy for the second. Indeed, Japanese bureaucrats' use of "foreign pressure" (*gaiatsu*) is legendary.[56] The MOFA's emphasis on maintaining American trust was not entirely convincing—after all, it was the Japanese government, not their American counterpart, that saw the solving of the territorial dispute as the precondition for normalizing relations with the Soviet Union. Oftentimes, alleged American concerns turned out not to have originated from American diplomats at Foggy Bottom. Instead, they were hatched by their Japanese colleagues at Kasumigaseki and then packaged as imported from America. *Gaiatsu* could be used not only as an impetus for change but also as an obstruction to change.

The MOFA's consistent obstructions could apply to Japan–Soviet Union/Russia relations in general. In the mid-1980s, Prime Minister Nakasone Yasuhiro proposed a "comprehensive approach" that would seek to reach a peace treaty concurrently while negotiating the territorial dispute. This proposal would depart from Japan's traditional approach of solving the territorial dispute as the precondition for any peace treaty. Japanese bureaucrats moved in quickly to crush such overtures. The MOFA defended its all-or-nothing intransigence as crucial for safeguarding the US-Japan alliance. Some Japanese diplomats went so far as to denounce Nakasone's proposal as "utterly ridiculous" (*kotomukei*) and to criticize Wada Haruki, a prominent scholar and a supporter of Nakasone's proposal, for having "the face of a Japanese but the heart of a Soviet" (*nichimen soshin*).[57] Meanwhile, the MOFA dismissed the Soviet leader Mikhail Gorbachev's conciliatory speech in 1986, fearing Moscow would "eat and run"—that is, receive economic aid but default on any commitment to solving the territorial dispute.[58] Pro-America and anti-USSR formed the two sides of the same coin for the MOFA, serving the common purpose of warding off challengers to its authority in policy making.

Another example that highlights the tension between politicians and the MOFA centers on Japan-China relations. For a long time, rumors have circulated in the Japanese media of a so-called *Chaina-sukūru* (China School) segment in the Japanese government, especially in the foreign ministry. The term "China School" originated from the Chinese language-training program housed by the ministry. Later the Japanese press picked up the term to describe officials and politicians who prioritize the importance of Japan-

China relations and emphasize the need to reach compromises with the Chinese government.

Representative figures include political veterans like Tanaka Makiko, daughter of the late prime minister Tanaka Kakuei and also Prime Minister Koizumi Jun'ichiro's first foreign minister. Soon after taking office, Tanaka angered Taiwan by suggesting it would not be a bad idea for them to follow Hong Kong's footsteps of returning back to China. Prime Minister Fukuda Yasuo and Kato Koichi, who served as cabinet office secretary and as party secretary of the ruling LDP, are also commonly perceived as pro-China and thus members of the China School. In fact, Kato made a series of speeches to voice his objection to Koizumi's annual visits to the Yasukuni Shrine on the grounds that the action may further antagonize China. This led to a rightwing nationalist burning down Kato's house and adjoining office in August 2006. Other prominent members of this group include consecutive chiefs of the Asian and Pacific Affairs Bureau's China Division and Japanese ambassadors to China, for example, Makita Kunihiko, Anami Koreshige, Tanino Sakutaro, Miyamoto Yūji, Niwa Uichiro, and the current ambassador Yokoi Yutaka.

The term "China School" carries a negative connotation. Its members are portrayed as being excessively soft to the Chinese government. Some critics could go so far as to condemn members of this segment as treasonous to Japan.[59] In the past, members of this segment endured not just public shaming but also marginalization from the top. In August 2005, in a highly unusual gesture, Ambassador Anami telegraphed Koizumi and urged him not to further antagonize Japan-China relations by visiting the controversial Yasukuni Shrine.[60] Koizumi apparently snubbed Anami's desperate appeal, and his visit to the shrine went undisturbed in October.

Tensions between the MOFA and politicians are not strictly ideological—it could happen between the MOFA and whoever is in charge of the government. In 2012, when the premiership was in the hands of the Democratic Party of Japan (DPJ), an episode similar to the Koizumi-Anami feud happened—this time between Ambassador Niwa and Prime Minister Noda Yoshihiko. Niwa was a member of the China School in a broader sense. He was not a career bureaucrat; instead, he was a businessman. Joining the giant trading company Itochu at the age of twenty-two, he worked for the company for forty-eight years, climbing all the way from a salaryman to the company's president, overseeing approximately eighty thousand employees and total assets of US$600 million. Itochu has particularly benefited from trading with China, thanks to its operational strength in sectors like textiles, machines, and minerals. Niwa traveled to China numerous times and had a vibrant personal network in the country. By choosing him, the DPJ government apparently wanted to use the "hotter" economic aspect of bilateral relations to warm up the "cooler" politics.

Yet, when Niwa attempted to make a difference, he ran into thick walls in both Beijing and Tokyo. In his memoir, he discussed his frustrations with the Japanese government in greater detail. After all, given the dire situation of Sino-Japanese relations, Niwa was anticipating Chinese hostility. But the Japanese backstabbing was more disheartening. In 2012, the DPJ government decided to nationalize the Senkaku/Diaoyu Islands, over which China also claimed sovereignty. While firmly supporting Japan's sovereign control, Niwa contacted the Japanese prime minister's office multiple times, urging Noda to hold off the announcement before a summit with Chinese president Hu Jintao. Yet, as Niwa lamented, "My words fell to deaf ears."[61] Not surprisingly, the Chinese canceled the meeting. Even after leaving his post, Niwa remained bitter over this snub. He accused the Noda government of being irresponsible for the safety of the Japanese in China. He further chastised: "I still don't know why Noda rushed to make the announcement—did he have intelligence that I, as the ambassador to China, did not possess?"[62]

The Russian case and the Chinese case reveal that vexation is not a one-way street. Bad feelings are mutual between politicians and bureaucrats. If anything, it is that politicians have become bolder in recent years. They are no longer satisfied with being herded by the country's elite bureaucrats. Instead, they have begun to drain or bypass what they perceive as the inefficient and timid bureaucratic swamp. The urge to take on the country's elitist bureaucracy is bipartisan. The DPJ came to power in 2009 by riding on popular resentment of bureaucratic politics—a resentment that did not go unnoticed in my conversations with multiple Japanese diplomats. Though most conversations were in small groups or in one-on-one situations, Japanese diplomats' responses were universal, with a mixture of opposition and dismissal not strikingly different from how Sir Humphery Appleby sounded in *Yes Minister*—the DPJ government does not know what it is doing. It is too idealistic or naive, and its crowd-pleasing ideas will fail.[63]

The Japanese bureaucrats were partly correct. The DPJ government was indeed marked by a string of weak leaders and policy failures. But the return of a familiar face, Abe Shinzo, and establishment politics have not soothed the tensions between bureaucrats and politicians. In fact, Abe was actively promoting so-called multilevel, multidimension diplomacy, sending his close allies as personal go-betweens to handle vital relations. While personal envoys have always existed, Abe institutionalized such arrangements, creating the position of special adviser for foreign affairs to the prime minister

(*Gaiko tokubetsu hosakan*). Kawai Katsuyuki, the lawmaker who assumed this position, played a key role in arranging Abe's meeting with Donald Trump on November 18, 2016, ten days after Trump's upset victory in the US presidential election. As a reporter close to Kawai recorded, the preparatory meeting for this summit was attended by Abe, Kawai, and a few high-ranking MOFA officials, including the Japanese ambassador Sasae Ken'ichiro, the director of MOFA's North America Bureau Mori Takeo, and head of the National Security Council Yachi Shotaro. Kawai not only led the meeting but also held off sharing crucial documents with other diplomats. He later went to Abe's hotel room to hand over the documents. As the reporter summarized, Abe's "multi-level/dimensional diplomacy" is a euphemism for prime minister–led foreign policy making.[64] Distrust between the administrative and political camps is deep-rooted. Now, leaders like Abe have chosen to step up. They are attempting to be the herder rather than the herded.

The Public as Powerful Undercurrent

At my university, I teach a seminar class titled "Politics of Reconciliation." One case it explores is the Rape of Nanking, a topic that few American students are aware of. On one occasion, an American student told me that after she learned about the case she had a conversation with a Japanese high school student on a homestay with her family. The American student asked her Japanese guest about her thoughts on the mutual hostility between Japan and China. "What was her answer?" I asked. "She said we [Japanese] don't dislike them [Chinese]. They just dislike us," my American student answered.

The answer from the Japanese student did not surprise me. I have received similar answers from Japanese students I have talked to in America and in Japan. Such an answer embeds sentiments of both grievance and innocence. It implies that many people in Japan feel that "we," the Japanese, should not be blamed for the hostile relations between Japan and China. "They," the Chinese, have chosen to dislike or even hate "us." The bitter, belligerent emotion flows one way from China to Japan. Since it is a one-way street, the implication is that Japan, on the receiving end, can do little to reverse such negative sentiments harbored by the Chinese.

Answers offered along this line strike me as half-accurate. Let me first address the inaccurate part of this popular perception. The fact is that hostility has become mutual. As figure 5.1 reveals, Japanese public response to the question of how friendly they felt toward China had its first big drop in 1989,

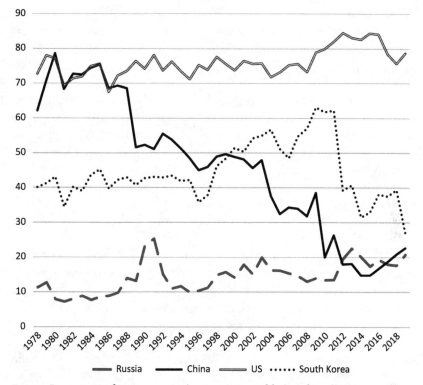

Fig. 5.1. Percentage of Japanese popular perception of feeling friendliness toward Russia, China, America, and South Korea (1978–2019). (*Data source:* Japanese Cabinet Office, Gaiko ni kansuru yoron chosa [Survey on Diplomacy], https://survey.gov-online.go.jp/r01/401-gaiko/index.html)

in the wake of the Tian'anmen Massacre. Since then, the "friendliness" trajectory has been dropping precipitously. Popular hostility toward China has become so widespread that in 2016, for the first time, China replaced Russia as the one country the Japanese public felt most unfriendly toward. The Japanese have certainly been well aware of Chinese hostility and responded with similarly negative sentiment. But, poll numbers from China show that the percentage of the Chinese public who feel friendly toward Japan has increased significantly in recent years. In 2013, only 5.9 percent of Chinese stated they felt very friendly toward Japan. In 2017, 31.4 percent chose this answer. The Japanese trajectory, on the other hand, fluctuated between 14 percent to 18 percent during the same period. So, one may even argue that now hostility has been tipped toward the Japanese side.

At a time when more and more Chinese feel that they like Japan and millions of Chinese tourists are flocking to the country, the Japanese popular perception of China has remained hostile. Even the Chinese tourists are not always welcomed. Their spending power is so impressive that it has created a new Japanese word: *bakugai*, or explosive buying. Japanese media began chastising the phenomenon called *kanko kogai*, or tourist pollution. Chinese tourists in particular have stirred up Japanese hostility, derision, and condescension. After video footage of Chinese tourists brawling at an airport in Hokkaido over a flight delay was made public, social media in Japan were flooded by angry, sometimes racist, posts calling the Chinese "barbarians," "criminals," "monkeys," and "livestock."[65] Some assumed the moral high ground of teaching the Chinese good manners, touting that tourists who came to Japan and learned Japanese manners would bring them back to their countries, thus exporting Japan's cultural charm overseas.

Hokkaido tourism authorities published booklets in Chinese and English to remind tourists of manners of all kinds, from moral issues to bodily functions. They include warnings of not to steal cutlery from restaurants, not to be late for appointments, and not to break wind or belch in public. One Chinese resident protested that such publications exclusively in foreign languages constituted targeted discrimination. Later, the tourism authority changed the booklet's wording.[66] The flooding of Chinese tourists, while economically welcoming, has heightened cultural clashes for more and more Japanese. In many cases, superficial exchanges like serving Chinese customers have deepened rather than lessened stereotypes.

But the Japanese complaint that the Chinese choose to dislike them has its accurate components. In terms of genesis, the Chinese dislike or hatred of Japan was encouraged or even manufactured by the Chinese government, as it was relying on nationalism as a new foundation for regime legitimacy. In recent years, as chapter 4 reveals, anti-Japan hatred has turned into a billion-yuan cultural industry. It has thus acquired its own economic logic. On the flip side, though, if the Chinese government chose to de-escalate or switch the direction of its propaganda, Chinese public opinion could change fast. A current example is the Chinese government's quite positive coverage of Japanese aid to help China combat the Covid-19 crisis. Beijing is offering effusive remarks to Japan to create a "positive atmosphere" for a scheduled visit by Xi Jinping. The tactic also helped the Chinese public focus its wrath on America.

On the Japanese side, negative feelings are somewhat more resilient. They demonstrate an inertia: that is, they are not as wildly fluctuating as the ones in China, partly thanks to the country's democratic institution. The Japanese government does not have the mechanism to mandate the country's media to cover China in a positive light. There is also no Japanese equivalent of the Chinese anti-Japan TV dramas and movies. As one analysis suggests, however, recent Japanese war-centric movies have had a tendency to soften the country's image as an aggressor. A most talked-about movie was *Eternal Zero*, which focused on kamikaze pilots near the end of the war. By raking in US$84 million, the movie was a huge commercial success. But the revenue would be dwarfed by the US$874 million yielded by the Chinese nationalist movie *Wolf Warrior 2*.

This contrast reveals another accurate component of the Japanese complaint: it is related to not only *what* people think about but also *how intensely* they think about it. In other words, is foreign policy a topic that attracts huge public interest? In a democracy, where people have the electoral power to hold officials accountable and a government cannot dictate what the public *must* be interested in, people have a natural tendency to care about local issues, followed by national and international ones. In 2019, a Pew Research Center survey showed that the American public's top five policy priorities are the economy (70 percent), health-care costs (69 percent), education (68 percent), terrorism (67 percent), and Social Security (67 percent). Despite that the trade war with China is intensifying, only 39 percent chose "global trade" as a priority, making the issue the lowest one among the eighteen issues identified.[67] A Gallup survey in December 2018 asked Americans to identify the "top problem" for the country. Among the thirteen problems identified by at least 3 percent of respondents, none was about US foreign policy. All the problems were domestic.[68]

Americans are not unique in prioritizing issues close to home, though the minimal presence of international issues did strengthen the impression that Americans see their country as a world onto itself. In a similar survey in Japan, foreign policy made it onto the list of priorities, but the results still clearly lean on domestic or local issues.

As the figure shows, security and foreign policy sat toward the lower end of the priority list. Issues that the majority of Japanese people feel their leaders should focus on are all domestic and unique to the country's situation—economic recovery, welfare, and education. Even for China, where poll numbers on political issues are not entirely reliable, the government's survey results show that all top ten issues are domestic.

Hence, the Japanese public is simply following the universal pattern of caring about themselves, their loved ones, their neighborhoods, their cities and prefectures, their nation, and the world, in that order. On contested foreign policy issues that attract sensational media coverage, for example, Japan's

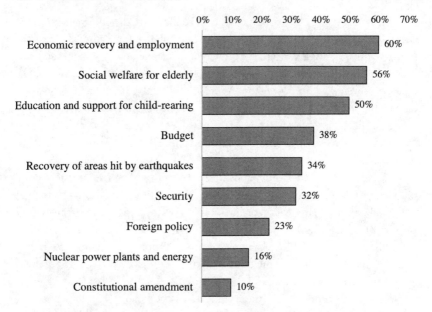

Fig. 5.2. "What should Prime Minister Abe's priorities be?" (May 2018). (*Data Source: Asahi Shimbun*, Seisaku no yusendo "kenpo kaisei" wa saikai Asahi yoron chosa [Asahi survey: priority of policies: constitutional amendment lowest priority], May 1, 2018; accessed at https://www.asahi.com/articles/ASL4R4HT4L4RU ZPS006.html [August 20, 2019].)

bitter territorial disputes with China over the Senkaku/Diaoyu Islands, with South Korea over the Takeshima/Dokto Islands, and with Russia over the Kuril Island/Northern Territories, public awareness of these issues is high, all in the 90 percent range. But public interest is comparatively low. In 2019, the ratio of people who indicated they follow the disputes with China and South Korea to those who did not was about two to one. Another survey in 2017 showed that about one in three did not know Senkaku was part of Okinawa Prefecture. More than 40 percent could not identify the island's accurate location.[69] The public is clearly *aware* of Japan's major diplomatic hot spots, and their views are overwhelmingly supportive of the government's position. However, they do not think intensely about them. Foreign countries probably matter more in terms of food, fashion, culture, and sightseeing rather than intergovernmental disputes. This is even true for Sino-Japanese relations. Despite China's abysmal popularity in Japan as a country, its cultural aspects remain attractive. The number of Japanese visits to China peaked in 2011 at over 3.65 million. Since then, the deterioration of bilateral relations

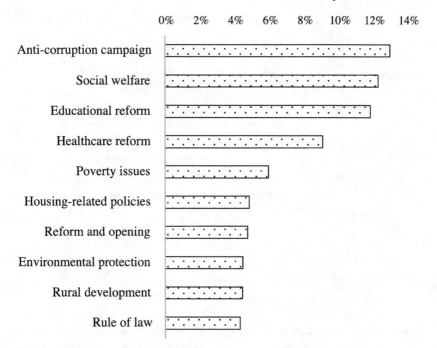

Fig. 5.3. Top ten issues the Chinese public identifies as priorities (February 2018). (*Data source: Sohu News*, "2018 quanguo lianghui zhaokai zaiji, na 'shidaredian' qunzhong zuiguanzhu!" [Right before 2018 national two conventions to start, what are the top ten issues people care the most?], March 1, 2018; https://www.sohu.com/a/224659820_121220)

has indeed been accompanied by a decline in Japanese tourists bound for China. Still, in 2016, with over 2.58 million Japanese visits to China, the country was the second most popular destination for outbound Japanese tourism. Only the United States attracted more visitors from Japan.[70]

In April 2018, a Japanese person named Iwata Takanori published a picture book on China's anti-Japan TV dramas. Entitled *A Reader of China's Anti-Japan Drama: Unintentionally Anti-Japan, Patriotic Comedies*, the book became a best seller on the Japanese Amazon.com.[71] Another major Japanese book seller, Kinokuniya, ran out of stock of the book in June 2018. Customers would have to wait for one to three weeks for their orders to be delivered. Iwata is no political pundit or scholar. He is an IT worker with a passion for Chinese language and culture. He began to watch these dramas as a way to learn Chinese but soon became fascinated by their portrayals of Japan and the Japanese. The book collected images from twenty-one Chinese anti-

Japan TV dramas and analyzed their inaccuracies. But Iwata's purpose was investigative rather than political. Many of his tweets are about Chinese scenery, items he bought in China, and language learning tips. Even when commenting on Chinese mistakes in these dramas, he would often offer technical speculations on why such errors occurred. Ironically, China's anti-Japan TV dramas now have acquired an economic logic even in Japan. The Chinese are the ones who feel humiliated by Iwata's book. Many netizens commented that this book has made the Chinese "lose face" to the Japanese—a scenario they had long feared such dramas could produce. Many also expressed amazement at the meticulous research an ordinary Japanese could put into writing this book. To them, the book served as another example of Japan's famed diligence and craftsmanship.[72]

So, if foreign policy is an issue that the Japanese public tends to have clear opinions on but does not think intensely about, what then is the public's impact on foreign policy making? The public's role may be latent, but its power is fundamental at both the macro- and microlevels. This is particularly the case for a democracy like Japan. As a country based on the rule of law, the Japanese public could exert tremendous influence on changing or maintaining the country's fundamental path. On the US-Japan alliance, for example, the Cabinet Office's annual survey has presented a highly stable public opinion: over 85 percent of the public surveyed in the past twenty years has consistently labeled relations with America as "extremely important" (*hijoni taisetsu*). In the past two years, when the public was asked whether these relations will be "very important" in the future, approximately 80 percent chose "yes." By contrast, only approximately 2 percent chose "no." Hence, when Japanese leaders seek to strengthen the country's alliance with America, they have solid public opinion to support them. The path chosen by Yoshida has continued to be the national consensus six decades later. On another fundamental issue, namely, constitutional amendment, public opinion has been divided and fluctuating. For almost the entire 1990s and the 2010s, those who favored revising the constitution consistently outnumbered those who opposed it—the gap ranged between a few percentage points in the early 1990s to over 40 percent in 2004. Since then, however, the gap has been narrowing. One survey by the *Asahi Shimbun* in May 2020 showed that 72 percent felt that amending the constitution should not be a priority, in contrast to 22 percent who felt otherwise.[73] Another poll showed that 88 percent of the public saw the pacifist constitution as playing a positive role in Japan's postwar development.[74]

Though locked in a tug of war, the opposition forces are more fired up. They saw Abe's implementation of the National Security Law as antidemocratic. Thousands of protesters took to the streets in Tokyo, Osaka, and other cities in 2016 and 2017, holding "no war" and "peace" signs and rejecting what they perceived as a return to militarism. I personally witnessed one such protest in July 2017. At a campaign stop in Tokyo's Akihabara district, as the prime minister was offering an endorsement speech for a female candidate, hundreds of angry protesters were chanting, "Abe, quit!" and "Go home!" Angered by the chanting, Abe raised his voice and said: "We cannot lose to people like this!" These protestors presented a sharp visual contrast to Abe's supporters, many of whom were waving Japanese *hinomaru* national flags. Abe's candidate would later lose.

Though presented on a much smaller scale, the scene was somewhat reminiscent of public opposition in 1960, when tens of thousands of people poured onto the streets of Tokyo to protest Prime Minister Kishi Nobusuke, Abe's grandfather, for railroading the renewal of the US-Japan Security Treaty. What triggered such massive popular resistance was not just the content of the treaty—it was also Kishi's heavy-handed approach and his little regard for the democratic process, which reminded many people of the militarist style of governance. Now, Kishi's grandson is facing the same criticism. Such dissenting voices from the masses are important. Though the practice of Japan's postwar pacifist constitution has long been buried, its spirit remains vibrant. Abe's push for the constitutional revision has, in effect, alerted and energized those who oppose it. The regime, buttressed by pacifist norms, values, and identities, remains enduring. It restricts leaders' efforts to stretch the interpretation of Japan's most fundamental piece of law to serve their agendas.

At the microlevel, as people living in an affluent democracy, the Japanese public could contribute to improving relations with other countries through their personal effort. To have a passport ranked as the world's most powerful one, according to the number of countries its holders can access without a visa, certainly helps.[75] For a long time Japan has had a small but active community of foreign-bound volunteers. In 2014, compared with 30 percent of volunteers working in neighborhood management and 22 percent active in youth development, the combined total percentage of Japanese volunteers working in foreign- or international-related issues was 8.6 percent.[76] One leading volunteer organization, the Japan International Cooperation Agency, has fourteen local offices throughout Japan and ninety-six offices overseas. As of February 2018, the organization had sent over seventy thousand volunteers to nearly ninety countries on every continent with human inhabitance. Even in China, a country that Japan no longer offers official development aid to and one known for its tense relations with Japan, more than seven hundred volunteers from this one organization alone worked there. They often go to poor and remote parts of the country to help local development, especially in education and health care.[77] One volunteer, Sakai Junko, reported with great pride how she taught the Yi people in Liangshan, a desolate region in Sichuan Province, basic hygiene skills like brushing teeth. When running water was cut off, Sakai and the students used shoulder poles to fetch water to continue this daily personal hygiene practice. Since 1980, more than seven thousand Japanese volunteers have come to plant trees in the Gobi Desert.[78] To green China has become a generational mission for some Japanese families. It is people like Sakai and the tree-planting volunteers who have kept the flame of trust and friendship burning even during the most difficult times.

This is not to say that the Japanese public's role in foreign policy is always positive. When politicians talk about the importance of people-to-people exchanges, they often make their appeals to young people. This was true for Hu Yaobang in 1984, when he invited three thousand young Japanese to China. This was true for Barack Obama in 2009, when he launched the "100,000 Strong" initiative to boost the number of American students studying in China. Poll numbers have also shown that despite the strong hostility that the Japanese public harbors toward China, young people between the ages of eighteen and twenty-nine have consistently constituted the least hostile group to China. This pattern applies to Japanese perceptions of Russia and South Korea, too.[79] Young people in Japan are also the least resistant to the idea of making the country more welcoming to immigrants. A 2012 survey showed that among young people between the ages of eighteen and twenty-nine, the ratio of those who support allowing more immigrants into Japan to those opposing it was two to one. The national average, though, was a one to one ratio.

However, this is where Japan is facing its most daunting challenges. Japan is among the most rapidly aging countries in the world. Young people as a group will have an ever-shrinking presence in the country. Even more worrisome, though, is a growing trend of the country's youth directing their visions increasingly inward. On this issue, it is worth sharing the critical reflections of Japan's CEO-turned-ambassador Niwa Uichiro. Niwa titled his book on his ambassadorial tenure *China's Great Dilemma*. The last chapter of the book, though, is on Japan's great dilemma. Niwa laments that young people in Japan are losing the competitive and curious spirit that used to guide their parents' and grandparents' generations. Citing a multinational survey on youth development, Niwa points to a dispiriting picture in Japan. On answering the question "Do you want to achieve something great in your life?" 89 percent of Chinese high school respondents and 75 percent of South Korean high school respondents offered a positive answer. By contrast, 46 percent of Japanese students said "yes," while 54 percent said "no."[80] Niwa also called out a song, "The Only Flower in the World," as revealing Japan's loss of its combative pursuit of excellence. The lyrics go:

> I saw all the flowers lined up on display
> The shop full of colors and scented embrace
> We all have a blossom we like more than the rest
> But I think, with flowers, they are all the best
> No fighting or envy they never contend
> But smile in the sunlight and sway in the wind
> They all know their mission; it fills them with pride
> Everyone is different yet all are alike
>
> I wonder why people must always compare
> And judge one another it seems so unfair
> To place color, status, and looks to the test
> How can these show us who's the best?

The song, sung by the all-boy band SMAP, was immensely popular among the young. To Niwa, however, it was a swan song of a Japan that chose to give up: having been mired in economic malaise for over two decades, the country decided to stop trying. It chose to become self-complacent by seeing everyone, including itself, as the only beautiful flower in the world. Yet, as Niwa warned, the world is still a competitive place. Such self-pitying would only lead to Japan's further marginalization.

The Japanese ambassador's evidence may seem anecdotal, but data have indeed presented a picture that Japanese youth participation in overseas educational adventures is shrinking. Take America as an example: the country has been consistently the biggest market for Japanese students. In 2001, there were close to 60,000 Chinese students and 46,497 Japanese students studying in America. Thirteen years later, the number of Chinese students increased to more than 270,000, a growth of 457 percent. By contrast, the number of Japanese students went down to 19,334, a decrease of 60 percent.

One popular explanation offered from the Japanese side is that hiring season in the country collides with the academic calendars of most American colleges, creating a huge disadvantage for those who study abroad. This explanation sounds more like an excuse, for it cannot explain the steady decline of Japanese students studying on American campuses, even when there is no change to the hiring season in Japan, not to mention that some

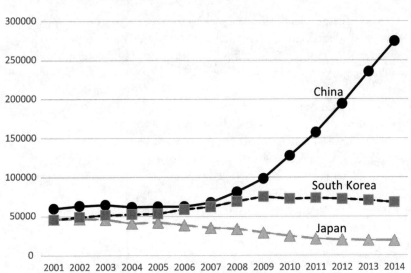

Fig. 5.4. Number of Chinese, South Korean, and Japanese students in America (2001–14). (*Data source:* "Kakkoku no zaibei ryugakuseisu no sui to nihonjin ryugakusei" [Number of international students in America and students from Japan] accessed at https://wag-study-aborad.com [August 20, 2018].)

Japanese firms are beginning to implement more flexible hiring mechanisms to attract those who study overseas. In fact, among all the East Asian and Southeast Asian countries surveyed, Japan and Taiwan are the only two countries that have experienced steady declines in the number of students studying in America. Taiwan's drop from 28,556 in 2001 to 21,266 in 2014 was less dramatic than that of Japan.[81] Niwa may be right after all—Japanese people may continue to go to other countries as tourists, but their curiosity in learning in-depth about others and exposing themselves to cultural unknowns is dwindling, as attested to by the declining number of Japanese students willing to study overseas.

In 1854, an American fleet led by Commodore Matthew Perry dropped anchors at Shimoda near Edo Bay. Yoshida Shoin, a pre-Meiji intellectual, presented a letter to the Americans asking to be allowed aboard so that he could go to the West and study. After being rejected, Yoshida climbed up to one of the American ships at night, only to be refused by the American troops a second time. Even when captured and put in a cage, Yoshida still managed to hand over a note to Perry asking for his permission to allow him to see the West. This spirit is indeed long gone. With over 2.4 million people working as "freeters" (part-timers) and another 850,000 working as NEETS (young people not in employment, education, or training), the prospect looks far from encouraging for Japan's youth. No wonder many seek solace in humming to the tune of the "The Only Flower in the World."

Political Buns and Ozymandias' Shadow

This book employs a tripartite analytical framework and examines various roles that leaders, bureaucrats, and the masses play in jointly shaping Chinese foreign policy. As a dynamic process, foreign policy making is constantly conditioned by factors exogenous and endogenous at the macro- and micro-levels: contingencies, leadership personalities, organizational identities, and public sentiments driven by both emotional and materialistic considerations. As David Lampton points out, these forces form an interactive web.[82] Their trajectories meet and create nodes—critical points where policies are contested, formulated, and executed. Such an interactive web applies to not only China but also other countries with different regime types.

The Chinese journey winds back to a junction where history meets the present. Under the leadership of Xi Jinping, the country's new motto is one about the Chinese Dream. What makes one vision a grand national dream and another a fantasy lies in legitimacy; that is, there needs to be consensual confidence shared by all major actors—leaders, bureaucrats, and the masses—on the worthiness and feasibility of this pursuit. The bigger context seems to be offering a favorable environment for China's pursuit of its greatness: the postwar world order based on liberal democracy and free trade has been under attack by no other than its leader, the United States. The Trump administration's emphasis on "America First" and trade protectionism, however, is nothing new in the global context. In fact, if anything, by implementing these slogans, the world's hegemon has finally succumbed to a trend in the making for decades. America's retrenching could create an opening for China to assert its own leadership. In January 2017, three days before Trump was to be sworn in and shred global trade deals, Chinese president Xi Jinping traveled to Davos, Switzerland, to attend the World Economic Forum, an annual invitation-only elitist gathering where political, economic, and societal leaders address key issues of globalization. Xi sounded almost philosophical in his speech as he told the audience, "Honey melons hang on bitter vines; sweet dates grow on thistles and thorns."[83] In a not so subtle zinging, Xi also warned America that "pursuing protectionism is like locking oneself in a dark room. While wind and rain may be kept outside, that dark room will also block light and air. No one will emerge as a winner in a trade war."[84] As *Bloomberg News* puts it, Xi's speech marked a historical role reversal: a Communist Party leader had now become the new "Davos Man"—a champion of free trade—as America was engulfed by populist angst.[85]

The new Davos Man, though, is also a paranoid man. China may seem to be exuding confidence and optimism as it faces outward, but relations among crucial domestic actors, particularly those between the leadership and the masses, are only superficially quiet. In my own conversations with Beijing cab drivers, who are known for their acerbic take on Chinese politics, it was not unusual for the dream metaphor to be mocked as a fantasy. Many of them would also refer to China's most powerful leader by various derogatory nicknames, the most popular one being "Xi the Bun" or just "the Bun." Xi got this nickname as a result of a much-publicized visit to a Beijing chain restaurant in December 2013, where he ordered some buns. A flurry of state media coverage, along with the president's own portly appearance, led to the coinage of this term. Predictably, typing the nickname in Chinese in the search engine Baidu did not return any results as of September 2020. A similar search performed on Google, however, generated more than 675,000 results. Some netizens borrowed the name of the chain restaurant, Qingfeng, and used it as the imperial-style era name for Xi's reign, calling the year 2018 the starting year of the Qingfeng Era—a mockery of the Chinese president's decision to eliminate presidential term limits. Needless to say, a search of the phrase "starting year of Qingfeng Era" in September 2020 returned nothing relevant on Baidu but produced more than 29 million results on Google, almost universally related to Xi's elimination of presidential terms.

Of course, when a leader is climbing to demigod status, all the glories go to him but all the errs belong to someone else. In early 2020, when the Covid-19 crisis was engulfing the country, Xi's name all but disappeared in the media for much of February. Meanwhile, transient but intense public outcries erupted following the death of Li Wenliang, a whistleblowing doctor who was silenced by the Wuhan police authorities for "spreading rumors." Yet, as the situation improved, Xi returned to dominate headline news on a daily basis. In May, the leader felt emboldened enough to turn to Hong Kong to strip its autonomy, when much of the West was reeling from the Covid-19 losses. In September, Xi presided over a grand ceremony of awarding the country's top honors to four citizens for their outstanding contributions to fighting the Covid-19 epidemic. Inquiries into its origin and punishments for incompetent officials, however, remain murky. Chinese netizens have long mocked that the party always tries to "turn a funeral into a wedding" to cover their failures.[86] Unfortunately, they are right.

The Chinese Communist Party and the man in charge of it are torn between two forces: a desire to achieve greatness and a paranoia of being toppled down. Such conflicting sentiments are certainly not unique to Chinese leaders or to this era. Two hundred years ago, English poet Percy Shelley lamented the faded glory of Ozymandias, the Greek name for ancient Egypt's most celebrated king, Ramesses the Great, with the following sonnet:[87]

"My Name is Ozymandias, King of Kings;
Look on my works, ye Mighty, and despair!"
Nothing beside remains. Round the decay
Of that colossal wreck, boundless and bare
The lone and level sands stretch far away

We are living in an era when steamed buns can become political and contemporary Ozymandias-like figures are making another try at securing eternal fame and fear. In China, tensions between society and the state are right underneath the surface. As the country and its leader seek greatness around the world, its greatest weakness is coming from within. Its spectacular soft power failure at wooing its own people—the people of Hong Kong and the Uyghurs locked in concentration camps in Xinjiang—stands as powerful proof of the dearth of its attractions.

Such a realization brings me back to the great novel *Dream of the Red Chamber*. The word "dream" in the story is not about the future. It is about the past. The dream is sighing and sobbing about a world lost forever. During their heydays, the two families in the story had all the glory, influence, and affluence they wanted. Their fortune and power could rival those of a nation. Not one of the hundreds of figures in the story is singularly responsible for the two families' downfalls. Yet, as the reader treks from one chapter to the next, constantly marveling at all the extravagancies, a sense of decay at every level also begins to seep in. And then, to use the words of the author, Cao Xueqin, "just like that, all of a sudden, the grand mansion falls."

When the Chinese president proclaimed to the world that he had a Chinese Dream, he and his ghostwriter more likely had Martin Luther King Jr. rather than Cao Xueqin on their minds, let alone Ozymandias. But, with all the tensions and political backsliding, there is no guarantee that the dream that China pursues is not a future-oriented vision but rather a prelude to political decay. And China is not alone in facing such a danger—bad dreams could be conceived in the Red Chamber or the White House.

Notes

Chapter 1

1. Cao, *Hong Lou Meng* [Dream of the red chamber], chapter 4.
2. Ling Shao, "Can Big Data Find Out Cao Xueqin's Exact Years of Birth and Death?"
3. Almond, "Separate Tables: Schools and Sects in Political Science."
4. Almond, "Separate Tables: Schools and Sects in Political Science," 828.
5. Almond, "Separate Tables: Schools and Sects in Political Science," 840.
6. Jin Chen, "How Mao Zedong read the Dream of Red Chamber as history," accessed at http://history.people.com.cn/n/2014/0207/c372327-24292696-2.html, May 7, 2020.
7. Jin Chen, "How Mao Zedong read the Dream of Red Chamber as history."
8. Yi Wang, "Mao Zedong on Dream of Red Chamber," accessed at http://dangshi.people.com.cn/n/2015/0622/c85037-27189350-2.html, May 7, 2020.
9. Yi Wang, "Mao Zedong on Dream of Red Chamber."
10. Chen, "Stories of Mao Zedong and 'Dream of Red Chamber'" [Mao Zedong yu hongloumeng de gushi], *People's Daily Net*, November 12, 2006, accessed at http://dangshi.people.com.cn/n1/2019/0313/c85037-30973083.html, September 18, 2020.
11. Geertz, *The Interpretation of Cultures*, 9.
12. Lampton, *Following the Leader*, 85.
13. Singer, "The Levels-of-Analysis Problem in International Relations."
14. Waltz, "Anarchic Orders and Balances of Power."
15. Gruber, *Ruling the World*.
16. Waltz, *Man, the State, and War*.
17. Singer, "The Levels-of-Analysis Problem in International Relations," 81.
18. On leadership perception, see Jervis, *How Statesmen Think*; on state autonomy, see Gilpin, *The Political Economy of International Relations*; on bureaucracy, see Allison and Halperin, "Bureaucratic Politics: A Paradigm and Some Policy Implications."
19. Gourevitch, "Second Image Reversed," 901.
20. Gourevitch, "Second Image Reversed," 904.
21. Putnam, "Diplomacy and Domestic Politics: The Logic of Two-Level Games."
22. Gourevitch, "International Trade, Domestic Coalitions and Liberty."

23. Jin and Jiang, "Xinhua guoji shiping: maoyizhan meiyou yingjia" [Xinhua brief comment on international issues: Trade war has no winners], Xinhua News Agency, March 7, 2018, accessed at http://www.xinhuanet.com/world/2018-03/08/c_11225 06988.htm, June 2, 2018.

24. As of July and August 2018, reports on how the trade war has hurt American economic sectors appear almost on a daily basis on China's major web portals like *Sina.com* and *news.qq.com*.

25. Hu defended his argument in an interview with a reporter from China News Service, claiming China's comprehensive surpassing of America has been supported by data. See "Hu Angang huiying 'Zhongguo quanmian chaoyue meiguo' lun: you zhishichanquan shujuku zuo lunzheng" [Hu Angang responds to 'China Comprehensively Surpassing America' argument, claiming it is supported by intellectual property database], *China News Service*, April 1, 2018, accessed at https://www.sohu.com/a/226960041_115479, April 25, 2020.

26. Egger, "Farmers the First Casualties in Trump's Trade War," accessed at https://www.weeklystandard.com/andrew-egger/u-s-farmers-hardest-hit-in-trump-trade-war-with-china, August 2, 2018.

27. Goffman, "The Interaction Order."

28. Goffman, "The Presentation of Self in Everyday Life," 120.

29. Jervis, *The Logic of Images in International Relation*.

30. Adler-Nissen, "Stigma Management in International Relations"; Carson, "Facing Off and Saving Face"; Schimmefennig, "Goffman Meets IR."

31. Jervis, *How Statesmen Think*.

32. Weiss, "Authoritarian Signaling, Mass Audiences, and Nationalist Protest in China."

33. Quoted in Piven et al., *The Worse-Case Scenario Almanac*, 10.

34. Nicholson, "The Continued Significance of Positivism?"

35. Nye, "Only China Can Contain China."

36. Ikenberry, "The End of Liberal International Order?"

37. Stephens, "A Beijing Cabby's View of the World."

38. Quoted in Xiaoshi Wang, "Fukuyama's Reflections and the Buildup of National Governing Capability," accessed at http://opinion.people.com.cn/n/2014/1023/c1003-25892618.html, September 19, 2020.

39. "The World's Most Powerful Man: Xi Jinping Has More Clout than Donald Trump. The World Should Be Wary," *The Economist*, October 14, 2017; accessed at https://www.economist.com/leaders/2017/10/14/xi-jinping-has-more-clout-than-donald-trump.-the-world-should-be-wary, May 19, 2018.

40. Buckley, "As China's Woes Mount, Xi Jinping Faces Rare Rebuke at Home."

41. White House, "National Security Council," https://www.whitehouse.gov/nsc/

42. Cohen and Merica, "Unlike Tillerson, Trump Says Pompeo 'Always on Same Wavelength.'"

43. Yan and Yan, "How the Chinese Nation Completely Rid the Risk of Being Stripped of the Membership of the Globe," accessed at http://theory.people.com.cn/n1/2016/0801/c40531-28599851.html, September 18, 2018.

44. Zheng Wang, "National Humiliation, History Education, and the Politics of Historical Memory."

45. For a more nuanced, historicized analysis of Chinese nationalism, see Gries, *China's New Nationalism*.

46. Shirk, *Fragile Superpower*.

47. Lee, "Western Australia's Mining Boom Ebbs along with China's Economy," accessed at http://www.latimes.com/business/la-fi-australia-china-mining-20150111-story.html, August 18, 2018.

48. Australian Government Department of Foreign Affairs and Trade, "Composition of Trade Australia 2018–19," accessed at https://www.dfat.gov.au/sites/default/files/cot-2018-19.pdf, April 27, 2020.

49. The video remains accessible at https://twitter.com/SkyNewsAust/status/939310385798057984?s=20 as of September 10, 2020.

50. Johnson, "The State and Japanese Grand Strategy," 216.

51. For an American comparison, see Davidson, *Foreign Policy, Inc.*

52. Niwa, *China's Great Dilemmas*, 219–20.

Chapter 2

1. *Daily Show with Jon Stewart*, November 11, 2014, accessed at http://www.cc.com/video-clips/75oamz/the-daily-show-with-jon-stewart-diplomatic-for-the-people-s-republic--apec, May 19, 2018.

2. Chen, "Zhou Enlai Proactively Prepares for the Making of Diplomatic Corps for New China," accessed http://cpc.people.com.cn/GB/64162/64172/85037/85038/5869507.html, on May 6, 2020.

3. Elliott, "Prince Upsets Chinese with 'Appalling Waxworks Jibe," accessed at https://www.independent.co.uk/news/uk/politics/prince-upsets-chinese-with-appalling-waxworks-jibe-326844.html, May 19, 2018.

4. Bader, "Order from Chaos," accessed at https://www.brookings.edu/blog/order-from-chaos/2015/09/17/chinese-state-visits-are-always-hard-a-historical-perspective/, May 6, 2020.

5. Both the video and comments can be viewed at https://www.youtube.com/watch?v=Zur6ASgexGw, accessed May 19, 2018.

6. The reference of Hu Jintao as "petty daughter-in-law" is widely used by Chinese internet users, including Hu's supporters or sympathizers, for example, "Leitingshou-duan chu Bo, Hu Jintao yizhen shengwei" [Hu Jintao establishes his authority by eliminating Bo Xilai in blitzkrieg], accessed at http://dailynews.sina.com/gb/chn/chnnews/ausdaily/20120321/02313247360.html, May 19, 2018.

7. Rogin, "China's President Lashed Out," accessed at http://foreignpolicy.com/2011/01/12/wikileaked-chinas-next-president-lashed-out-in-mexico-against-well-fed-foreigners/, May 20, 2018.

8. Personal translation of Xi Jinping's remarks to the staff at the Chinese embassy in Mexico, February 11, 2011; the video remained accessible at https://youtu.be/uZv0B28Gx-c as of September 4, 2020.

9. Machiavelli, "How Prince Keeps Faith."

10. Mearsheimer, "Structural Realism," 82.

11. Mearsheimer, "Structural Realism," 77.

12. Mearsheimer, "Back to the Future: Instability in Europe after the Cold War."

13. Tanaka and Tahara, *Country and Diplomacy*, 164.

14. Abe, "Japan Is Back," accessed at https://japan.kantei.go.jp/96_abe/statement/201302/22speech_e.html, May 6, 2020.

15. Habib, "South Africa: The Rainbow Nation and Prospects for Consolidating Democracy."

16. Hammelt, "Zapiro and Zuma."

17. Follesdal and Hix, "Why There Is a Democratic Deficit in the EU."

18. Judge and Piccolo, "Transformative and Transactional Leadership."

19. Spence, "The Mystery of Zhou Enlai," accessed at http://www.nybooks.com/articles/2009/05/28/the-mystery-of-zhou-enlai/, September 6, 2018.

20. *Liang, Time Bygone like a Song*, accessed at http://phtv.ifeng.com/program/tfzg/200905/0513_2950_1155097_1.shtml, May 6, 2020.

21. A similar account may still be found in Chen, *Mao Zedong and Nixon in 1972*, accessed at https://www.2002n.com/book/history/maozedongnixon/4850.html, September 4, 2020.

22. Barrass, "The Art of Calligraphy in Modern China," accessed at http://www.britishmuseum.org/research/search_the_collection_database/term_details.aspx?bioId=138943, September 6, 2018.

23. Liu, "Mao Zedong's Amazing Monkey King Complex," accessed at http://history.sina.com.cn/his/zl/2013-10-31/101172811.shtml, September 6, 2018.

24. Pengbai Wang, "How Peng Dehuai Was Doomed," accessed at https://m.sohu.com/n/388208272/?pvid=000115_3w, May 6, 2020.

25. Butterfield, "Mao Tse-Tung: Father of Chinese Revolution."

26. Sun, "China as Funhouse Mirror."

27. Snow, "A Reporter Got This Rare Interview with Chairman Mao," accessed at https://newrepublic.com/article/119916/edgar-snow-interview-china-chairman-mao-zedong, September 6, 2018.

28. Li, "1978: Re-approach Southeast Asia," accessed at http://tt.cssn.cn/zzx/gjzzx_zzx/201408/t20140811_1287210.shtml, May 6, 2020.

29. *People's Daily*, April 20, 1965.

30. "Looking into the Massacres of Indonesia's Past," BBC, June 2, 2016, accessed at https://www.bbc.com/news/world-asia-36431837, September 6, 2018.

31. *People's Daily*, September 26, 1968.

32. Zhou, *Diplomatic Career in Strange Times*, 20–26.

33. Xue, "Reflections on China's Aid to Africa before Reform and Open-door Era," 107.

34. Xue, "Reflections on China's Aid to Africa before Reform and Open-door Era," 103.

35. University of Southern California US-China Institute, "Mao Zedong Meets Richard Nixon, February 21, 1972," accessed at https://china.usc.edu/mao-zedong-meets-richard-nixon-february-21-1972, September 9, 2018.

36. University of Southern California US-China Institute, "Mao Zedong meets Richard Nixon, February 21, 1972."

37. Snow, "Interviews with Mao Tse-tung," accessed at https://www.marxists.org/reference/archive/mao/works/1936/11/x01.htm, September 11, 2018.

38. China Soviet Republic, "Constitutional Guidelines of the Chinese Soviet Repub-

lic, Article Fourteen" accessed at https://baike.baidu.com/item/%E4%B8%AD%E5%8
D%8E%E8%8B%8F%E7%BB%B4%E5%9F%83%E5%85%B1%E5%92%8C%E5%9B
%BD%E5%AE%AA%E6%B3%95%E5%A4%A7%E7%BA%B2, September 6, 2020.

39. Li, "Historical Leaps from Standing Up to Becoming Rich and to Becoming
Strong," accessed at http://theory.people.com.cn/n1/2017/0906/c40531-29517810.
html, September 11, 2018.

40. Yan and Yan, "How the Chinese Nation Completed Rid the Risk of Being
Stripped of Membership of the Globe," accessed at http://theory.people.com.cn/
n1/2016/0801/c40531-28599851.html, September 11, 2018.

41. Yi, "Lee Kuan-Yew Adamantly Declines Gift Book from Hua Guofeng and Causes
Embarrassment," accessed at http://culture.dwnews.com/history/news/2015-03-
18/59642043.html, September 11, 2019.

42. "What's the Big Idea? Lee Kuan Yew at 90," *The Economist*, accessed at https://
www.economist.com/blogs/banyan/2013/09/singapore-s-elder-statesman, September
13, 2018.

43. Jiachang, Chen, *LKY Whom I Knew*, 449.

44. Zhou, "Remembering Hua Guofeng," accessed at http://news.sohu.
com/20130514/n375845856.shtml, September 12, 2018.

45. Zhou, "Remembering Hua Guofeng."

46. Oon, "The Dragon and the Little Red Dot."

47. Yinan Chen, "Malaysian Communist Party's China-Based Radio Station,"
accessed at http://www.yhcqw.com/30/9925.html, May 6, 2020.

48. He, "Mutual Affection between Two Heroes: Lee Kuan Yew and Deng Xiaoping,"
accessed at http://phtv.ifeng.com/a/20150331/41031184_0.shtml, May 6, 2020.

49. Chinese Communist Party Central Archive Bureau, *Annuals of Deng Xiaoping*,
368.

50. "Saqie'er yu Deng Xiaoping tapan shoucuo, zai renmin daihuitang qian shuaijiao"
[Hit by negotiation setback, Thatcher falls after meeting with Deng Xiaoping], *Jinghua
Shibao*, April 9, 2013, accessed at http://hb.sina.com.cn/news/n/2013-04-09/103565858.
html, May 6, 2020.

51. Schiavenza, "When Margaret Thatcher Came to China."

52. Schiavenza, "When Margaret Thatcher Came to China."

53. "Jiexi: weishenme zhongguo zuiai zai lianheguo tou qiquanpiao" [Explanation:
Why does China love to vote abstention at UN?], *Dakung Pao*, August 4, 2015, accessed
at http://news.takungpao.com/world/exclusive/2015-08/3098361_app.html?tkpc=4,
May 6, 2020.

54. Personal experience.

55. "Rang 'touxianglun' chengwei guojie laoshu" [Let the "surrender" voice become
public enemy], *Xinhua Net*, June 8, 2019, accessed at https://www.thepaper.cn/newsDe
tail_forward_3636015 on May 6, 2020.

56. "Xi Jinping's Eight Arguments on 'gui ju'" [Xi Jinping balun guiju], *Xinhua Net*,
October 25, 2014, accessed at http://www.xinhuanet.com/politics/2014-10/25/
c_1112975663.htm, September 18, 2018.

57. Savic, "Behind China and Russia's 'Special Relationship,'" accessed at https://the
diplomat.com/2016/12/behind-china-and-russias-special-relationship/, September 6,
2020.

58. Perlez, "Stampede to Join China's Development Bank Stuns Even Its Founder,"

accessed at https://www.nytimes.com/2015/04/03/world/asia/china-asian-infrastruc
ture-investment-bank.html, September 17, 2018.

59. Dreyer, "China's Dream, Japan's Nightmare," accessed at https://japan-forward.
com/chinas-dream-japans-nightmare/, September 17, 2018.

60. Battin, "The Basic Annals of Xiang Yu," accessed at https://ethicsofsuicide.lib.
utah.edu/selections/sima-qian/, September 4, 2020.

61. Mao Zedong, "Seven-Character Pome: The PLA Captures Nanjing," accessed at
https://allpoetry.com/The-PLA-Captures-Nanjing, September 22, 2018.

62. Xi, "Speech at the Ceremony Commemorating the 100th Birthday of Hu Yaobang," accessed at http://www.xinhuanet.com/politics/2015-11/20/c_1117214229.
htm, September 17, 2018.

63. Lu, "Interview of Hu Yaobang," accessed at http://blog.creaders.net/u/3843/
201511/240988.html, September 18, 2018.

64. Lu, "Interview of Hu Yaobang," accessed at http://blog.creaders.net/u/3843/
201511/240988.html, September 18, 2018.

65. Ma, "Deng Xiaoping and Hu Yaobang's Views of Japan," accessed at https://www.
china-week.com/html/3427.htm, September 22, 2018.

66. "Riben yulun zan Hu Yaobang" [Japanese media praise Hu Yaobang], *Voice of
America Chinese News*, December 9, 2005, accessed at https://www.voachinese.com/a/a-
21-w2005-12-09-voa13-58376692/1079265.html, September 22, 2018.

67. Whiting, *China Eyes Japan*, 1–8.

68. Chinese Communist Party Central Archive Bureau, *Annuals of Deng Xiaoping*,
1192–93.

69. "Koshi hihan rokukōmoku no kōsai" [Details of six indictments on Hu], *Yomiuri
Shimbun*, January 23, 1987.

70. Lu, "Interview of Hu Yaobang."

71. "Li Keqiang zongli rennei shouci fangri" [Li Keqiang visits Japan for the first time
as premier], *Xinhua Net*, May 10, 2018, accessed at http://www.sohu.com/a/23117
8886_100103081, September 18, 2018.

72. Boucher, "Press Statement on the Death of Zhao Ziyang," accessed at https://2001-
2009.state.gov/r/pa/prs/ps/2005/40987.htm, September 22, 2018.

73. Yang, "Why Did Zhao Ziyang Collaborate with Chen Yun on Criticizing Hu
Yaobang?" accessed at https://www.aboluowang.com/2016/0424/728563.html, September 22, 2018.

74. Yang, "Why Did Zhao Ziyang Collaborate with Chen Yun on Criticizing Hu
Yaobang?"

75. Nathan, *Chinese Democracy*, 176.

76. Song, "A Silkworm Who Keeps Spinning until Death," accessed at http://cpc.
people.com.cn/GB/69112/75843/75872/5166226.html, May 7, 2020.

77. Gao, *Zhou Enlai's Final Years*, accessed at https://hkx.eu/history/41672.html,
May 6, 2020.

78. Ruijin Zhou, "Deng Xiaoping Praises Zhu Rongji as Leader Who Understands
Economics," accessed at http://finance.sina.com.cn/china/20130813/015416424359.
shtml, September 22, 2018.

79. "Jiujie rendai yici huiyi: Zhu Rongji zongli deng da zhongwai jizhe wen" [Premier
Zhu Rongji etc. hold press conference at the first plenary session of the 9th National
People's Congress], *People's Daily*, March 20, 1998, accessed at http://www.people.com.
cn/GB/shizheng/7501/7558/20020225/673502.html, on September 22, 2018.

80. "Jiujie rendai yici huiyi: Zhu Rongji zongli deng da zhongwai jizhe wen."

81. "Jiujie rendai yici huiyi: Zhu Rongji zongli deng da zhongwai jizhe wen."

82. Ling, "What Happened on the 'Darkest Day' of Zhu Rongji's 1999 Visit to America?," accessed at http://news.ifeng.com/history/zhongguoxiandaishi/detail_2013_08/23/28937328_0.shtml, September 22, 2018.

83. "A Premier's Legacy," *Wall Street Journal*, March 18, 2002, accessed at https://www.wsj.com/articles/SB1016401811933065440, September 18, 2018; "Zhu Rongji zhuangjiweichou chagngran tui" [Zhu Rongji to retire with dream unfulfilled], *Apple Daily* (Hong Kong), February 2003, accessed at https://hk.news.appledaily.com/international/daily/article/20030225/3138811, September 22, 2018.

84. Saich, "What Does General Secretary Xi Jinping Dream About?," 4.

85. Li, "Xi Jinping de yizhou" [Xi Jinping's one week], accessed at https://news.sina.com.cn/c/xl/2020-09-07/doc-iivhuipp2892237.shtml, September 6, 2020.

Chapter 3

1. For one prominent example, see "Cui Yongyuan zale? Zhemejiu buchulai?" [What happened to Cui Yongyuan? Why has he disappeared for so long?], *Radio Free Asia*, March 6, 2019, accessed at https://www.rfa.org/mandarin/zhuanlan/wangluoboyi/aw-03062019153704.html, May 7, 2020.

2. "Taiwan meiti zan Wang Yi zhangxiang yingjun jushoutouzu poxiang Zhou Enlai" [Taiwanese media praise Wang Yi for good-looking and mimicking Zhou Enali], *People's Daily Network*, July 29, 2008, accessed at https://news.sohu.com/20080729/n258449629_1.shtml, May 7, 2020.

3. "Guomin nanshen Wang Yi, yong yingjun he caihua zhengfu shijie" [National male hottie Wang Yi uses good look and talent to conquer the world], *Global Times Network*, August 10, 2015, accessed at https://m.huanqiu.com/article/9CaKrnJOmF7, May 7, 2020.

4. Kassam, "Chinese Minister Vents Anger when Canadian Reporter Asks about Human Rights," accessed at https://www.theguardian.com/law/2016/jun/02/chinese-foreign-minister-canada-angry-human-rights-question, September 2, 2020.

5. The video remains accessible as of May 2020 at https://www.youtube.com/watch?v=qikBsQ1h4S8

6. The video remains accessible as of May 2020 at https://www.youtube.com/watch?v=qikBsQ1h4S8

7. Kassam, "Justin Trudeau 'Dissatisfied' with How Chinese Minister Treated Journalist," *The Guardian*, June 3, 2016, accessed at https://www.theguardian.com/world/2016/jun/03/justin-trudeau-wang-yi-canadian-journalist-amanda-connolly, May 8, 2020.

8. Baodong Li, "A Reporter's Witness," accessed at https://news.sina.cn/gn/2016-06-03/detail-ifxsvenx3228168.d.html?from=wap, May 8, 2020.

9. Baodong Li, "A Reporter's Witness."

10. The criticism first appeared at https://zhidao.baidu.com/question/1927728385748635467.html before being removed.

11. Melinda Liu, "China's New Negotiator, Foreign Minister Wang Yi," accessed at https://www.newsweek.com/chinas-new-negotiator-foreign-minister-wang-yi-62953, May 6, 2020.

12. Ng, "China's New Foreign Minister Wang Yi," accessed at https://www.scmp.com/news/china/article/1192238/expert-japan-becomes-chinas-new-foreign-minister, May 8, 2020.

13. Minfeng Chen, "Frank Hsieh Meets Wang Yi," accessed at http://www.boxun.com/news/gb/china/2012/10/201210071713.shtml, May 8, 2020.

14. Pomfret, "US Takes a Tougher Tone with China," accessed at https://www.washingtonpost.com/wp-dyn/content/article/2010/07/29/AR2010072906416.html, May 8, 2020.

15. "Guanyuan chuohao pandean: Yang Jiechi bei lao Bushi chengwei 'laohu Yang'" [Summary of nicknames for officials: Yang Jiechi known as "Tiger Yang" by Bush senior], *News Sina Network*, October 31, 2013, accessed at http://news.sina.com.cn/c/sd/2013-10-31/111128582058.shtml, May 8, 2020.

16. Taylor, "China's Ambassador to Sweden Calls Journalists Critical of Beijing Lightweight Boxers Facing a Heavyweight," accessed at https://www.washingtonpost.com/world/2020/01/21/chinas-ambassador-sweden-calls-journalists-critical-beijing-lightweight-boxers-facing-heavyweight/, May 7, 2020.

17. "'Waijiao diyi tiantuan' nvshen Hua Chunying huigui, jiebang Lu Kang ren waijiaobu xinwensi sizhang" [Hua Chunying, goddess of China's "top diplomatic godlike troupe," returns and succeeds Lu Kang as director of information of foreign ministry], *Phoenix TV*, July 22, 2019, accessed at http://ent.ifeng.com/c/7oWDk1bj9jd, May 7, 2020.

18. Wenhui Li, "Why Are China's Diplomats All Turning into Wolf-Warrior-Style Ambassadors?" accessed at https://www.chinatimes.com/cn/realtimenews/20200508001918-260409?chdtv, May 8, 2020.

19. Fifield, "China Wasn't Wild for Pompeo before the Virus. It's Really Gunning for Him Now," *Washington Post*, April 31, 2020, accessed at https://www.washingtonpost.com/world/asia_pacific/china-mike-pompeo-coronavirus-wuhan-lab/2020/04/30/1c9c8e8a-8acb-11ea-9759-6d20ba0f2c0e_story.html, on September 2, 2020.

20. Partial results have been published in Sun, "Growing Diplomacy, Retreating Diplomats."

21. Chinese Ministry of Foreign Affairs Councilor Service Net, "275 Xiaoshi! Yici zhenzheng de cheqiao xingdong" [275 Hours! An account of a real evacuation of Chinese citizens], August 30, 3017, accessed at http://cs.mfa.gov.cn/gyls/lsgz/lqbb/t1488501.shtml, May 8, 2020.

22. Hermann and Hermann, "Who Makes Foreign Policy Decisions and How: An Empirical Inquiry."

23. Zheng, *Grand Situation*, 1–8, 85–97.

24. "Chairman of Everything," *The Economist*, April 2, 2016, accessed at https://www.economist.com/china/2016/04/02/chairman-of-everything, May 8, 2020.

25. The Chinese Central Government Net, "Comprehensively Strengthen the Party's Organizational Construction," accessed at http://www.gov.cn/xinwen/2018-07/05/content_5303861.htm, May 8, 2020.

26. Morgenthau, Thompson, and Clinton, *Politics Among Nations*.

27. Keohane, *After Hegemony*.

28. Schwartz, "Henry Kissinger: Realism, Domestic Politics, and the Struggle against Exceptionalism in American Foreign Policy."

29. Beauchamp, "Bernie Sanders Is Right: Hillary Clinton Praising Henry Kissinger

Is Outrageous" accessed at https://www.vox.com/world/2016/2/12/10979304/clin ton-sanders-kissinger, May 9, 2020.

30. Jian, "China's 'Old Buddy' Diplomacy Dies a Death," accessed at http://www. atimes.com/atimes/China/NJ26Ad03.html, January 14, 2016.

31. Switzer, "Nixon, the Balance of Power, and Realism," accessed at http://nation alinterest.org/feature/nixon-the-balance-power-realism-11048, May 28, 2015.

32. Swaine, "Perceptions of an Assertive China," 10.

33. Tom Cotton, "Tom Cotton: We Should Buy Greenland," accessed at https:// www.nytimes.com/2019/08/26/opinion/politics/greenland-trump.html, May 9, 2020.

34. Johnston, "How New and Assertive Is China's 'New Assertiveness.'"

35. Sørensen, "Is China Becoming More Aggressive?"

36. Weber, *Economy and Society*, 1391.

37. Allison, "Conceptual Models and the Cuban Missile Crisis."

38. Bendor and Hammond, "Rethinking Allison's Models."

39. "Announcement on Organizational Structure of the State Council," *Chinese Communist Party News Network*, accessed at http://renshi.people.com.cn/n/2013/0321/ c139617-20871999.html, May 28, 2015.

40. For the ranked composition of the State Council in 2003, see http://news.xinhua net.com/zhengfu/2003-09/09/content_1071285.htm; for data in 1998, see http:// wenku.baidu.com/view/adc0272d2af90242a895e5ca.html; for data in 1993, see http:// www.360doc.com/content/15/0417/13/7499155_463872013.shtml; for data in 1988, see http://www.law-lib.com/LAW/law_view.asp?id=93047, all accessed May 24, 2015.

41. Yingchun He, "Party Secretary of Chinese Foreign Affairs University: Premier Zhou's Sixteen-Character Diplomatic Requirement Becomes School Motto," accessed at http://edu.people.com.cn/n/2014/0729/c1006-25365254.html, May 24, 2015.

42. Yingchun He, "Party Secretary of Chinese Foreign Affairs University."

43. Chang and Lv, "To Create Enduring and Faithful Soul Among Diplomatic Troops," accessed at http://www.qstheory.cn/zl/bkjx/201306/t20130620_241614. htm, May 24, 2018; Jiechi Yang, "Speech on the Seventh Inauguration Ceremony of Chief Diplomats to Be Stationed Overseas, and the Open-Ministry Day to the Public," accessed at https://www.fmprc.gov.cn/web/ziliao_674904/zt_674979/ywzt_675099/ 2009zt_675493/gzkfr_675539/t575233.shtml, May 25, 2015.

44. Chinese Foreign Ministry, "Foreign Ministry Public Announcement of 2019 Entrance Examination, Interview, and Phycological Assessment," accessed at https:// www.fmprc.gov.cn/mfa_chn/wjb_602314/gbclc_603848/tzgg_660725/t1629847. shtml, May 10, 2020.

45. Kang, "Memory of China's 'Diplomatic Godfather' Qian Qichen," accessed at http://news.southcn.com/community/shgc/200312100588.htm, May 10, 2020.

46. Kang, "Memory of China's 'Diplomatic Godfather' Qian Qichen."

47. Wu, Zheng, and Yan, "Qian Qichen: Diplomatic Godfather Who Talks to Saddam," accessed at http://www.chnxp.com/dazhongwenxue/2015-1/188373.html, June 3, 2015.

48. "Qiao Guanhua bei 'sirenbang' neiding 'fuzongli' zhihou" [Qiao Guanhua's life after secretly chosen by Gang of Four as vice premier], *People's Daily Network*, June 14, 2004, accessed at http://www.people.com.cn/GB/wenhua/1088/2569611.html, May 25, 2015.

49. Shirk, *Fragile Superpower*.

50. The popular phrase "Shanghai Clique" (Shanghai bang) was used to describe Jiang Zemin's effort of promoting those who had worked with him in order to tame Hu Jintao after Jiang's formal retirement. The influence of the Shanghai Clique only began to recede after Xi Jinping took power. For a book-length analysis, see Wong and Zheng, *China's Post-Jiang Leadership Succession*.

51. Li, Sato, and Sicular, *Rising Inequality in China*.

52. "Strait Time: 'Buzheteng' nanyi, guanfang yingwengao gancui tiaoguo" [Haixian shibao: *Buzheteng* is hard to translate; official text simply skips the phrase], *Phoenix TV Network*, January 7, 2009, accessed at http://news.ifeng.com/opinion/detail_2009_01/07/1338099_0.shtml, May 10, 2020.

53. Zhengang Ma, "Waijiaoguan kuyule" [A diplomat's joys and sorrows], *Foreign Policy Advisory Group*, accessed at http://fpag.fmprc.gov.cn/chn/wyzj2/sgsw/t720286.htm, May 30, 2015.

54. Jiechi Yang, "Speech at the MFA Internal Conference on Logistical Management," accessed at http://www.ggj.gov.cn/hqzzs/zgjghq/2012/201206/201206/t20120612_277865.htm, May 30, 2015.

55. Fang, "Proposal of Setting Up National Security Committee Starts during Jiang Zemin Era," accessed at http://i.ifeng.com/news/sharenews.f?aid=73962154, May 30, 2015.

56. National Security Council, accessed at https://www.whitehouse.gov/administration/eop/nsc/, May 28, 2015.

57. Tiezzi, "Xi Jinping: China's Hope and Change President?," accessed at http://thediplomat.com/2013/11/xi-jinping-chinas-hope-and-change-president/, July 16, 2015.

58. Perlez, "New Chinese Panel Said to Oversee Domestic Security and Foreign Policy," accessed at http://www.nytimes.com/2013/11/14/world/asia/national-security-committee-china.html?_r=0, July 16, 2015.

59. "Wu Yi Ranked 2 among the Most Powerful Women in 2004, 2005 and 2007," *Forbes*, August 30, 2007; accessed at http://www.forbes.com/lists/2007/11/biz-07women_Wu-Yi_2CR9.html, June 10, 2015.

60. Chao Yang, "A Review of the Study of Military Diplomacy of New China in the Last Decade"; Ji, "The PLA and Diplomacy."

61. Shu, "Characteristics of Chinese Military Diplomacy in New Era," 42.

62. Deng, "Military Must Follow the Nation's Grand Agenda," 99–128; Fravel, "Shifts in Warfare and Party Unity," 74.

63. "Hu Jintao chanshu zhongguo xin anquanguan" [Hu Jintao iterates China's 'new security' concept], *Xinhua News Agency*, September 25, 2009, accessed at http://news.sina.com.cn/w/2009-09-25/080016356545s.shtml, May 29, 2015.

64. Mao, "Problems of War and Strategy," 224.

65. A most recent example of the party leadership's effort of reigning the military can be witnessed in Xi Jinping's major structural changes to the PLA announced in December 2015. See Yu, "Chinese President's Military Overhaul Tightens Communist Party's Control," accessed at https://m.washingtontimes.com/news/2015/dec/3/inside-china-xi-jinpings-military-overhaul-tighten/, May 11, 2020.

66. Allison, *Essence of Decision*, 26.

67. "Xinzhongguo de jiangjundashimen: lianxi waiyu, xuechi xican, shuigubuan ximengsi" [General-turned-ambassadors of New China: practice foreign languages, learn

to eat Western meals, yet remains uncomfortable with sleeping on mattress], *Xinhua News Agency*, November 14, 2014, accessed at http://dangshi.people.com.cn/n/2014/1013/c85037-25821070.html, January 22, 2016.

68. Xiliang Liu, "Reflection of a Chinese Translator after Six Decades," accessed at http://www.tac-online.org.cn/tran/2009-09/27/content_3162451.htm, May 26, 2015.

69. Bao Li, "Chinese Minister of Defense to Attend Shangri-la Dialogue after Years of Absence," accessed at https://www.voachinese.com/a/us-china-defense-chiefs-to-face-off-shangri-la-20190521/4925130.html, May 11, 2020.

70. Gittings, "General Zhu Goes Ballistic," accessed at http://www.wsj.com/articles/SB112165176626988025, May 29, 2015.

71. The *New York Times* attributed the quote to General Xiong Guankai. Chas Freeman, the person Xiong was speaking to, denied Xiong had said this. However, Freeman admitted that toward the end of the meeting, in a heated exchange of arguments, someone from the Chinese military delegation reminded American members that China could hit back at Los Angeles as a deterring measure. See Jeffrey Lewis, "Gertz and Xiong: A Love Torn Asunder," accessed at http://lewis.armscontrolwonk.com/archive/433/gertz-and-xiong-a-love-torn-asunder, May 29, 2015.

72. Personal interview, August 4, 2004.

73. Rourke, *Bureaucracy and Foreign Policy*, 49–50.

74. "Is Chinese Military Prepared to Fight?" *Liaowang Zhongguo* [Outlook China], April 2, 2015, accessed at http://www.outlookchina.net/html/news/201504/7984.html, May 11, 2020.

75. "Xi Jinping chuxi zhongyang waishi gongzuo huiyi bing fabiao zhongyaojianghua" [Xi Jinping attends Central Conference of Foreign Affairs and delivers important speech], *Xinhua News Agency*, November 29, 2014, accessed at http://news.xinhuanet.com/politics/2014-11/29/c_1113457723.htm, May 30, 2015; "Xi Jinping: Nuli kaichuang zhongguo tese daguo waijiao xinjumian" [Xi Jinping: Work hard to create new era of great power diplomacy with Chinese characteristics], *Xinhua News Agency*, June 23, 2018, accessed at http://www.xinhuanet.com/politics/2018-06/23/c_1123025806.htm, May 11, 2020.

76. "Zhongyang waishi gongzuo huiyi zaijing juxing, Hu Jintao zuo zhongyao jianghua" [Central Conference of Foreign Affairs opens in Beijing; Hu Jintao delivers important speech], *Xinhua News Agency*, August 23, 2006, accessed at http://news.xinhuanet.com/politics/2006-08/23/content_4999294.htm, May 30, 2015.

77. Dong, "Xinrenzhu Bajisitan dashi beijing hen teshu" [New ambassador to Pakistan has unique background], Phoenix Net, accessed at https://m.us.sina.com/gb/china/phoenixtv/2020-09-11/detail-ifzzxynp3787317.shtml on September 20, 2020.

78. Shirk, *Fragile Superpower*.

79. "Waijiaobu fauyanren qushi: youren song gaipian anshi biaotai tairuan" [Anecdotes of MFA spokespersons: ministry receives calcium pills as symbol of weakness], *Beijing Youth Daily*, December 16, 2013, accessed at http://news.qq.com/a/20131216/000719.htm, on July 25, 2015.

80. Mockeries of the MFA as the "Ministry of Protests" are numerous. They have appeared even on forums hosted by the *People's Daily*. See, for example, "Waijiaobu yinggai gaiming jiao kangyibu" [MFA should be renamed Ministry of Protests], accessed at http://bbs1.people.com.cn/post/6/1/2/123581184.html, May 29, 2015.

81. "China's School Bus Donation to Macedonia Derided," *The Telegraph*, November

28, 2011, accessed at http://www.telegraph.co.uk/news/worldnews/asia/china/8920865/Chinas-school-bus-donation-to-Macedonia-derided.html, May 30, 2015.

82. "Waijiaobu huiying maqidun xiaocheshijia" [MFA responds to incident of bus donation to Macedonia], *Phoenix TV Network*, November 28, 2011, accessed at http://news.ifeng.com/mainland/detail_2011_11/28/10961023_0.shtml, May 30, 2015.

83. "Japanese Visas Issued in Shanghai Hit Record High in 2014," *Japan Times*, January 9, 2015, accessed at http://www.japantimes.co.jp/news/2015/01/09/national/japanese-visas-issued-in-shanghai-hit-record-high-in-2014/#.VaxxgXiprzI, July 19, 2015.

84. "Daluyoukebaozeng yongguang rilingguanqianzhengzhi gaifalinshitiezhi" [Explosive increase of mainland visitors leads to exhaustion of visa stamps for Japanese consulate; temporary stamps issued as remedy], *Cankaoxiaoxi Network*, March 17, 2015, accessed at http://news.sohu.com/20150317/n409890310.shtml, January 22, 2016.

85. US State Department, "Non-immigrant Visas Issued by Issuing Office," accessed at https://travel.state.gov/content/dam/visas/Statistics/AnnualReports/FY2019AnnualReport/FY19AnnualReport-TableXIX.pdf, May 11, 2020.

86. "Xiecheng zengsu da hangye zengsu de sanbei" [C-Trip's growth rate triples growth rate for the whole industry], *Huaxi Dushibao* [Western China city daily], November 9, 2018, accessed at https://e.thecover.cn/wapepaper/html/20181109/92683.html, May 11, 2020.

87. Personal conversation, March 12, 2012.

88. Wang and Li, "The Historical Evolution in the Number of Chinese Diplomats and the New Agenda in the Building of Chinese Diplomatic Capability," accessed at http://world.people.com.cn/n1/2017/0913/c1002-29533476.html, May 11, 2020.

89. "Diaocha: zhongyang guojia jiguan gongwuyuan liushi" [Investigation: brain drain of public employees at national administration], *21st Century Economic Herald* [21shiji jingji daobao], accessed at http://www.c007.com/shdc/3094.htm, May 30, 2015.

90. Hao, "Top Ten Most Competitive Public Sector Entry Examinations in 2018," accessed at http://edu.people.com.cn/n1/2017/1106/c1053-29629343.html, May 11, 2020.

91. Xue, "Chinese Diplomacy Faces Threat of Bureaucraticism," accessed at http://translate.chinadaily.com.cn/article-305056-1.html; the article became retrievable again on this website in September 2016, only to disappear again shortly thereafter.

92. The Chinese Communist Party Central Committee, "Zhonggong zhongyan guanyu quanmian shenhua gaige ruogan zhongdawenti de jueding" [The CCP Central Committee's decisions on several important issues related to completely deepening reform," accessed at http://www.gov.cn/jrzg/2013-11/15/content_2528179.htm, September 3, 2020.

93. Perlez and Huang, "Diplomat's Death Reignites Debate over China's Role in the World," *New York Times*, June 25, 2016, accessed at https://www.nytimes.com/2016/06/25/world/asia/china-wu-jianmin.html?_ga=2.98945758.196622261 01.1599163615-1295488605.1590092225, September 3, 2020.

94. Stewart, "Gates: China Confirms Stealth Jet Test-Flight," accessed at https://www.reuters.com/article/us-china-defence-fighter/gates-china-confirms-stealth-jet-test-flight-idUSTRE70A19B20110111?pageNumber=2, May 11, 2020.

95. Personal interview, March 20, 2012.

Chapter 4

1. Willy Lam, "China's Hawks in Command," accessed at https://www.wsj.com/articles/SB10001424052702304211804577500521756902802, August 18, 2018; accessed on September 21, 2020.

2. "Zhuming junshi lilunjia, junshi pinglunjia Zhang Zhaozhong jiangjun tan dangqian zhongguo mianlin de anquan xingshi" [Famous military theorist, military commentator Admiral Zhang Zhaozhong: contemporary security situation facing China], *Iqiyi TV*, accessed at http://www.iqiyi.com/w_19rt6rx07l.html, August 18, 2018.

3. "'Zhanglve huyouju juzhang' douyou naxie yuce zhide yijiang?" [Which predictions offered by the 'Director of Fool-you Agency' are worth reading?], *Sohu News*, October 14, 2017, accessed at https://www.sohu.com/a/198065869_100040597, August 18, 2017.

4. Lam, "China's Hawks in Command."

5. Boyuan Chen, "Navy Rear Admiral Clarifies 'Smog Defense' Theory," accessed at http://www.china.org.cn/china/2014-02/25/content_31586077.htm, August 18, 2018.

6. "Zhang Zhaozhong wumai fangdaodan zaopiping wangyou xinve ta shi 'zuipao'" [Netizens bash Zhang Zhaozhong's "anti-missle smog" argument as ridiculous verbal loose cannon], *Sohu News*, May 6, 2016, accessed at http://news.sohu.com/20160506/n447927172.shtml, August 18, 2018.

7. "Zhagn Zhaozhong 'haidaichanqianting' xiangfa huode guojiazhuanli" [Zhang Zhaozhong's 'submarine-entangling seaweed' idea becomes patented], *Sohu News*, October 28, 2016, accessed at http://news.sohu.com/20161028/n471655014.shtml, August 18, 2018.

8. Zhaozhong Zhang, "Meiguo haijun shizhi zhilaohu bingbukepa" [US navy is a paper tiger not to be feared], BTV interview, 2015, accessed at http://bbs.tianya.cn/post-20-613959-1.shtml, August 18, 2018.

9. The cartoon can be viewed at http://www.ntdtv.com/xtr/gb/2013/03/28/a870698.html

10. Nan Li, "From Ridicule to Respect," accessed at http://www.bjreview.com/Lifestyle/201612/t20161230_800084536.html, May 19, 2018.

11. Xueqing Li, "Rear Admiral's Rally Cry to Youth Gets Lost in Laughter," accessed at http://www.sixthtone.com/news/709/rear-admiral%20s-rally-cry-youth-gets-lost-laughter, May 19, 2018.

12. "Clinton's Words on China: Trade Is the Smart Thing," *New York Times*, March 3, 2000, accessed at https://www.nytimes.com/2000/03/09/world/clinton-s-words-on-china-trade-is-the-smart-thing.html, May 12, 2020.

13. Brady, *Marketing Dictatorship*.

14. Brady, *Marketing Dictatorship*, chapter 5.

15. Stockmann, *Media Commercialization and Authoritarian Rule in China*, 4.

16. Lam, *Chinese Politics in the Era of Xi Jinping: Renaissance, Reform, or Retrogression*, 124.

17. Stockmann, *Media Commercialization and Authoritarian Rule in China*, 6; Minzner, *End of an Era: How China's Authoritarian Revival Is Undermining Its Rise*.

18. Smith, "The Unstoppable Rise of the Chinese Traveler," accessed at https://www.telegraph.co.uk/travel/comment/rise-of-the-chinese-tourist/, August 18, 2018.

19. Smith, "The Unstoppable Rise of the Chinese Traveler."

20. Ramzy, "Chinese Reporter Accused of Slapping Man at Political Event in Britain," accessed at https://www.nytimes.com/2018/10/02/world/asia/chinese-reporter-slap-britain.html, May 12, 2020.

21. On the Stockholm case, see Kuo, "China Accuses Sweden of Violating Human Rights over Treatment of Tourists," accessed at https://www.theguardian.com/world/2018/sep/17/china-accuses-sweden-of-violating-human-rights-over-treatment-of-tourists, May 12, 2020; on the New Zealand case, see Tan, "Police Seek Identities of People Involved in Hong Kong Protest that Turned Violent at Auckland University Campus," accessed at https://www.nzherald.co.nz/nz/news/article.cfm?c_id=1&objectid=12254396, May 12, 2020.

22. Christopher M. Duncan and Peter Seinberger, "Plato's Paradox? Guardians and Philosopher-Kings," *American Political Science Review* 84, no. 4 (December 1990): 1317–22.

23. Mapendere, "Track One and a Half Diplomacy and the Complementarity of Tracks."

24. Tsaliki, Frangonikolopoulos, and Huliaras, *Transnational Celebrity Activism in Global Politics.*

25. "Alibaba's Ma Meets Trump, Promises to Bring One Million Jobs to U.S.," *Reuters*, January 9, 2017, accessed at https://www.reuters.com/article/us-usa-trump-alibaba-idUSKBN14T1ZA, May 21, 2018.

26. "Alibaba Jack Ma's Promise of 1 Million U.S. Jobs Now in Jeopardy," *Sina Tech*, April 10, 2018, accessed at https://pandaily.com/alibaba-jack-mas-promise-of-1-million-u-s-jobs-now-in-jeopardy, May 22, 2018.

27. Corera, *Shopping for Bombs.*

28. "An Act of Dubious Diplomacy: Jesse Jackson Goes to Syria," *Time*, January 9 1984, accessed at http://content.time.com/time/magazine/article/0,9171,952291,00.html, August 10, 2019.

29. Will, "Jesse Jackson in Syria," accessed at https://www.washingtonpost.com/archive/opinions/1984/01/01/jesse-jackson-in-syria/70338f87-4d17-465d-8ed3-37205a95f9d3/?utm_term=.f6c34f8e6700, August 10, 2019.

30. Smothers, "Reagan Praises Navy Flier and Jackson," *New York Times*, January 5, 1984, accessed at https://www.nytimes.com/1984/01/05/world/reagan-praises-navy-flier-and-jackson.html, August 10, 2019.

31. Nakamura, "White House Denounces Dennis Rodman's Trip to North Korea," accessed at https://www.washingtonpost.com/news/post-politics/wp/2013/03/04/white-house-denounces-dennis-rodmans-trip-to-north-korea/?utm_term=.9c15 8337a257, May 22, 2018.

32. "Dennis Rodman Gets His 'Gangnam Style' Mixed Up in Pyongyang," *Reuters*, February 26, 2013, accessed at https://www.reuters.com/article/entertainment-us-korea-north-rodman/dennis-rodman-gets-his-gangnam-style-mixed-up-in-pyongyang-idUS BRE91P04X20130227, May 22, 2020.

33. Conversation with student protestors, May 1999.

34. Lei, "Anti-America yet Yearning for America?" accessed at http://blog.boxun.com/hero/201508/leisheng/65_1.shtml, May 23, 2018.

35. Lei, "Anti-America yet Yearning for America?"

36. Fangxiang Li, "On Mao Zedong's Experience at Beida during His Youth: Analysis

of Several Issues," accessed at https://www.guancha.cn/WenZhai/2014_09_18_268542.shtml, May 15, 2020.

37. Snow, *Red Star over China*, 173.

38. Snow, *Red Star over China*, 173–74.

39. Jiang, *Mao Zedong and Chiang Kai-shek: Negotiations and Decisive Confrontations*, 120.

40. Mao, "Song Zongyu Yilang Dongxing" [Farewell to Zongyu Yilang as he departs for the east], April 1918, accessed at http://www.people.com.cn/GB/shizheng/8198/30446/30453/2220887.html, May 24, 2018.

41. Snow, *Red Star over China*, 173.

42. Mao "On Coalition Government," 257.

43. Mao, "Preface and Postscript to Rural Surveys," 12.

44. "Mao Zedong de 'renkouguan': zhiyao youren jiuyou qiji" [Mao Zedong's view on population: miracles can happen as long as there are humans], *Sohu History Channel*, accessed at http://history.sohu.com/s2015/jihuashengyu/index.shtml, May 23, 2018.

45. "Zhouzongli 1000gongjin dingji bayou kuandai Nikesong beihou de gushi" [Stories behind Premier Zhao's 1000-kilogram top-grade abalone dinner for Nixon], *Phoenix News*, November 23, 2011, accessed at http://news.ifeng.com/history/vp/detail_2011_11/23/10843077_1.shtml, May 23, 2018.

46. "Zhou Enlai yiye dongyuan 80wan minzhong saoxue: Nikesong bei zhenhan" [Zhou Enlai mobilizes 800,000 to sweep snow, leaving Nixon dazzled], *Sohu News*, accessed at http://mil.sohu.com/20150415/n411301891.shtml, May 23, 2018.

47. "China Admits 320,000 Troops Fought in Vietnam," *Reuters*, May 16, 1989, accessed at https://news.google.com/newspapers?nid=1350&dat=19890516&id=HkRPAAAAIBAJ&sjid=_gIEAAAAIBAJ&pg=3769,1925460, May 23, 2018.

48. "Bi Shengming geng zhengui de baoshu" [A Treasure book more valuable than life], *People's Daily*, December 24, 1966.

49. Callahan, "Identity and Security in China."

50. Jin Zhang, "Foreign Ministry Spokesperson States China Has No Relations with Maoists in Nepal," accessed at http://news.sina.com.cn/c/2005-02-04/03225038185s.shtml, May 26, 2018.

51. "Mao's Theory on Atomic Bomb: They Can't Kill Us All," *United Press International*, October 17, 1964, accessed at https://www.upi.com/Archives/1964/10/17/Maos-theory-on-atomic-bomb-They-cant-kill-us-all/1653831424805/, May 24, 2018.

52. Zheng, "Adjustment of China's Africa Policy in the Early 1980s," 91.

53. Chinese Ministry of Commerce, "Statistics on China-Africa bilateral trade in 2017," accessed at http://english.mofcom.gov.cn/article/statistic/lanmubb/AsiaAfrica/201803/20180302719613.shtml, August 21, 2018.

54. Lyman, "China's Rising Role in Africa," accessed at https://www.cfr.org/report/chinas-rising-role-africa, August 21, 2018.

55. Yan and Yan, "How the Chinese Nation Completely Rid the Risk of Being Stripped of the Membership of the Globe," accessed at http://theory.people.com.cn/n1/2016/0801/c40531-28599851.html, August 21, 2018.

56. Wu, "Three-Decade-Long Changing Trajectory of Ways Young Students Express Patriotism in the Era of Reform and Open-Door Policy."

57. "Bashiniandai liuxuesheng de zhengzha: gui yu bugui? Geren xingfu haishi jiaguo qinghuai?" [Students of the 1980s: to return or to stay? To pursue personal happiness or

motherland complex], *Sohu News*, June 12, 2017, accessed at http://www.sohu.com/a/148096624_170104, August 21, 2018.

58. "Gaige kaifang 30nian: huzhao cong cengcengshenpi zouxiang anxu shenling" [Three decades of reform and open-door policy: passports from requiring layers of approvals to need-based issuance], *Jinghua Shibao*, November 4, 2008, accessed at http://www.chinanews.com/gn/news/2008/11-04/1436222.shtml, August 21, 2018.

59. "Gaige kaifang 30nian: huzhao cong cengcengshenpi zouxiang anxu shenling."

60. Athanasiadis, "Westerners and Chinese Alike Criticize Beijing Opening Ceremonies," accessed at https://www.worldpoliticsreview.com/articles/2569/westerners-and-chinese-alike-criticize-beijing-opening-cermonies, May 28, 2018.

61. South Park Studios, *The China Problem*, accessed at http://southpark.cc.com/full-episodes/s12e08-the-china-probrem, May 26, 2018.

62. Liu and Van Leuven, "A Study of the Unification of Western Public Opinion on China from the News Frame Adopted by AP, AFP and DPA in the Coverage of Beijing Olympic Opening Ceremony," 31.

63. Jon Stewart, *The Daily Show With Jon Stewart*, November 12, 2014, accessed at http://archive.org/details/COM_20141113_022700_The_Daily_Show_With_Jon_Stewart/start/87/end/147?q=beijing, May 26, 2019.

64. Jiaxing Chen, "As Everyone Collects Firewood, Flame Will Rise Higher and Higher," accessed at http://cpc.people.com.cn/n/2013/0116/c78779-20213599.html, May 26, 2018.

65. Lim, "Second Day of Anti-Japan Protests Rock China," accessed at https://www.npr.org/2012/09/16/161228298/chinese-flood-streets-in-anti-japan-demonstrations, May 25, 2018.

66. Chinese Communist Party Central Archive Bureau, *Annuals of Deng Xiaoping*, 1192–93.

67. "Koshi hihan rokukomoku no kosai" [Details of six indictments of Hu], *Yomiuri Shimbun*, January 23, 1987.

68. Student recollection, "Shanghai/Hefei 86 xuechao" [Shanghai/Hefei 86 student movement], *Independent Review*, April 22, 2002, accessed at http://www.duping.net/XHC/show.php?bbs=11&post=407158, May 25, 2018.

69. Student recollection, "Shanghai/Hefei 86 xuechao."

70. National Educational Committee, "Guanyu Nanjing Hehai Daxue '12.24' shijian de jingguo ji chuliqingkuang" [On the trajectory and consequences of Nanjing Hehai University's 'December 24' incident], January 4, 1989; accessed at http://blog.boxun.com/hero/201302/xsj14/1_1.shtml, May 25, 2018.

71. "Zhonggongzhongyang zhengzhijuchangwei, guojia fuzhuxi Hu Jintao fabiao dianshijianghua" [Chinese Politburo Standing Committee Member Vice President Hu Jintao delivers televised speech], *People's Daily*, May 10, 1999, accessed at http://www.people.com.cn/item/ldhd/hujint/1999/jianghua/jh0001.html, May 24, 2018.

72. "Renminwang ping jinri fanriyouxing: ying yifalixing biaoda aiguo reqing" [*People's Daily*'s brief commentary on anti-Japan protest: it needs to be based on legal, sensible patriotism], *People's Daily Net*, October 25, 2010, accessed at http://bbs.tianya.cn/post-284-225530-1.shtml, May 25, 2018.

73. Shirk, *Fragile Superpower*.

74. Brady, *Marketing Dictatorship*; Stockmann, *Media Commercialization and Authoritarian Rule in China*.

75. Yan, "China U-turn after Outcry over Revoking Residency Rights," accessed at http://www.scmp.com/news/china/society/article/2138916/shanghai-u-turn-after-outcry-over-revoking-residency-rights, May 25, 2018.

76. Cui, "Three Decades of Allowing Cross-Strait Family Reunion," accessed at http://www.chinatimes.com/cn/realtimenews/20170913000922-260407, May 25, 2018.

77. Jiachang Chen, *LKY Whom I Knew*, 449–50.

78. Jiachang Chen, *LKY Whom I Knew*, 445.

79. "Sheping: Baigong zhi Zhongguo xiepo meigongsi caishi hushuobadao" [Editorial: White House's criticism on China bullying foreign countries is baseless], *Global Times*, May 6, 2018, accessed at https://opinion.huanqiu.com/article/9CaKrnK8gQu, May 28, 2018.

80. "Jizhouhangkong jiang Taiwan Zhongguo binglie qiangguo xuesheng kangyi canzao dalian" [Jeju Air lists Taiwna next to China; student's protest rejected], *Liberty Times Net* (Taiwan), April 16, 2018, accessed at http://news.ltn.com.tw/news/world/breakingnews/2396729, May 25, 2018.

81. Ding, "Jeju Air Apologizes for Listing Taiwan Next to China, but Netizens Do Not Accept Its Apology," accessed at http://world.huanqiu.com/exclusive/2018-04/11892498.html, May 25, 2018.

82. "Mercedes Apologises to China after Quoting Dalai Lama," *The Telegraph*, February 7, 2018, accessed at https://www.telegraph.co.uk/news/2018/02/07/mercedes-apologises-china-quoting-dalai-lama/, May 31, 2018.

83. Shepardson, "US Condemns China for 'Orwellian Nonsense,'" accessed at https://www.reuters.com/article/us-usa-airlines-china-exclusive/u-s-condemns-china-for-orwellian-nonsense-over-airline-websites-idUSKBN1I60NL, May 29, 2018.

84. "44jia hangkonggongsi ganggaizheng de cuowu Tesila que fanle" [Soon after 44 airlines corrected mistakes, Tesla erred], *Sohu News*, May 29, 2018, accessed at http://www.sohu.com/a/233365466_519108, May 30, 2018.

85. "Taimei: jubao Lin Xinru 'taidu' de shi Taiwanren huoshe touzijiufen" [Taiwanese media: Ruby Lin's accusation stems from Taiwanese due to investment dispute], *Guancha Net*, January 19, 2018, http://m.guancha.cn/local/2018_01_09_442399.shtml

86. Horwitz, "Why a Washed-Up Pop Star Is Suddenly the Most Hated Man in Taiwan," accessed at https://qz.com/597272/why-a-washed-up-pop-star-is-suddenly-the-most-hated-man-in-taiwan/, May 26, 2018.

87. Chou's apology video clip accessed at https://www.youtube.com/watch?time_continue=55&v=t57URqSp5Ew, May 26, 2018.

88. Chan, "Teen Pop Star Chou Tzu-u's Apology for Waving Taiwan Flag Swayed Young Voters for DPP," accessed at https://www.scmp.com/news/china/policies-politics/article/1902195/teen-pop-star-chou-tzu-yus-apology-waving-taiwan-flag, May 28, 2018.

89 "Zhou Ziyu incident: Zhongguo guotaiban yu tai luweihui fenbie huiying" [Chou Tzu-yu Incident: responses from China's Taiwan Affairs Office and Taiwan's Mainland Affairs Office], *BBC Chinese*, January 16, 2016, accessed at http://www.bbc.com/zhongwen/simp/china/2016/01/160116_taiwan_chou_tzu_yu_reax, May 28, 2018.

90. The video remains accessible at https://www.youtube.com/watch?v=2Ji1RrgWSqA as of May 2020.

91. Gao, "'Crotch Bomb' Scene in Anti-Japan War Drama Is Blasted by Chinese Online Users as 'Lewd, Bizarre,'" accessed at https://www.scmp.com/news/china/soci

ety/article/1802970/crotch-bomb-scene-anti-japan-war-drama-blasted-chinese-online, May 21, 2018.

92. Yuan Luo, "Boyi Dianyudao" [Strategic competition over Diaoyu Islands], *Phoenix TV*, August 27, 2012, accessed at http://news.ifeng.com/opinion/phjd/sjdjt/detail_2012_08/27/17117673_0.shtml, May 21, 2018.

93. Xiaobo Liu, "Zhu Chenghu Merely a Miniature of Mao Zedong," accessed at https://www.boxun.com/news/gb/pubvp/2005/09/200509010336.shtml, August 24, 2018.

94. Canrong Jin, "Uncertainty and Challenges for Chinese Diplomacy in 2018," taped speech viewable at https://www.youtube.com/watch?v=BQJ3Yqq0SeY

95. Canrong Jin, "Xifang keneng bushi gengnianqi, youdian laonianchidai" [West is not having menopause but more likely dementia], *Guancha Net*, May 15, 2020, accessed at https://mil.news.sina.com.cn/china/2020-05-15/doc-iircuyvi3200886.shtml, May 17, 2020.

96. Weiwei Zhang, "My View of China," accessed at http://www.aisixiang.com/data/78189.html, May 21, 2018.

97. "Chair Mao's Grandson: China's Most-Mocked Man," *CBS News*, March 13, 2013, accessed at https://www.cbsnews.com/news/chairman-maos-grandson-chinas-most-mocked-man/, May 21, 2018.

98. Jian Hao, "Why Are TV Shows about the War against Japan So Popular in China?," accessed at http://www.eeo.com.cn/ens/2013/0329/241916.shtml, May 24, 2018.

99. "Hengdian qunzhongyanyuan pianchou buru fuwuyuan; 8xiaoshi gongzi 40yuan" [Paid at 40 yuan for eight hours, salary for amateur actors lower than that for waiters], *Sohu News*, July 18, 2013, accessed at http://business.sohu.com/20130718/n382011942.shtml, May 21, 2018.

100. "Zhewei Ribenyanyuan juyan 'kangri shenju'" [Japanese actor refuses to play in anti-Japan farcical dramas], *Global Time*, April 25, 2018, accessed at http://wemedia.ifeng.com/57948544/wemedia.shtml, May 21, 2018.

101. "Kangrishenju: henhuang henbaoli hennaocan chenguanjianci" [Anti-Japan farcical dramas: extremely obscene, extremely violent, extremely stupid listed as key words], *China News Service*, May 21, 2015, accessed at https://cul.sohu.com/20150521/n413464673.shtml, May 21, 2018; see also Hao, "Why Are TV Shows about the War against Japan So Popular in China?"

102. Mo Chen, "How Small-Town Hengdian Has Evolved to Host 18 Million Visits per Year," accessed at https://www.jiemian.com/article/1696725.html, August 24, 2018.

103. "10juzu chunjie zai Hengdian da'guizi'" [Ten 'anti-Japanese devil' dramas in production at Hengdian during Chinese New Year], *QQ News*, February 17, 2013, accessed at http://wxn.qq.com/cmsid/ENT2013021700011600, May 21, 2018.

104. "Yige qunzhong yanyuan yitian 'si'le baci" [One amature actor "killed" eight times in one day], *People's Daily Net*, February 23, 2013, accessed at http://culture.people.com.cn/n/2013/0203/c22219-20416620.html, May 21, 2018.

105. "Xi Jinping xinzheng: qibujiang hou youyou shiliutiao" [Xi Jinping's new politics: 16-clause to follow seven-do-not-talk-about], *BBC Chinese*, May 28, 2013, accessed at https://www.bbc.com/zhongwen/simp/china/2013/05/130528_china_thought_control_youth, May 17, 2020.

106. "Wu Bangguo gongzuobaogao: zhengzhong biaoming wuge bugao" [Wu Bang-

guo issues work report: solemnly indicates five "do-not-adopts"], *Xinhua News Agency*, March 10, 2011, accessed at http://news.ifeng.com/mainland/special/2011lianghui/content-0/detail_2011_03/10/5071450_0.shtml, May 30, 2018.

107. Zhu, Zheng, and Wang, "Hot Topics in the Field of Theoretical Construction in 2013," accessed at http://theory.people.com.cn/n/2014/0113/c143843-24096298.html, May 24, 2018.

108. Gan and Zhuang, "Why a Chinese Communist Party Branch at the University of California, Davis, Was Disbanded," accessed at https://www.scmp.com/news/china/policies-politics/article/2120707/why-chinese-communist-party-branch-university, May 24, 2018.

109. UIUC Chinese Communist Party cell information accessed at https://www.peacehall.com/news/gb/china/2018/04/201804231939.shtml; Chiba Chinese Communist Party cell information accessed http://blog.sina.com.cn/s/blog_79e6bfad0100q1ha.html

110. Hu, "Do Not Let 'Farcial Dramas' to Consume History of Anti-Japanese War," accessed at http://paper.people.com.cn/rmrb/html/2018-05/02/nw.D110000renmrb_20180502_5-05.htm, August 30, 2018.

111. Box Office Mojo, "All Time Box Office," accessed at http://www.boxofficemojo.com/alltime/domestic.htm, May 30, 2018.

112. "'Wolf Warrior 2' Promotes How China Will Always Protect Its Nationals," *China Daily*, August 2, 2017, accessed at http://www.chinadaily.com.cn/culture/2017-08/02/content_30332014.htm, May 30, 2018.

113. "Sanjia zhongguo dashiguan fasheng: jichang buxuyao 'zhanlang'shi aiguo" [Three Chinese embassies warn that airports are no place for wolf-warrior style patriotism], *Xinhua News Agency*, February 1, 2018, http://www.xinhuanet.com/2018-02/01/c_1122351291.htm

Chapter 5

1. Chinese Communist Party Central Archive Bureau, *Selected Works by Xi Jinping on Realizing Chinese Dream of Great Rejuvenation*.

2. Lam, *Chinese Politics in the Era of Xi Jinping*.

3. Mingfu Liu, *The China Dream: Great Power Thinking and Strategic Posture in the Post-American Era*.

4. Jiajun Zhang, "Two Admirals Oppose China Pursuing the World's Top Military Power," accessed at https://mil.huanqiu.com/article/9CaKrnJn4wf, May 19, 2020.

5. Xu, *The New Tianxia: Rebuilding China's Internal and External Order*.

6. Saich, "What Does General Xi Jinping Dream About?"

7. Xi, "Keynote Speech at the World Economic Forum," accessed at https://america.cgtn.com/2017/01/17/full-text-of-xi-jinping-keynote-at-the-world-economic-forum, May 16, 2020.

8. Remarks by President Obama and President Xi Jinping of the People's Republic of China after bilateral meeting, June 8, 2013.

9. Shi, "Seven Major Differences between the China Dream and the American Dream," accessed at http://comments.caijing.com.cn/2013-05-27/112830491.html, September 13, 2013.

10. Cai, "CCTV's Unprecedented Attacks on America," accessed at http://hx.cnd. org/2019/07/30/, May 19, 2020.

11. CCTV Editorial, "Renlei gongdi; Qiangu maming" [Enemy of the state; someone whose name shall be condemned for thousands of years], April 27, 2020; accessed at http://finance.sina.com.cn/wm/2020-04-27/doc-iirczymi8703138.shtml, May 18, 2020.

12. "Yangshi meiri yima: meiguo zhengke 'koutulianhua' 'tunge xuanfeng'" [CCTV's daily curse: American politicians pretend they could spit lotus or gulp down a tornado], *China News*, May 17, 2020, accessed at http://news.creaders.net/china/2020/05/17/2225767.html, May 18, 2020.

13. Guy Taylor, "Secretary of State John Kerry Outlines Vision for 'Pacific Dream' Asia," *Washington Times*, April 13, 2013, accessed at www.washingtontimes.com/news/2013/apr/15/kerry-outlines-vision-pacific-dream-asia/, August 20, 2019.

14. Daniel Workman, "Australia's Top Trading Partners," *World's Top Exports*, May 3, 2020, accessed at http://www.worldstopexports.com/australias-top-import-partners/, May 19, 2020.

15. Australian Bureau of Statistics, "Chinese Tourism in Australia—Statistics," accessed at http://www.worldstopexports.com/australias-top-import-partners/, May 19, 2020.

16. Tourism Australia, "International Tourism Snapshot," March 31, 2019, accessed at https://www.tourism.australia.com/content/dam/assets/document/1/7/1/k/b/2008235.pdf, May 19, 2020.

17. Department of Education, Skills and Employment, Australian Government, "Student Numbers," database accessed at https://internationaleducation.gov.au/research/DataVisualisations/Pages/Student-number.aspx, May 19, 2020.

18. "Australia Faces 'Unprecedented' Economic Hit from Coronavirus: RBA," *Reuters*, May 18, 2020, accessed at https://www.reuters.com/article/us-australia-economy-rba-minutes/australia-faces-unprecedented-economic-hit-from-coronavirus-rba-minutes-idUSKBN22V06Z, May 19, 2020.

19. Turner, "How a China Slowdown Could Hit the Economy," accessed at https://www.afr.com/policy/economy/how-a-china-slowdown-would-hit-the-economy-20190620-p51zkv, May 19, 2020.

20. Martino, "Pauline Hanson's Maiden Speech: Has Australia Been 'Swamped by Asians'?" accessed at http://www.abc.net.au/news/2016-09-14/pauline-hanson-maiden-speech-asian-immigration/7645578, May 20, 2020.

21. Rucker and Parker, "How Trump Made Up with Australia's Prime Minister after a 'Most Unpleasant Call,'" accessed at https://www.washingtonpost.com/politics/how-trump-made-up-with-australias-prime-minister-after-a-most-unpleasant-call/2018/02/22/e1c4a4c2-1737-11e8-b681-2d4d462a1921_story.html?utm_term=.c4df9a865061, June 5, 2018.

22. Ruwitch and Packham, "In Shanghai, Australia Minister Sees Limits to Tackling Irritants in Ties," *Reuters*, May 18, 2018, accessed at https://www.reuters.com/article/us-australia-china/in-shanghai-australian-minister-sees-limits-to-tackling-irritants-in-ties-idUSKCN1IJ0XA, May 20, 2020.

23. Guanwen Chen, "Challenge China: Australia Self-Exaggerates Its Importance by Announcing Actions in South China Sea," accessed at https://news.qq.com/a/20160127/021159.htm, May 20, 2020.

24. "Zhongguo guoyoumeti cheng Aodaliya chengwei 'fanhua jixianfeng'" [China's state media call Australia "anxious anti-China deputy"], *ABC Chinese News*, February 18, 2018, accessed at https://www.abc.net.au/chinese/2018-02-27/chinese-media-says-aus tralia-has-become-an-anti-china-pioneer/9489734, May 20, 2020; Shi Yun, "Weish-enme Aodaliya dui Zhongguo quefa haogan" [Why does Australia lack positive feelings about China?], *Zhihu Net*, January 19, 2018, accessed at https://zhuanlan.zhihu.com/p/33123444, May 19, 2020.

25. Baxendale, "Kevin Rudd Accuses Malcolm Turnbull of Offending China."

26. Duran and Needham, "Australia and China Spat over Coronavirus Inquiry Deep-ens," May 18, 2020, accessed at https://www.reuters.com/article/us-health-coronarivus-australia/australia-and-china-spat-over-coronavirus-inquiry-deepens-idUSK BN22V083, September 21, 2020.

27. Jennifer Hewett, "Business Is Nervous about the Turnbull Government's Anti-China Rhetoric," *Financial Review*, April 13, 2018, accessed at http://www.afr.com/opin ion/columnists/business-is-nervous-about-the-turnbull-governments-antichina-rheto ric-20180413-h0yppt, September 17, 2020.

28. Embassy of the People's Republic of China in the Commonwealth of Australia, "Transcript of Ambassador Cheng Jiye's Interview with Australian Financial Review Political Correspondent Andrew Tillett," April 27, 2020, accessed at http://au.china-embassy.org/eng/sghdxwfb_1/t1773741.htm, May 20, 2020.

29. The video remains accessible at https://twitter.com/SkyNewsAust/status/939310385798057984?s=20 as of September 10, 2020.

30. Baxendale, "Kevin Rudd Accuses Malcom Turnbull of Offending China."

31. Guo, "Australian PM Proclaims Australia Has Stood Up; China Says Such Remarks Are Self-Hurting," accessed at http://news.cctv.com/2017/12/11/ARTIeMd 0BDUqvz9zTjc3aZWG171211.shtml, May 19, 2020.

32. Grant, "Malcolm Turnbull's China Strategy Absolutely All Over the Place,' Kevin Rudd Says," accessed at http://www.abc.net.au/news/2018-02-11/kevin-rudd-slams-malcolm-turnbull-over-china-strategy/9420064, May 19, 2020.

33. "Jianggexiaohua Aodaliya renmin zhanqilaile" [Here's a joke—Australian people have stood up!], *Global View* (China), December 11, 2017, accessed at http://www.glo balview.cn/html/global/info_21708.html, May 19, 2020.

34. Xiuhui Li, "Why Is Australia So Concerned about China's Political Interference?," accessed at https://www.thenewslens.com/article/85179, May 20, 2020.

35. Yoshida, *Yoshida Shigeru: Last Meiji Man*, 49.

36. Yoshida, *Yoshida Shigeru: Last Meiji Man*, 49.

37. Yoshida, *Yoshida Shigeru: Last Meiji Man*, 38.

38. Sun, *Japan and China as Charm Rivals*, 31–32.

39. Sun, *Japan and China as Charm Rivals*, 88.

40. "Yoshida Shigeru Zo" [Portrait of Yoshida Shigeru], *Tosa Rekishi Sanpo* [A stroll in Tosa history], accessed at https://tosareki.gozaru.jp/tosareki/satokaida/yoshida_shigeru.html, May 21, 2020.

41. Hirano, "China Wary of Haotyama's 'East Asian Community,'" accessed at https://www.japantimes.co.jp/news/2009/10/03/national/china-wary-of-hatoyamas-east-asian-community/, May 21, 2020.

42. Miks, "Who Hatoyama Could've Been," accessed at https://thediplomat.com/2010/06/who-hatoyama-could-have-been-2/, May 21, 2020.

43. Onishi, "Koizumi Visits War Shrine, as He Pledged," accessed at https://www.nytimes.com/2005/10/17/world/asia/koizumi-visits-war-shrine-as-he-pledged.html, May 21, 2020.

44. Lieberman, "Maybe Trump Is Not Mentally Ill. Maybe He's Just a Jerk," accessed at https://www.nytimes.com/2018/01/12/opinion/trump-mentally-ill.html, May 12, 2018.

45. "'Abe seiken wa fashisuto' 'Uyoku naikaku yorusanai' kokkai mae demo sarani kagekini" ["Abe administration is fascist" "Rightwing cabinet not allowed" protests in front of Diet goes increasingly disruptive], *Sankei Shimbun*, September 18, 2015, accessed at https://www.sankei.com/politics/news/150918/plt1509180081-n1.html, May 21, 2020.

46. "Gaikokan no shushin daigaku towa" [On graduating schools for diplomats], *Shukatsu no mirai* [Toward employment], April 20, 2020, accessed at https://shukatsu-mirai.com/archives/70251, May 22, 2020.

47. Japanese Ministry of Foreign Affairs, "Saiyo shonin nado kihonhoshin ni motozuku ninyo no jokyo (Heise 24 nendo)" [Overview of recruitment and promotion statistics based on principle rules], January 31, 2014, accessed at https://www.mofa.go.jp/mofaj/files/000025838.pdf, May 22, 2020.

48. Johnson, *MITI and the Japanese Miracle*, 138.

49. Gerald Curtis, "The Role of the Diet in Policymaking and Legislation," accessed at http://afe.easia.columbia.edu/at/jp_diet/govtjd03.html, May 22, 2020.

50. Pilling, "The Perils of Japan's Andy Warhol,'" accessed at https://www.ft.com/content/1347ab18-b5ff-11df-a048-00144feabdc0, May 22, 2020.

51. Yamaguchi, *Fights Under Surface*, 118

52. Part of the research has been published by Sun, "Frozen Dilemma."

53. Rich, "Meeting Between Japan and Russia Ends with Stalemate on Disputed Island," accessed at https://www.nytimes.com/2016/12/16/world/asia/japan-russia-abe-putin.html?_r=0, April 27, 2017.

54. Hara, "Norms, Structures, and Japan's 'Northern Territories' Policy," 77.

55. Hasegawa, *The Northern Territories*, 2:225.

56. Schoppa, *Bargaining with Japan*.

57. Hasegawa, *The Northern Territories*, 2:231, 252.

58. Hasegawa, "Japanese Misperceptions of the Soviet Union during the Gorbachev Period," 52.

59. Niwa, *China's Great Dilemma*.

60. "Shushoni sanpaichūshi gushin, Anami zenchūgokudaishi ga" [Former ambassador to China Anami appeals to PM to stop visiting (Yasukuni)], *Kyodo News Agency*, August 12, 2006, accessed at http://news.goo.ne.jp/news/kyodo/seiji/20060812/20060812a1270.html, August 20, 2018.

61. Niwa, *China's Great Dilemma*, 145.

62. Niwa, *China's Great Dilemma*, 150.

63. Personal conversations with multiple Japanese diplomats, November 2009 and April 2010.

64. Yamaguchi, *Fights Under Surface*, 104–5.

65. Such critical posts, including those using racial slurs, remain accessible at http://5chb.net/r/newsplus/1482754616/ as of on September 12, 2020.

66. Ryall, "Why Are Japanese So Condescending to Chinese Tourists?," accessed at http://www.scmp.com/week-asia/society/article/2058280/why-are-japanese-so-condescending-chinese-tourists, May 23, 2020.

67. Pew Research Center, "Public's Policy Priorities for 2019," accessed at https://www.pewresearch.org/fact-tank/2019/02/04/state-of-the-union-2019-how-americans-see-major-national-issues/pp_2019-01-24_political-priorities_0-02/, August 18, 2019.

68. Reinhart, "Healthcare, Immigration Down as Most Important Problem," accessed at https://news.gallup.com/poll/245513/healthcare-immigration-down-important-problem.aspx, May 23, 2020.

69. Japanese Cabinet Office, "Senkaku shoto ni kansuru tokubetsu yoronchosa" [Special survey on Senkaku Islands], accessed at https://survey.gov-online.go.jp/tokubetu/h25/h25-senkaku.html, September 17, 2020.

70. JTB Tourism Research and Consulting, "Nihonjin haigai ryoko doko" [Trajectory of Japanese outbound tourism], accessed at https://www.tourism.jp/tourism-database/stats/outbound/, August 19, 2018.

71. Iwata, *A Reader of China's Anti-Japan Drama*.

72. Henley & Partners Passport Index, accessed at https://www.henleypassportindex.com/passport, May 23, 2020.

73. "Gaiken giron 'isogu hitwsuyo nai' 72%, Asah Shimbun yoron chosa" [Asahi Shimbun survey: "no need to speed up constitutional amendment debate" 72%], *Asahi Shimbun*, May 3, 2020, accessed at https://www.asahi.com/articles/ASN5271Z3N4ZUZPS005.html, May 23, 2020.

74. https://blog.goo.ne.jp/raymiyatake/e/51a90827a31defcad1ed393e7a01a1fc

75. https://www.passportindex.org/byRank.php

76. Data drawn from Borapura SDG's homepage, https://volunteer-platform.org/vpf-blog/statistics/26659/, August 19, 2018.

77. "Zai Zhongguo de Ribenzhiyuanzhe" [Japanese volunteers in Japan], *People's Daily Network*, accessed at https://japan.people.com.cn/xielidui/xielidui.htm, August 19, 2018.

78. "Zai zhongguo shamo zhongshu de jiwei Ribenren" [Several Japanese who are planting trees in China's deserts], August 1, 2016, *Sino Blog*; accessed at http://blog.sina.com.cn/s/blog_5cfc58cb0102ww5i.html, August 19, 2018.

79. Japanese Cabinet Office, "Gaiko ni kansuru yoron chosa" [Survey on diplomacy], accessed at https://survey.gov-online.go.jp/r01/r01-gaiko/index.html, September 17, 2020.

80. Niwa, *China's Great Dilemma*, 219.

81. "Kakkoku no zaibei ryugakuseisu no sui to nihonjin ryugakusei" [Number of international students in America and students from Japan], accessed at https://wag-study-aborad.com, August 20, 2018.

82. Lampton, *Following the Leaders*, 85.

83. "Full Text of Xi Jinping Keynote at the World Economic Forum," *CGTN America*, January 17, 2017, accessed at https://america.cgtn.com/2017/01/17/full-text-of-xi-jinping-keynote-at-the-world-economic-forum, May 23, 2020.

84. "Full Text of Xi Jinping Keynote at the World Economic Forum."

85. "China's Xi Takes on Trump in Rebuttal against Protectionism," *Bloomberg News*, January 17, 2017, accessed at https://www.bloomberg.com/news/articles/2017-01-17/china-s-xi-urges-davos-elite-to-solve-excesses-of-globalization, May 23, 2020.

86. Voice of America, "Wangmin huyu guanmei buyao ba sangshi dang xishi ban" [Netizens call on official media not to turn funeral into wedding], April 6, 2010, accessed at https://www.voachinese.com/a/article-201004006-cctv-disaster-news-89987802/465553.html, September 12, 2020.

87. Shelly, "Ozymandias," accessed at https://www.poetryfoundation.org/poems/46565/Ozymandias, September 12, 2020.

Bibliography

A list of media sources appears at the end of this bibliography.

Abe, Shinzo. "Japan Is Back." Policy Speech by Prime Minister Shinzo Abe at the Center for Strategic and International Studies (CSIS), February 22, 2013.

Adler-Nissen, Rebecca. "Stigma Management in International Relations: Transgressive Identities, Norms, and Order in International Society." *International Organization* 69, no. 1 (2014): 143–76.

Allison, Graham. "Conceptual Models and the Cuban Missile Crisis." *American Political Science Review* 63 (1969): 689–718.

Allison, Graham. *Essence of Decision: Explaining the Cuban Missile Crisis*. New York: Pearson, 1999.

Allison, Graham T., and Morton H. Halperin. "Bureaucratic Politics: A Paradigm and Some Policy Implications." *World Politics* 24 (Spring 1972): 40–79.

Almond, Gabriel. "Separate Tables: Schools and Sects in Political Science." *PS: Political Science and Politics* 21, no. 4 (Autumn 1988): 828–42.

Athanasiadis, Iason. "Westerners and Chinese Alike Criticize Beijing Opening Ceremonies." *World Politics Review*, August 14, 2008.

Australian Government, Department of Foreign Affairs and Trade. "Composition of Trade Australia, 2018–19," January 2020.

Bader, Jeffrey. "Order from Chaos: Chinese State Visits Are Always Hard: A Historical Perspective." *Brookings Institute's Series on Xi Jinping's State Visit*, September 17, 2015.

Barrass, Gordon. *The Art of Calligraphy in Modern China*. Berkeley: University of California Press, 2002.

Battin, Margaret Pabst, ed. *The Ethics of Suicide: Historical Sources*, 1st ed. Oxford: Oxford University Press, 2015.

Baxendale, Rachel. "Kevin Rudd Accuses Malcom Turnbull of Offending China." *The Australian*, April 30, 2018.

Beauchamp, Zack. "Bernie Sanders Is Right: Hillary Clinton Praising Henry Kissinger Is Outrageous." *Vox*, February 12, 2016.

Bendor, Jonathan, and Thomas H. Hammond. "Rethinking Allison's Models." *American Political Science Review* 86, no. 2 (1992): 301–22.

Boucher, Richard. "Press Statement on the Death of Zhao Ziyang." US Department of State, January 18, 2005.

Brady, Anne-Marie. *Marketing Dictatorship: Propaganda and Thought Work in Contemporary China*. Plymouth, UK: Roman & Littlefield, 2008.

Buckley, Chris. "As China's Woes Mount, Xi Jinping Faces Rare Rebuke at Home." *New York Times*, July 31, 2018.

Butterfield, Fox. "Mao Tse-Tung: Father of Chinese Revolution." *New York Times*, September 10, 1976.

Cai, Li. "Xinwenlianbo kongqian nudui Meiguo, Zhongguo dui xifang de renzhi zaici fasheng fangxiangxing bianhua" [CCTV's unprecedented attacks on America: China's new directional change to its perception of the West]. *China News Digest International*, July 30, 2019.

Callahan, William. "Identity and Security in China: The Negative Soft Power of the China Dream." *Politics* 25, no. 3–4 (2015): 216–29.

Cao, Xueqin. *Hong Lou Meng* [Dream of the red chamber]. Beijing: Renmin Wenxue Press, 1982.

Carson, Austin. "Facing Off and Saving Face: Covert Intervention and Escalation Management in the Korean War." *International Organization* 70, no. 1 (2016): 103–31.

Chan, Minnie. "Teen Pop Star Chou Tzu-u's Apology for Waving Taiwan Flag Swayed Young Voters for DPP." *South China Morning Post*, January 17, 2016.

Chang, Qing, and Qiqing Lv. "Laozhu waijiao duiwu de xinyang zhihun" [To create enduring and faithful soul among diplomatic troops]. *Sixiang Zhengzhi Gongzuo Yanjiu* [Research of political propaganda work], June 20, 2013.

Chen, Boyan. "Navy Rear Admiral Clarifies 'Smog Defense' Theory." China.org.cn, February 14, 2015.

Chen, Dunde. *Mao Zedong he Nikesong zai 1972* [Mao Zedong and Nixon in 1972]. Beijing: Jiefangjun wenyi chubanshe, 1997.

Chen, Guangwen. "Tiaozhan Zhongguo Aodaliya zibuliangli yaozai nanhai dongshou" [Challenge China: Australia self-exaggerates its importance by announcing actions in South China Sea]. *QQ News*, January 27, 2016.

Chen, Jiachang. *LKY Whom I Knew*. Singapore: Linzi Chuan Mei, 2015.

Chen, Jiaxing. "Zhongren shichai huoyangao" [As everyone collects firewood, the flame will rise higher and higher]. *People's Daily*, January 16, 2013.

Chen, Jin. "Mao Zedong zenyangba hongloumeng dang lishi dude" [How Mao Zedong read the Dream of the Red Chamber as history]. *Chinese Communist Party History Online Archive*, 2013.

Chen, Lifen. "Zhou Enlai weiyu chounmou zhu xinzhongguo waijiao jiliang" [Zhou Enlai proactively prepares for the making of diplomatic corps for New China]. *People's Daily Network*, November 1, 2013.

Chen, Minfeng. "Xie Changting yehi Wang Yi fouren you jiu'er gongshi" [Frank Hsieh meets Wang Yi in the evening and denies 92 consensus]. *Radio France Internationale*, October 7, 2012.

Chen, Mo. "Nianyoukeliang 1800wanrenci de Hengdian xiaozhen shi ruhe fazhanzhijinde" [How small-town Hengdian has evolved to host 18 million visits per year]. *Jiemian*, October 21, 2017.

Chen, Si. "Stories of Mao Zedong and 'Dream of Red Chamber'" [Mao Zedong yu hongloumeng de gushi], *People's Daily Network*, November 12, 2006.

Chen, Yi'nan. "Shezai zhongguo de magong guangbo diantai" [Malaysian Communist Party's China-based radio station]. *Yanhuang Chunqiu* 8 (2015).

China Soviet Republic, *Zhonghua suweiai xianfa dagang* [Constitutional Guidelines of the China Soviet Republic], January 1934.

Chinese Central Government. "Quanmian tuijin dang de zhuzhi tixi jianshe" [Comprehensively strengthen the party's organizational construction]. www.gov.cn, July 6, 2018.

Chinese Communist Party Central Archive Bureau. *Deng Xiaoping nianpu* [Annuals of Deng Xiaoping]. Vol. 1, 1975–1997. Beijing: Central Archives Press, 2004.

Chinese Communist Party Central Archive Bureau. *Xi Jinping guanyu shixian zhonghuaminzu weidafuxing de zhongguomeng lunshu zhaibian* [Selected works by Xi Jinping on realizing chinese dream of great rejuvenation]. Beijing: Central Archives Press, 2013.

Chinese Communist Party Central Committee. "Zhonggong zhongyan guanyu quanmian shenhua gaige ruogan zhongdawenti de jueding" [The CCP Central Committee's decisions on several important issues related to completely deepening reform." Accessed at http://www.gov.cn/jrzg/2013-11/15/content_2528179.htm, November 15, 2013.

Chinese Communist Party News Network. "Guowuyuan guanyu jigou shezhi de tongzhi" [Announcement on organizational structure of the State Council]. *Chinese Communist Party News Network*, March 21, 2013.

Chinese Ministry of Foreign Affairs. "Waijiaobu 2019niandu kaoshi luyong gongwuyuan zhuanye nengli ceshi, mianshi he xinli sushi ceshi gonggao" [Foreign Ministry public announcement of 2019 entrance examination, interview, and psychological assessment]. Chinese Ministry of Foreign Affairs, January 18, 2019.

Chinese Ministry of Foreign Affairs Councilor Service Net. "275 Xiaoshi! Yici zhenzheng de cheqiao xingdong" [275 hours! An account of a real evacuation of Chinese citizens]. *Chinese Ministry of Foreign Affairs Councilor Service Net*, August 30, 2017.

Cohen, Zachary, and Dan Merica. "Unlike Tillerson, Trump Says Pompeo 'Always on Same Wavelength.'" *CNN*, March 13, 2018.

Corera, Gordon. *Shopping for Bombs: Nuclear Proliferation, Global Insecurity, and the Rise and Fall of the A.Q. Khan Network*, Oxford: Oxford University Press, 2006.

Cotton, Tom. "Tom Cotton: We Should Buy Greenland." *New York Times*, August 26, 2019.

Cui, Cidi. "Liang'an kaifang 30nian Wu Po-hsiung: Chiang Ching-kuo qinzi jueding" [Three decades of allowing cross-strait family reunion; Wu Po-hsioung: Chiang Ching-kuo's personal decision]. *China Times*, September 13, 2017.

Davidson, Lawrence. *Foreign Policy, Inc.: Privatizing America's National Interest*. Lexington: University of Kentucky Press, 2009.

Deng, Xiaoping. "Jundui yao fucong zhengge guojia jianshedaju" (Military must follow the nation's grand agenda). In *Deng Xiaoping Wenxuan Disanjuan* [Selected works of Deng Xiaoping], vol. 3. Beijing: People's Publishing House, 1993.

Ding, Jieyun. "Jiang Zhongguo he Taiwan binglie de Jizhouhangkong daoqianle, dan wangyou haoxiang bingbumaizhang" [Jeju Air apologizes for listing Taiwan next to China, but netizens do not accept its apology]. *Huanqiu Network* (Xinhua News Agency), April 20, 2018.

Dong, Xin. "Xinren zhu Bajisitan dashi Beijing hen teshu" [New ambassador to Pakistan has unique background], *Phoenix News*, September 11, 2011.

Dreyer, June Teufel. "China's Dream, Japan's Nightmare." *Japan Forward*, July 11, 2017.

Duran, Paulina, and Kirsty Needham. "Australia and China Spat over Coronavirus Inquiry Deepens." *Reuters*, May 18, 2020.

Egger, Andrew. "Farmers the First Casualties in Trump's Trade War." *Washington Examiner*, July 9, 2018.

Elliott, Francis. "Prince Upsets Chinese with 'Appalling Waxworks' Jibe." *Independent*, November 13, 2005.

Fang, Ledi. "Zhongguo choushe guoanwei Jiang Zemin shidai ceng youci tiyi" [Proposal of setting up National Security Committee starts during Jiang Zemin era]. *Dakung Pao*, November 12, 2012.

Fifield, Anna. "China Wasn't Wild for Pompeo before the Virus. It's Really Gunning for Him Now." *Washington Post*, April 30, 2020.

Follesdal, Andreas, and Simon Hix. "Why There Is a Democratic Deficit in the EU: A Response to Majone and Moravcsik." *Journal of Common Market Studies* 44, no. 3 (2006): 533–62.

Fravel, M. Taylor. "Shifts in Warfare and Party Unity: Explaining China's Changes in Military Strategy." *International Security* 42, no. 3 (Winter 2017–18): 37–83.

Gan, Nectar, and Pinghui Zhuang. "Why a Chinese Communist Party Branch at the University of California, Davis, Was Disbanded." *South China Morning Post*, November 20, 2017.

Gao, Kathy. "'Crotch Bomb' Scene in Anti-Japan War Drama Is Blasted by Chinese Online Users as 'Lewd, Bizarre.'" *South China Morning Post*, May 19, 2015.

Gao, Wenqian. *Wannian Zhou Enlai* [Zhou Enlai's final years]. New York: Mingjing Chubanshe, 2003.

Geertz, Clifford. *The Interpretation of Cultures*. New York: Basic Books, 1973.

Gilpin, Robert. *The Political Economy of International Relations*. Princeton: Princeton University Press, 1987.

Gittings, Danny. "General Zhu Goes Ballistic." *Wall Street Journal*, July 18, 2005.

Goffman, Erving. "The Interaction Order: American Sociological Association, 1982 Presidential Address." *American Sociological Review* 48, no. 1 (February 1983): 1–17.

Goffman, Erving. "The Presentation of Self in Everyday Life." In *Sociology: Exploring the Architecture of Everyday Life*, edited by David M. Newman and Jodi O'Brien, 120–30. Los Angeles: Pine Forge Press, 2008.

Gourevitch, Peter. "International Trade, Domestic Coalitions and Liberty: Comparative Responses to the Crisis of 1873–1896." *Journal of Interdisciplinary History* 8, no. 2 (Autumn 1977): 281–313.

Gourevitch, Peter. "Second Image Reversed: The International Sources of Domestic Politics." *International Organization* 32, no. 4 (Autumn 1978): 881–912.

Grant, Stan. "Malcolm Turnbull's China Strategy 'Absolutely All Over the Place,' Kevin Rudd says." *ABC News* (Australia), February 11, 2018.

Gries, Peter. *China's New Nationalism: Pride, Politics, and Diplomacy*. Berkeley: University of California Press, 2005.

Gruber, Lloyd. *Ruling the World: Power Politics and the Rise of Supranational Institutions*. Princeton: Princeton University Press, 2000.

Guo, Fang. "Aozongli xuancheng Aozhou 'zhanqilaile' Zhangfang: yousun zishenxingx iang" [Australian PM proclaims Australia has stood up; China says such remarks are self-hurting]. *Global Times*, December 11, 2017.

Habib, Adam. "South Africa: The Rainbow Nation and Prospects for Consolidating Democracy." *African Journal of Political Science* 2, no. 2 (1997): 15–37.

Hammelt, Daniel. "Zapiro and Zuma: A Symptom of an Emerging Constitutional Crisis in South Africa." *Political Geography* 29, no.2 (2010): 88–96.

Hao, Jian. "Why Are TV Shows about the War against Japan So Popular in China?" *China Buzz*, March 29, 2013.

Hao, Mengjia. "2018nian guojia gongwuyuan kaoshi booming jingzheng zuijilie shida zhiwei" [Top ten most competitive public sector entry examinations in 2018]. *People's Daily Network*, November 6, 2017.

Hara, Kimie. "Norms, Structures, and Japan's 'Northern Territories' Policy." In *Norms, Interests, and Power in Japanese Foreign Policy*, edited by Yoichiro Sato and Keiko Hirata. New York: Palgrave MacMillan, 2008.

Hasegawa, Tsuyoshi. "Japanese Misperceptions of the Soviet Union during the Gorbachev Period." In *Misperceptions between Japan and Russia*, edited by Semyon Verbitsky, Tsuyoshi Hasegawa, and Gilbert Rozman. Pittsburgh: University of Pittsburgh Press, 2000.

Hasegawa, Tsuyoshi. *The Northern Territories Dispute and Russo-Japanese Relations*. Vol. 1, *Between War and Peace, 1697–1985*; Vol. 2, *Neither War nor Peace, 1985–1998*. Berkeley: International and Area Studies, University of California, Berkeley, 1998.

He, Liangliang. "Li Guangyao he Deng Xiaoping yingxiong xi yingxiong" [Mutual affection between two heroes: Lee Kuan Yew and Deng Xiaoping]. Interview script for the program Shishi Liangliang Dian [News highlights], *Phoenix News*, March 30, 2015.

He, Yingchun. "Waijiao xueyuan dangwei shuji: Zhou zongli 16zi waijiao yaoqiu cheng xiaochun" [Party secretary of China Foreign Affairs University: Premier Zhou's sixteen-character diplomatic requirement becomes school motto]. *People's Daily Network*, July 29, 2014.

Hermann, Margaret G., and Charles F. Hermann. "Who Makes Foreign Policy Decisions and How: An Empirical Inquiry." *International Studies Quarterly* 33 (December 1989): 361–87.

Hirano, Ko. "China Wary of Haotyama's 'East Asian Community.'" *Japan Times*, October 3, 2009.

Horwitz, Josh. "Why a Washed-Up Pop Star Is Suddenly the Most Hated Man in Taiwan." *Quartz*, January 20, 2016.

Hu, Haisheng. "Bierang kangrishenju xiaofei kangzhanshi" [Do not let "farcial dramas" to consume history of anti-Japanese war]. *People's Daily Network*, May 2, 2018.

Ikenberry, G. John. "The End of Liberal International Order?" *International Affairs* 94, no. 1 (2018): 7–23.

Iwata, Takanori. *Chugoku konichi dorama dohon: izusezaru hannichi, aikoku komedia* [A reader of China's anti-Japan drama: Unintentionally anti-Japan, patriotic comedies]. Tokyo: Publib Publishing, 2018.

Jervis, Robert. *How Statesmen Think: Psychology of International Politics*. Princeton: Princeton University Press, 2017.

Jervis, Robert. *The Logic of Images in International Relations*. Princeton: Princeton University Press, 1970.

Ji, You. "The PLA and Diplomacy: Unraveling Myths about the Military Role in Foreign Policy Making." *Journal of Contemporary China* 23, no. 86 (2014): 236–54.

Jian, Junbo. "China's 'Old Buddy' Diplomacy Dies a Death." *Asia Times,* October 26, 2012.

Jiang, Yongjing. *Mao Zedong yu Jiang Jieshi de tanda yu juezhan* [Mao Zedong and Chiang Kai-shek: Negotiations and decisive confrontations]. Taipei: Taiwan Shangwu Publishing, 2014.

Jin, Minmin and Jiang Yujuan, Xinhua guoji shiping: maoyizhan meiyou yingjia" [Xinhua brief comment on international issues: Trade war has no winners], *Xinhua News Agency*, March 7, 2018.

Johnson, Chalmers. *MITI and the Japanese Miracle: The Growth of Industrial Policy, 1925–1975.* Palo Alto, CA: Stanford University Press, 1982.

Johnson, Chalmers. "The State and Japanese Grand Strategy." In *The Domestic Bases of Grand Strategy,* edited by Richard Roscrance and Arthur A. Stein. Ithaca: Cornell University Press, 1993.

Johnston, Alastair Iain. "How New and Assertive Is China's 'New Assertiveness?,'" *International Security* 37, no. 4 (Spring 2013): 7–48.

Judge, Timothy A., and Ronald F. Piccolo. "Transformative and Transactional Leadership: A Meta-analytical Test of Their Relative Validity." *Journal of Applied Psychology* 89, no. 5 (2004): 755–68.

Kang, Kai. "Memory of China's Diplomatic Godfather Qian Qichen." *Xinwen Zhoukan* [News weekly], December 10, 2003.

Kassam, Ashifa. "Chinese Minister Vents Anger When Canadian Reporter Asks about Human Rights." *The Guardian,* June 2, 2016.

Kassam, Ashifa. "Justin Trudeau 'Dissatisfied' with How Chinese Minister Treated Journalist." *The Guardian,* June 3, 2016.

Keohane, Robert O. *After Hegemony: Cooperation and Discord in the World Political Economy.* Princeton: Princeton University Press, 1984.

Kuo, Lily. "China Accuses Sweden of Violating Human Rights over Treatment of Tourists." *The Guardian,* September 17, 2018.

Lam, Willy. "China's Hawks in Command." *Wall Street Journal,* July 1, 2012.

Lam, Willy Wo-Lap. *Chinese Politics in the Era of Xi Jinping: Renaissance, Reform, or Retrogression.* New York: Routledge, 2015.

Lampton, David. *Following the Leader: Ruling China, from Deng Xiaoping to Xi Jinping.* Berkeley: University of California Press, 2014.

Lee, Don. "Western Australia's Mining Boom Ebbs along with China's Economy." *Los Angeles Times,* January 11, 2015.

Lei, Sheng. "Fanbei que benmei? Kankan zan you duoshao 'fenmeidoushi' yiminmeiguo" [Anti-America yet yearning for America? Let's count how many "anti-America warriors" emigrated to America]. *Boxun Blog Forum,* August 24, 2015.

Li, Bao. "Queci duonian zhongguo fangzhang jiang chuxi xianggelila duihuahui, zhubanzhe cheng gaoduqidai" [Chinese minister of defense to attend Shangri-la Dialogue after years of absence; host expresses high hopes]. *Voice of America,* May 21, 2019.

Li, Baodong. "Wang Yi nuchu jianada jizhe xianchang muji: zaichangren guzhangdian zan" [A reporter's witness: Wang Yi's fierce refutation of Canadian reporter: people clap hands and applause]. *Xinhua News Agency,* June 3, 2016.

Li, Fangxiang. "Guanyu qingnian Mao Zedong Beida jingli de jige wenti bianxi" [On Mao Zedong's experience at Beida during his youth: analysis of several issues]. *Makesi zhuyi yanjiu* [Journal of Marxism studies], September 17, 2014.

Li, Nan. "From Ridicule to Respect." *Beijing Review,* January 5, 2017.

Li, Shi, Hiroshi Sato, and Terry Sicular, eds. *Rising Inequality in China: Challenges to a Harmonious Society.* Cambridge: Cambridge University Press, 2013.

Li, Ting, et al. "Xi Jinping de yizhou" [Xi Jinping's one week]. China Central Television, September 6, 2020.

Li, Wenhui. "Weishenme zhongguo zhuwaishijie dou chengwei zhanlang dashi?" [Why are China's diplomats all turning into wolf-warrior-style ambassadors?]. *Voice of America,* May 8, 2020.

Li, Xiuhui. "Weishenme Aozou name danxin Zhongguo ganzheng" [Why is Australia so concerned about China's political interference?] *News Lens,* December 11, 2017.

Li, Xueqing. "Rear Admiral's Rally Cry to Youth Gets Lost in Laughter." *Six Tone,* April 3, 2016.

Li, Ya'nan. "1978: chongxin renshi dongnanya: zailun 20 shiji 70 niandaimo zhongguo yu dongmeng kaizhan anquanhezuo de shuangchong yiyi" [1978: Re-approach Southeast Asia: Re-examine the 1970s' China-ASEAN security cooperation's dual implications]. *Beijing Shehui Kexue* [Beijing social science journal] 3 (2014).

Li, Zhen. "Xi Jinping 7.26 zhongyao jianghua jingshen xilie jiedu zhi wu: Cong zhanqilai, fuqilai dao qiangqilai de lishixing feiyue" [Historical leaps from standing up to becoming rich and to becoming strong: The fifth interpretation of Xi Jinping's important July 26 speech]. *People's Daily Network,* September 6, 2017.

Liang, Tao. *Suiyue Ruge* [Time bygone like a song]. Beijing: Zhongyang bianyi chubanshe, 2013.

Lieberman, Jeffrey A. "Maybe Trump Is Not Mentally Ill. Maybe He's Just a Jerk." *New York Times,* January 12, 2018.

Lim, Louisa. "Second Day of Anti-Japan Protests Rock China." *National Public Radio,* September 16, 2012.

Ling, Zhijun. "1999nian Zhu Rongji fangwei 'zuihei'an yitian' fashengle shenme" [What happened on the "darkest day" of Zhu Rongji's 1999 visit to America?]. *Phoenix TV Network,* August 23, 2013.

Liu, Jixing. "Mao Zedong nairenxunwei de 'Sun Wukong qingjie'" [Mao Zedong's amazing Monkey King complex"]. *Xinhua Net,* November 3, 2013.

Liu, Melinda. "China's New Negotiator, Foreign Minister Wang Yi." *Newsweek,* March 25, 2013.

Liu, Mingfu. *The China Dream: Great Power Thinking and Strategic Posture in the Post-American Era.* CN Times Book, 2015.

Liu, Xiliang. "Zhongguo fanyijie 60nian huimo" [Reflection of a Chinese translator after six decades]. *Zhongguo fanyi* [Chinese translation], published online by Translators Association of China, September 2009.

Liu, Xiaobo. "Zhu Chenghu buguo shige xiao Mao Zedong" [Zhu Chenghu merely a miniature of Mao Zedong]. *Boxun News,* September 1, 2005.

Liu, Xiaoyan, and Nancy Van Leuven. "A Study of the Unification of Western Public Opinion on China from the News Frame Adopted by AP, AFP and DPA in the Coverage of Beijing Olympic Opening Ceremony." *Journalism and Mass Communication Studies* 4 (2010).

Lu, Keng. "Hu Yaobang fangwenji" [Interview of Hu Yaobang]. *Baixing,* June 1985.

Lyman, Princeton. "China's Rising Role in Africa." Council on Foreign Relations, July 21, 2005.

Ma, Licheng. "Deng Xiaoping he Hu Yaobang de duiriguang" [Deng Xiaoping and Hu

Yaobang's views of Japan]. *Zhongguo Baodao Zhoukan* [China weekly report], January 13, 2009.

Machiavelli, Niccolo. "How Prince Keeps Faith." *The Prince,* translated by N. H. Thompson. Value Classic Reprints, 2016.

Mao, Zedong. "On Coalition Government (April 24, 1945)" and "Preface and Postscript to Rural Surveys (March and April 1941)." In *Selected Works of Mao Tse Tung,* vol. 3. Beijing: Foreign Language Press, 1967.

Mao, Zedong. "Qilü:Renminjiefangjun jiefang Nanjing" [Seven-character poem: PLA captures Nanking]. Allpoetry.com; translator unknown.

Mao, Zedong. "Problems of War and Strategy." In *Selected Works of Mao Tse Tung,* vol. 2. Beijing: Foreign Languages Press, 1966.

Mapendere, Jeffrey. "Track One and a Half Diplomacy and the Complementarity of Tracks." *Culture of Peace Online Journal* 2, no. 1 (2006): 66–81.

Martino, Matt. "Pauline Hanson's Maiden Speech: Has Australia Been 'Swamped by Asians'?" *ABC News* (Australia), September 13, 2016.

Mearsheimer, John. "Back to the Future: Instability in Europe after the Cold War." *International Security* 15, no. 1 (1990): 5–56.

Mearsheimer, John. "Structural Realism." In *International Relations Theories: Discipline and Diversity*, edited by Tim Dunne, Milja Kurki, and Steve Smith, 3rd ed. Oxford: Oxford University Press, 2013.

Miks, Jason. "Who Hatoyama Could've Been." *The Diplomat,* June 2, 2010.

Minzer, Carl. *End of an Era: How China's Authoritarian Revival Is Undermining Its Rise.* New York: Oxford University Press, 2018.

Morgenthau, Hans, Kenneth Thompson, and David Clinton. *Politics Among Nations.* New York: McGraw-Hill Education, 2005.

Nakamura, David. "White House Denounces Denis Rodman's Trip to North Korea." *Washington Post,* March 4, 2013.

Nathan, Andrew. *Chinese Democracy.* New York: Knopf Doubleday, 2012.

Ng, Teddy. "China's New Foreign Minister Wang Yi." *South China Morning Post,* March 16, 2013.

Nicholson, Michael. "The Continued Significance of Positivism?" In *International Theory: Positivism and Beyond,* edited by Steven Smith, Ken Booth, and Marysia Zalewski, 128–45. Cambridge: Cambridge University Press, 1996.

Niwa, Uichiro. *Chugoku no daimondai* [China's great dilemma]. Kyoto: PHP Kenkyusho, 2014.

Nye, Joseph. "Only China Can Contain China." *Huffington Post,* March 11, 2015.

Onishi, Norimitsu. "Koizumi Visits War Shrine, as He Pledged." *New York Times,* October 17, 2005.

Oon, Clarissa. "The Dragon and the Little Red Dot: 20th Anniversary of China-Singapore Diplomatic Ties." *Strait Times,* October 2, 2010.

Perlez, Jane. "New Chinese Panel Said to Oversee Domestic Security and Foreign Policy." *New York Times,* November 13, 2013.

Perlez, Jane. "Stampede to Join China's Development Bank Stuns Even Its Founder." *New York Times,* April 2, 2015.

Perlez, Jane, and Yufan Huang. "Diplomat's Death Reignites Debate over China's Role in the World." *New York Times,* June 25, 2016.

Pilling, David. "The Perils of Japan's Andy Warhol." *Financial Times,* September 2, 2010.

Piven, Joshua, David Borgenicht, Piers Marchant, and Melissa Wagner. *The Worse-Case Scenario Almanac*. San Francisco: Chronicle Books, 2006.

Pomfret, Jon. "US Takes a Tougher Tone with China." *Washington Post,* July 30, 2010.

Putnam, Robert. "Diplomacy and Domestic Politics: The Logic of Two-Level Games." *International Organization* 42, no. 3 (Summer 1988): 427–60.

Ramzy, Austin. "Chinese Reporter Accused of Slapping Man at Political Event in Britain." *New York Times,* October 2, 2018.

Reinhart, R. J. "Healthcare, Immigration Down as Most Important Problem." *Gallup News,* December 18, 2018.

Rich, Motoko. "Meeting Between Japan and Russia Ends with Stalemate on Disputed Island." *New York Times,* December 16, 2016.

Rogin, Josh. "China's President Lashed Out in Mexico against 'Well-Fed Foreigners.'" *Foreign Policy,* January 12, 2011.

Rourke, Francis E. *Bureaucracy and Foreign Policy,* Baltimore: Johns Hopkins University Press, 1972.

Rucker, Philip, and Ashley Parker. "How Trump Made Up with Australia's Prime Minister after a 'Most Unpleasant Call.'" *Washington Post*, February 22, 2017.

Ruwitch, John, and Colin Packham. "In Shanghai, Australia Minister Sees Limits to Tackling Irritants in Ties." *Reuters,* May 18, 2018.

Ryall, Julian. "Why Are Japanese So Condescending to Chinese Tourists?" *South China Morning Post,* January 1, 2017.

Saich, Tony. "What Does General Secretary Xi Jinping Dream About?" In *Ash Center Occasional Papers*, edited by Tony Saich. Cambridge, MA: Ash Center for Democratic Government and Innovation, Harvard Kennedy School, 2017.

Savic, Bob. "Behind China and Russia's 'Special Relationship.'" *Diplomat*, December 7, 2016.

Schiavenza, Matt. "When Margaret Thatcher Came to China." *The Atlantic,* April 9, 2013.

Schimmefennig, Frank. "Goffman Meets IR: Dramaturgical Action in International Community." *International Review of Sociology* 12, no. 3 (2002): 417–37.

Schoppa, Leonard. *Bargaining with Japan What American Pressure Can and cannot Do.* Ithaca: Cornell University Press, 1997.

Schwartz, Thomas A. "Henry Kissinger: Realism, Domestic Politics, and the Struggle against Exceptionalism in American Foreign Policy." *Diplomacy and Statecraft* 22, no. 1 (2011): 121–41.

Shao, Ling. "Dashuju suandechu Cao Xueqin shengzu nian me" [Can big data figure out Cao Xueqin's exact years of birth and death?]. *Wenzhai Bao,* January 7, 2016.

Shelly, Percy Bysshe. "Ozymandias." As in the *Examiner*, January 11, 1818.

Shepardson, David. "US Condemns China for 'Orwellian Nonsense; over Airline Websites." *Reuters,* May 5, 2018.

Shi, Yuzhi. "Zhongguo meng qubie yu Meiguo meng de qi da tezheng" [Seven major differences between the China dream and the American dream]. *Renmin luntan,* May 27, 2013.

Shirk, Susan. *Fragile Superpower: How China's Internal Problems Could Derail Its Peaceful Rise*. Oxford: Oxford University Press, 2007.

Shu, Jinglin. "Xinshiqi zhongguo junshi waijiao de tedian" [Characteristics of Chinese military diplomacy in the new era]. *Xueshujiaoliu* [Academic exchange], S1 (2013): 42–44.

Singer, J. David. "The Levels-of-Analysis Problem in International Relations." *World Politics* 14, no. 1 (Oct. 1961): 77–92.

Smith, Oliver. "The Unstoppable Rise of the Chinese Traveler—Where Are They Going and What Does It Mean for Overtourism?" *The Telegraph,* April 11, 2018.

Smothers, Ronald. "Reagan Praises Navy Flier and Jackson." *New York Times,* January 5, 1984.

Snow, Edgar. "Interviews with Mao Tse-tung." In *China: The March toward Unity,* by Mao Tse-tung. New York: Workers Library, 1937.

Snow, Edgar. *Red Star over China: Classic Account of the Birth of Chinese Communism.* New York: Random House, [1938], 1944.

Snow, Edgar. "A Reporter Got This Rare Interview with Chairman Mao in 1965, Even Though China Was Entirely Closed to the West." *New Republic,* February 26, 1965.

Song, Renqiong. "Chuncan daosi si fangjin" [A silkworm who keeps spinning until death]. In *Women de Zhou Zongli* [Our premier Zhou]. Beijing: Zhongyang wenxian chubanshe, 1990.

Sørensen, Camilla T. N. "Is China Becoming More Aggressive? A Neoclassical Realist Analysis." *Asian Perspective* 37, no. 3 (2013): 363–85.

Spence, Jonathan D. "The Mystery of Zhou Enlai." *New York Review of Books,* May 28, 2009.

Stephens, Philip. "A Beijing Cabby's View of the World: The Chinese Are Complaining That They Have Domestic Politics to Consider Too." *Financial Time,* November 3, 2011.

Stewart, Phil. "Gates: China Confirms Stealth Jet Test-Flight." *Reuters,* January 10, 2011.

Stockmann, Daniela. *Media Commercialization and Authoritarian Rule in China.* Cambridge: Cambridge University Press, 2013.

Sun, Jing. "China as Funhouse Mirror: The Yomiuri Shimbun's Portrayal of the Cultural Revolution and Its Contemporary Implications." *Japanese Studies* 28, no. 2 (2008): 179–96.

Sun, Jing. *Japan and China as Charm Rivals: Soft Power in Regional Diplomacy.* Ann Arbor: University of Michigan Press, 2012.

Sun, Jing. "Growing Diplomacy, Retreating Diplomats—How Chinese Foreign Ministry Has Been Marginalized in Foreign Policymaking." *Journal of Contemporary China* (November 2016). http://dx.doi.org/10.1080/10670564.2016.1245895

Sun, Jing. "Why Japan Cannot Break the Stalemate in Its Relations with Russia: Tokyo's Frozen Dilemma." *Asian Survey,* 58, no. 5 (2018): 771–96. https://www.doi.org/10.1525/as.2018.58.5.771

Swaine, Michael. "Perceptions of an Assertive China." *China Leadership Monitor,* no. 32 (May 2010): 1–19.

Switzer, Tom. "Nixon, the Balance of Power, and Realism." *National Interest,* August 14, 2014.

Tan, Lincoln. "Police Seek Identities of People Involved in Hong Kong Protest That Turned Violent at Auckland University Campus." *New Zealand Herald,* July 31, 2019.

Tanaka, Hitoshi, and So'ichiro Tahara. *Kokka to gaiko* [Country and diplomacy]. Tokyo: Kodansha, 2007.

Taylor, Adam. "China's Ambassador to Sweden Calls Journalists Critical of Beijing Lightweight Boxers Facing a Heavyweight." *Washington Post,* January 21, 2020.

Tiezzi, Shannon. "Xi Jinping: China's Hope and Change President?" *The Diplomat,* November 19, 2013.

Tsaliki, Liza, Christos A. Frangonikolopoulos, and Asteris Huliaras, eds. *Transnational Celebrity Activism in Global Politics: Changing the World?* Bristol, UK: Intellect, 2011.

Turner, Sarah. "How a China Slowdown Could Hit the Economy." *Financial Review,* June 20, 2019.

University of Southern California, US–China Institute Online Archive. "Mao Zedong Meets Nixon, February 21, 1972; Declassified Transcript of the Beijing Meeting between China's Leader and America's. It Took Place in Mao's Living Quarters."

Waltz, Kenneth. "Anarchic Orders and Balances of Power." In *Neorealism and Its Critics,* edited by Robert Keohane. New York: Columbia University Press, 1986.

Waltz, Kenneth. *Man, the State, and War: A Theoretical Analysis.* New York: Columbia University Press, [1954, 1959], 2001.

Wang, Pengbai. "Peng Dehuai de eyun shi ruhe zhudingde" [How Peng Dehuai was doomed]. *Yanhuang Chunqiu* 10 (2002).

Wang, Xiaoshi. "Cong Fushan fansi tan guojia zhili nengli" [Fukuyama's reflections and the buildup of national governing capability]. *Global Times Net,* October 23, 2014.

Wang, Yi. "Mao Zedong tan hongloumeng: budu sanbian meiyou fayanquan" [Mao Zedong on Dream of the Red Chamber: One has no right to talk about it unless he has read it three times]. *Chinese Communist Party History Online Archive,* 2015.

Wang, Yizhou, and Xinda Li. "Cong waijiaoguan shuliang de lishi bianqian tan woguo waijiao nengli jianshe xinketi" [The historical evolution in the number of Chinese diplomats and the new agenda in the building of Chinese diplomatic capability]. *People's Daily Network,* September 13, 2017.

Wang, Zheng. "National Humiliation, History Education, and the Politics of Historical Memory." *International Studies Quarterly* 52, no. 4 (2008): 783–806.

Weber, Max. *Economy and Society: An Outcome of Interpretative Analogy.* Edited by Guenther Roth and Claus Wittich. Vol. 2. Berkeley: University of California Press, 1978.

Weiss, Jessica Chen. "Authoritarian Signaling, Mass Audiences, and Nationalist Protest in China." *International Organization* 67, no. 1 (2013): 1–35.

Will, George F. "Jesse Jackson in Syria." *Washington Post,* January 1, 1984.

Wong, John, and Yongnian Zheng, eds. *China's Post-Jiang Leadership Succession: Problems and Perspectives.* Singapore: World Scientific, 2002.

Wu, Guangxiang, Dayong Zheng, and Jing Yan. "Qian Qichen: yu Sadamu duihua de waijiao jiaofu" [Qian Qichen: Diplomatic godfather who talks to Saddam]. *Lingdao Wencui* [Leadership journal], no. 1 (2011).

Wu, Qiulan. "Gaige kaifang 30nian qingnian xuesheng aiguozhuyi biaoda de bianhuaguiji" [Three-decade-long changing trajectory of ways young students express patriotism in the era of reform and open-door policy]. *Chinese Youth Studies Journal,* no. 1 (2009): 21–24.

Xi, Jinping. "Keynote Speech at the World Economic Forum." Delivered at the annual World Economic Forum, Davos, Switzerland, January 17, 2017.

Xi, Jinping. "Zai jinian Hu Yaobang tongzhi tanchen 100 zhounian zuotanhuishang de jianghua" [Speech at the ceremony commemorating the 100th birthday of Hu Yaobang]. November 20, 2015.

Xu Jilin. *The New Tianxia: Rebuilding China's Internal and External Order.* Translated by Mark McConaghy, Tang Xiaobing, and David Ownby. *Reading the China Dream. com,* 2018. https://www.readingthechinadream.com/xu-jilin-the-new-tianxia.html

Xue, Li. "Zhongguo waijiao mianlin guanliaozhuyi weixie" [Chinese diplomacy faces threat of bureaucraticism]. *China Daily Network*, April 22, 2015.

Xue, Lin. "Dui gaige kaifangqian Zhongguo yuanfei de zhanlve fansi" [Reflections on China's aid to Africa before reform and open-door era]. *Dangdai shijie shehuizhuyi wenti* [Issues of contemporary world socialism], no. 1 (2013).

Yamaguchi, Noriyuki. *Anto* [Fights under the surface]. Tokyo: Gentosha, 2017.

Yan, Alice. "China U-turn after Outcry over Revoking Residency Rights." *South China Morning Post,* March 26, 2018.

Yan, An, and Haodong Yan. "Zhonghua minzu shi ruhe chedi baituo bei kaichu qiuji weixian de" [How the Chinese nation completely rid the risk of being stripped of the membership of the globe]. *Dang Jian* [Party construction], August 1, 2016.

Yang, Chao. "Jinshinian xinzhongguo junshiwaijiao yanjiu shuping" [A review of the study of military diplomacy of New China in the last decade]. *Gaoxiao Sheke Dongtai* [Social sciences perspective in higher education], no. 3 (2001): 19–26.

Yang, Jiechi. "Zai diqici zhuwaishijie renzhi yishi ji gongzhong kaifangri de jianghua" [Speech on the seventh inauguration ceremony of chief diplomats to be stationed overseas, and the open-ministry day to the public]. July 26, 2009.

Yang, Jiechi. "Zai waijiaobu neibu houqinguanli gongzuo huiyi shang de jianghua" [Speech at the MFA Internal Conference on Logistical Management]. June 2012.

Yang, Jisheng. "Zhang Ziyang wei shenme he Chenyun lianshou piping Hu Yaobang" [Why did Zhao Ziyang collaborate with Chen Yun on criticizing Hu Yaobang?]. In *Zhongguo gaige kaifang niandai de zhengzhidouzheng* [Political struggles in China's reform era]. Hong Kong: Tequ wenhua tushu youxiangongsi, 2011.

Yi, Qing. "Li Guangyao jujue Hua Guofeng zengshu yin quanchang ganga" [Lee Kuan Yew adamantly declines gift book from Hua Guofeng and causes embarrassment]. *Duowei News,* March 18, 2015.

Yoshida, Shigeru. *Yoshida Shigeru: Last Meiji Man,* edited by Hiroshi Nara. Plymouth, UK: Rowman & Littlefield, [1967], 2007.

Yu, Miles. "Chinese President's Military Overhaul Tightens Communist Party's Control." *Washington Times,* December 3, 2015.

Zhang, Jiajun. "Liang shaojiang fandui zhuiqiu shijie diyi junshiqiangguo" [Two admirals oppose China pursuing the world's top military power]. *Huanqiu Network,* March 3, 2010.

Zhang, Jin. "Waijiaobu fayanren biaoshi nibo'er maopai wuzhuang he zhongguo wuguan" [Foreign Ministry spokesperson states China has no relations with Maoists in Nepal]. *Jinghua shibao,* February 4, 2005.

Zhang, Weiwei. "Wo de Zhoongguo guan" [My view of China]. *Aisixiang,* September 24, 2014.

Zheng, Kejun. "Bashiniandai chuqi zhongguo duifei zhengce de tiaozheng" [Adjustment of China's Africa policy in the early 1980s]. In *Zhongguo Yu Feizhou* [China and Africa]. Beijing: Peking University Africa Studies Center, Peking University Press, 2000.

Zheng, Yongnian. *Dageju: Zhongguo jueqi yinggai chaoque qinggan he yishixingtai* [Grand situation: Rising China needs to transcend emotional and ideological obstacles]. Beijing: Dongfang chubanshe, 2014.

Zhou, Bin. "Suoyi Hua Guofeng" [Remembering Hua Guofeng]. *Xinmin Zhoukan,* May 14, 2013.

Zhou, Boping. *Feichangshiqi de waijiao shengya* [Diplomatic career in strange times]. Beijing: Shijie zhishi chubanshe, 2004.

Zhou, Ruijin. "Zhu Rongji ceng bei Deng Xiaoping chengzan wei 'dongjingji' lingdaoren" [Deng Xiaoping praises Zhu Rongji as leader who understands economics]. *Diyi Caijing Ribao,* August 13, 2013.

Zhu, Nianfeng, Liping Zheng, and Xueling Wang. "2013nian sixianglilun lingyu de redian wenti" [Hot topics in the field of theoretical construction in 2013]. *Hongqiwengao* [Red flag written works], January 13, 2014.

Media

ABC News (Australia), 2018.
ABC Chinese News (Australia), 2018.
Aiqiyi [爱奇艺视频网], 2018.
Apple Daily [蘋果日報], 2003.
Asahi Shimbun [朝日新聞], 2020.
The Australian, 2018.
Baixing [百姓], 1985.
BBC, 2016.
BBC Chinese [BBC 中文网], 2018.
Beijing Youth Daily [北京青年报], 2013.
Bloomberg News, 2017.
Boxun News [博讯新闻], 2015.
Cankaoxiaoxi Network [参考消息网], 2015.
CBS News, 2013.
CGTN America, 2017.
China Central Television, 2019–20.
China Daily, 2015.
China News Digest International, 2020.
China News Service [中国新闻社], 2018.
China Times [中時電子報], 2018.
Chinese Communist Party News Network [中国共产党新闻网], 2009–18.
CNN, 2018.
Daily Show with Jon Stewart, 2014.
Dakung Pao [大公報], 2012–15.
Diyi Caijing Ribao [第一财经日报], 2013.
Duowei News [多维新闻], 2015.
Dushikuaibao [都市快报], 2012.
The Economist, 2012–18.
Financial Times, 2011.
Gallup News, 2018.
Global Times Network [环球网], 2010–17.
Global View [环球视野], 2017.
Guancha Net [观察者网], 2016.
The Guardian, 2018.
Huaxi Dushibao [华西都市报], 2018.

Huffington Post, 2015.
Japan Times, 2015.
Jiemian [界面], 2017.
Jinghua Shibao [京华时报], 2004–13.
Kyodo News Agency, 2006.
Liaowang Zhongguo [瞭望中国], 2015.
Liberty Times [自由時報], 2018.
Los Angeles Times, 2015.
New Republic, 1965.
Newsweek, 2013.
New Tang Dynasty TV, 2013.
New York Review of Books, 2009.
New York Times, 1976–2018.
New Zealand Herald, 2019.
People's Daily Network [人民日报/人民网], 1965–2017.
Phoenix News Network, 2009–19.
QQ News [腾讯新闻], 2013–16.
Radio France Internationale, 2012–13.
Radio Free Asia, 2019.
Renmin Luntan [人民论坛], 2013.
Reuters, 1989–2020.
Sankei Shimbun [産経新聞], 2015.
Sina.com [新浪网], 2012–13.
Sohu.com [搜狐网], 2013–18.
South China Morning Post, 2013–18.
Time, 1984.
21st Century Economic Herald [21世纪经济导报], 2015.
Voice of America, 2005–20.
Wall Street Journal, 2002–12.
Washington Examiner, 2018.
Washington Post, 1984–2020.
Washington Times, 2015.
Wenzhai Bao [文摘报], 2016.
Xinhua News Agency [新华通讯社], 2006–18.
Yanhuang Chunqiu [炎黄春秋], 2002–18.
Yomiuri Shimbun [読売新聞], 1987.
Zhongguo Baodao Zhoukan [中国报道周刊], 2009.

Index

Note: Page numbers in *italic text* indicate figures or tables.